Camp free in B.C.

VOLUME ONE ~~~~~RN BRITISH COLUMBIA
From Trans-Can~~~~~ ~~~~~nwy 1 to the U.S. border.
From Vancouver island to the Rocky Mountains.

Explored and written by Kathy & Craig Copeland
Voice in the Wilderness Press, Inc. Riondel, British Columbia

Third Edition

First edition, March 1995
Second Edition, March 1997
Revised, updated Third Edition, June 1999

Published by   Voice in the Wilderness Press, Inc.
                P.O. Box 71, Riondel, British Columbia
                Canada V0B 2B0

Typesetting / Production / Maps by C.J. Chiarizia

Cover design by Matthew Clark

Photos by Kathy and Craig Copeland

Canadian Cataloguing in Publication Data

Copeland, Craig, 1955-
  Camp free in B.C.

  Includes index.
  Contents: V. 1. Southern British Columbia.
  ISBN 0-9698016-7-X

    1. Camping—British Columbia—Guidebooks.   2. British Columbia—Guidebooks.
  I. Copeland, Kathy, 1959- II. Title.
  GV191.46.B75C66 1999   796.54'09711   C99-910456-X

Printed and Bound in Canada by Transcontinental Printers

Over 50% recycled paper
including 100% post
consumer fibre

ACKNOWLEDGEMENTS

First, we thank you. We appreciate anyone who's adventurous enough to buy this book and get out in the wilds and use it.

We also thank both our parents. They continue to be understanding about our love of exploration, even though it keeps us from visiting them often.

And we thank each other. To create *Camp Free*, we endured arduously long drives on rough roads; days without exercise, showers or proper meals; arguments incited by discomfort and close quarters; the endless recording of niggling details, when we just wanted to cut loose; then months of sitting indoors, writing, while we ached to be outside. Each of us is deeply grateful for the other's extreme perseverance.

CONTENTS

SOUTHERN B.C.
CAMPING REGIONS

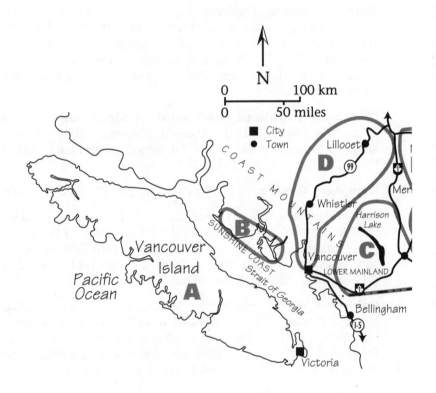

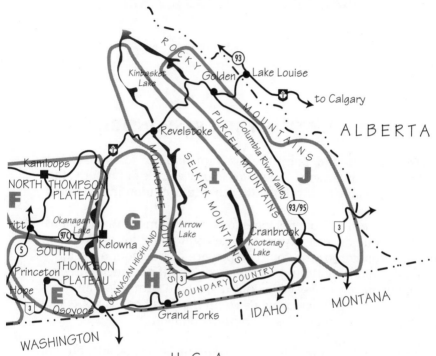

Philosophy, Strategies and Joys of Camping Free

British Columbia has more than 1,400 free campgrounds.

THE ANTIDOTE FOR CIVILIZATION

British Columbia has more than 1,400 free campgrounds—tucked into immense forests, in the shadows of noble mountains, beside dancing rivers, snuggled up to lakes grand and petite.

A few of these campgrounds are big, organized, groomed, much like provincial parks and nearly as popular. Others are tiny, rough hewn, seldom visited, almost certain to offer you solitude. Many are hidden just a short distance off paved roads. Some are deep in the woods. And most are free. Open year-round. No reservations required. They're provided by the B.C. Forest Service. Once you buy a low-cost, annual Camping Pass, you can pull into any of these campgrounds whenever you like. Just pick your site and camp. Only a handful of the most heavily-used campgrounds require a minimal per-night fee to help cover higher maintenance costs.

En route to any of these campgrounds, you'll savour a fresh perspective on the stunning geography of our glorious province. You'll be astonished at where B.C.'s seemingly endless network of backroads can take you. Just getting your tires off the pavement is fun. Though there's a lot to see from the highways, there's much more beyond. Even with *Camp Free's* detailed directions, you'll feel the excitement of discovery.

Nearly all these campgrounds are away from towns and highways, so you'll likely glimpse one of the locals: perhaps an owl or a coyote; maybe a bear or a moose. Even the common sight of a deer or a salmon can thrill and comfort, reminding you that despite the damage done, wilderness still exists and nature is alive and well. That's the joy of free-camping. Not just what you keep in your wallet, but what you take away in your heart.

Camping is CPR for your senses. It opens your eyes to the night sky, with stars so thick they look like clouds. It opens your ears to the music of wind in the trees, water rushing over rocks, or maybe absolute silence. It reacquaints you with the simple, sweet pleasure of not feeling cement under foot, not being confined by fences or walls, not complying with rules, and sometimes not having to look at another human being. It's the antidote for civilization.

Chilliwack River, from Eagles Roost campground

And *free* camping is *real* camping. It's an adventure—something sadly missing from most people's lives and impossible to find at commercial campgrounds. Neon signs? Reception offices? Pop machines? Hook-ups? TV antennas? Where's the adventure in that? It's hard to tell many campgrounds from RV dealerships these days. They're just parking lots. Even provincial-park campgrounds are often within earshot of a roaring highway.

You'll forgo conveniences at the campgrounds described in *Camp Free*. None have showers, flush toilets, or even running water. But what most people consider necessities are actually luxuries. Doing without can make you feel more complete. And camping, by definition, means contending with the elements—bugs, wind, rain, cold, heat. But if you're prepared and can shrug off minor discomfort, the elements can make you feel more alive.

If you go with an open mind and soft heart, *Camp Free* will guide you to a rousing experience. You'll be revitalized, able to calmly slip back into the shackles of civilization with renewed vigor. Your memory, your mental gallery, will be filled with vivid images—sustenance for the soul until your next outing. At the very least, you'll have a story to tell neighbours and co-workers who've never sought adventure beyond the nearest video store.

GET OUT WHILE YOU CAN

Twenty-five years ago, free-camping was so easy that a guidebook was unnecessary. A short drive from any city would reward you with lots of beautiful places to park where nobody would bother you. But rampant development and population growth have overtaken those of us who would flee. Now you have to drive hours, and still you'll be contending with country homes, resorts, farms and ranches that make it almost impossible to free-camp—unless you know where to go.

That's why we wrote this book: to tell you about B.C.'s extensive network of free Forest Service (FS) campgrounds, explain exactly where they are and how to get there, and encourage you to enjoy and protect them.

The need for a guidebook on free B.C. campgrounds became apparent to us in 1994. Although we'd traveled throughout the province for years, not until then did we stumble upon a free campground on the Nahatlatch River, west of Fraser Canyon. A few months later we found more free campgrounds along the Chilliwack River, in the Lower Mainland. We gave thanks to the Camping God. Then it struck us. During all our explorations, we were unaware of these free campgrounds; other people must be too. Our journey to create *Camp Free* had begun.

Too many people struggle to find places to pitch their tent or park their RV for a night without having to pay excessively for the privilege. Having camped in all kinds of weird, noisy, uncomfortable spots, we know the frustration. Many of those nights, we now realize, could have been far more pleasant, because established, free campgrounds were only minutes away. Today, we still see others repeating our mistakes. Near Sugar Lake, for example, we met a young European couple vacationing with their two kids, traveling across B.C. in a rented motorhome. They parked overnight at a pullout, just off the pavement, next to an ugly gravel pit. They settled for such a dismal spot because it was late, they were tired, and no other option was obvious. Too bad. Just across the highway, an unsigned, dirt road led to an official, free campground. Surrounded by trees, next to the Shuswap River, it was only a kilometer away. Had they known, they would have been safer and enjoyed their stay infinitely more.

With *Camp Free* in hand, you're now a fully-informed camper. This is the most comprehensive guide available to B.C.'s free campgrounds. But get out while you can. Camping is increasingly popular. Most campgrounds are being visited more frequently. Economic pressures have decreased FS budgets. The result: camping in B.C. is not as free as it once was, and that trend could continue.

At a few of the busiest campgrounds, the FS now charges a minimal per-night fee. It supplements the cost of garbage removal, pit-toilet pumping, and access improvement. Occasionally it helps pay for a patrol to keep the peace, or a repair necessitated by vandalism. And while the vast majority of free campgrounds remain free—no toll-boxes, no money-collecting hosts—the *right* to camp free is no longer gratis. The provincial government now asks that you buy a Camping Pass. All funds raised by Camping Pass sales go directly to campground maintenance. The annual Camping Pass costs $27 (1999) and is valid for an entire year beginning in spring. It allows you and your family (or a group of up to six friends) unlimited, free use of more than 1,400 FS campgrounds throughout the province. At the 30 or so campgrounds that charge per night, the annual Camping Pass entitles you to a 50% discount. Camping Passes are available at sporting goods stores and government agent offices. Or you can use the form in the back of this book to receive your Camping Pass by mail. It's a bargain even if you camp only a few times each summer. And it will help ensure that the campgrounds themselves remain forever free.

THE MAP IS NOT THE TERRITORY

Free campgrounds are rarely on paved roads. Signs announcing free campgrounds are never on paved roads. Only after you drive onto a backroad will you encounter a sign, typically *way* after. You might see signposts at the campgrounds. Even some campgrounds are unsigned. For these reasons, *Camp Free* is invaluable.

A highway sign like this could indicate the Forest Service road you're looking for is just ahead.

Researching *Camp Free*, we relied on FS Recreation Maps. Though helpful, they lack detail. They don't indicate the numerous switchbacks and junctions you'll encounter. They rarely label the roads that lead to campgrounds and don't specify where to turn off the highway. Using FS maps, we were reminded: the map is not the territory. And commercially published map books are little better. They too require the skills of an explorer and the instincts of a detective.

A sign or signpost marks
the entry to many Forest
Service campgrounds.

So, during field trips, we were often on edge. "How much farther?" "This can't be the right road." "Think we'll make it?" "No way there's a campground up here." Sometimes we felt like rats in a maze. But you won't. Following *Camp Free's* precise directions, you can relax and enjoy the drive knowing you *are* on the right road, your vehicle *can* make it, and there *is* a campground up there.

Camp Free is the only resource you need to find most of B.C.'s free campgrounds. FS Recreation Maps, however, can broaden your perspective. Call or visit the FS offices for the districts you'll be exploring. Ask if maps are available. The phone numbers and addresses are in the back of this book.

YOU'LL KNOW BEFORE YOU GO

Camp Free not only gives you directions to the campgrounds, it tells you what to expect when you arrive. How's the scenery? Is the area quiet or noisy? What outdoor activities are possible? Now you'll know before you go.

Example of the excellent Forest Service campgrounds throughout B.C.

Camp Free even rates each campground. Is it a worthwhile **destination** for an extended stay? Good enough for a **weekend** visit? Or useful only as an **overnight** pullout on your way to someplace else? *Camp Free* goes beyond the facts, offering opinions based on widely-accepted, common-sense criteria.

To help you confidently turn off major highways and forge onto dirt backroads, *Camp Free* states the distance to each campground and the quality of the road. **Easy** means it's a short way and the road is good. **Moderate** means it's 15 to 20 minutes from pavement, or the road is only fair. **Difficult** means it's a long way or the road is poor. Road surfaces, however, change over time—usually for the worse—so make your own assessment before proceeding.

Every campground in this book should be accessible in a two-wheel-drive (2WD) low-clearance car. *Camp Free* warns you where conditions could necessitate four-wheel-drive (4WD) or a high-clearance vehicle. *Camp Free* also advises big-rig pilots (motorhomes, 5th-wheels, trailers) if the access road might be troublesome, or the campground too small.

TURN LEFT AT THE BOULDER

"Any chance I'll get lost?" you ask.

Very little. *Camp Free* gives explicit directions that should make sense to you now, and will become perfectly clear en route. "Turn left at the boulder" will be a no-brainer once you're out there, in the shadow of a looming boulder the size of a house.

The forests and ex-forests of B.C. conceal a bird's nest of inter-laced dirt roads totaling more than 32,000 kilometers (20,000 miles). With only rudimentary FS maps to work with, the task of unsnarling all the details severely challenged our endurance and sanity. We believe we calculated all our meanderings accurately. We certainly gave it a supreme effort. But it's possible we goofed without knowing.

On the road, if the book seems unclear or you feel uncertain, try to bear with the directions. The description should be adequate to steer you to the campground regardless of a minor error. Look for the stated landmarks. Be intuitive. Poke your nose around the next corner. You'll find it. Remember: free-camping is an adventure. And when you get home, please mail, e-mail, or fax us your suggested corrections.

Find out what's happening. Do something about it.

YOU CAN MAKE A DIFFERENCE

The roads to most free campgrounds in B.C. are logging roads. Though logging practices have been irresponsible in the past, keep in mind these campgrounds wouldn't be there, so you probably wouldn't either, if logging companies hadn't built the roads. Ideally, the great wild lands of B.C. would be unscarred, preserved in their original majesty forever. Now the best we can do is get out there and look after what's left. It's a lazy king who never leaves the castle to survey his domain. Just be prepared for disappointment: your forests have been logged rapaciously.

Environmental integrity. Scenic value. Future viability. When you see a clearcut, it's hard to believe any of these were considerations. The good news is that improved forestry practices are helping to sustain our forests and save forestry jobs. But we all need to stand guard. An informed public is an empowered public. If you don't know or care enough to hold logging companies and the Ministry of Forests responsible for their actions, who will? Just by exploring the backroads, you can make a difference.

GO GIRL!

Many single women are afraid to camp alone. Perhaps you're among them. If so, your fear is understandable. But the following observations and suggestions should help ratchet your fear down to a reasonable level of concern. Because the reality is that you *can* safely enjoy solo camping at FS campgrounds. If you're drawn to the wilds, go girl! Don't limit yourself to walks in the city park. You'll probably find camping is actually safer. The worst that's likely to befall you is an onslaught of mosquitoes, or a cookie-coveting squirrel.

FS campgrounds are frequented primarily by couples and families. More travellers from across Canada and even from Europe are also now camping in B.C. They'll all be your neighbours while you're out there. Campers are generally kind, trustworthy, peaceful and likable. They're nature lovers, just like you. Most are happy to converse if you approach them but will otherwise respect your privacy. If you've never camped alone, on your first trip you'll probably make a comforting discovery: you're *not* alone.

When they notice you don't have a companion, other campers—usually a chivalrous, older gentleman—might approach and offer to be of service. "Need help starting that fire?" "Want a hand stringing up your tarp?" Don't assume they're chauvinists who doubt your competence. Such acts are almost always genuinely benevolent. If you welcome assistance, accept the offer. If you decline, be tactful and appreciative.

Common sense dictates that a single woman be cautious and vigilant. But that's true anywhere, not just camping. We all have to be somewhat on guard until we've assessed whatever situation we're entering. Here's how single women can do that at campgrounds:

• When reading *Camp Free* and choosing a campground, note what other campgrounds and towns are nearby and how to reach them. That way you'll already have a plan in case you're later unnerved and decide to move.

• Arrive before nightfall so you can see the campground and other campers. Drive slowly through before picking a camp-site. The presence of other women, even in a mixed group, is heartening, because they tend to be a calming influence. Try to camp near them.

• If the campground is empty, and you like solitude, stay. If others arrive after dark, listen and observe intently. Get a sense for who they are and how you feel about them. Trust your instincts. If the newcomers seem rude or belligerent, if their behaviour puts you on edge, quickly and quietly pack and leave.

• While settling in, talk to your fellow campers. Ask them questions about the lake, the stream, other campgrounds they recommend, anything to get them talking and revealing themselves. Establish a bond with just one couple and you'll relax. They'll probably comment on your solo status. If not, tell them you're on your own. It will heighten their awareness on your behalf.

After thoroughly assessing the situation, even if you feel at ease about camping alone, take these precautions:

• Sleep in your vehicle. It's safer than a tent. It will reduce your anxiety and allow you a better night's rest. A van is ideal, because you can move from bed to the driver's seat without exiting. A truck and camper (or shell) is good too. Some cars, particularly wagons, have enough space for a bed if you fold down the rear seat.

• Keep a canister of pepper spray handy but concealed. Its intended use is stopping a charging bear, so you can imagine how effective it would be against a mere human. Cayenne pepper, highly irritating to the nose and eyes, is the active ingredient. Without causing permanent injury, it disables the aggressor long enough to let you escape. Obviously, it's a last-resort defense. Use it only if you believe you're at serious risk. You can buy pepper spray—possibly labeled Bearguard, Counter Assault, OC-10, or Phazer—at outdoor stores.

During all our years camping in B.C., we've never met anyone scary or suspicious. We've never felt threatened or perceived any danger. That should reassure you. It's inevitable that you'll

Many 2WD backroads described in Camp Free *lead to grand vistas.*

react negatively to someone. Shabby clothes, a gruff voice, questionable hygiene—something will put you off. But our initial harsh judgments have repeatedly been shattered after a brief conversation reveals a gentle, caring soul beneath the stereotype. We hope your encounters will be equally positive.

HITTING THE DIRT

Inexperienced on backroads? Consider these suggestions before you hit the dirt. A little preparation can increase your confidence and safety.

• Carry more food and water than you think you'll need for your camping trip, in case of emergency. A first-aid kit is also a wise addition.

• Check your vehicle's fuel supply and engine fluid levels before leaving the highway.

• Always drive with your headlights on—even during daylight hours.

Drive defensively. You can encounter a speeding logging truck anytime, anywhere.

• Drive cautiously. You never know who's coming or what's up ahead. It's possible the road has been damaged recently by severe weather or other natural hazards.

• Be patient. Keep your speed moderate, unless the road is clearly flat and straight for a long way. Even then, holes or rocks might surprise you.

• Slow down on washboard roads. Go too fast and your dashboard will clack like a player piano. Worse, you could lose traction and slide out of control as your vehicle hops from one ripple to the next.

• Avoid the middle of the road. Always cling to the right side. Even if you haven't seen another vehicle for hours, one could appear at the worst possible moment. On dirt, reduced traction makes vehicles less responsive.

• Never block the road. If you stop, pull far enough off to allow industrial vehicles to pass at high speed.

• Yield to logging trucks or other industrial vehicles. As soon as you see one (a cloud of dust is a sure indicator) pull as far over as possible and let it proceed.

• Obey all posted restrictions. Some active logging roads are closed to the public from 5 a.m. Monday until 8 p.m. Friday. Don't be tempted to sneak in. The closure is for your own safety. Monster logging trucks are belting down those roads.

• Don't let the logging companies' warning signs scare you off the roads. Except when the

Don't let the signs scare you away. Just drive safely.

area is specifically closed to the public between certain hours, they're just telling you to be aware and drive safely. Sometimes you'll see lots of signs. It can be intimidating. But it doesn't mean you'll be fighting your way upstream against a constant flow of industrial traffic.

TWO-WHEELING IT

Driving a low-clearance 2WD car or RV? Don't worry. The roads in this book shouldn't present any serious obstacles. But if you encounter a stretch of rough, challenging road, these suggestions might help.

• Before leaving home, look at your vehicle's underbelly. Get on your knees and really see what's down there. Make note of where you have the least clearance and where you have the most, so you'll know how to straddle rocks.

• When the road looks questionable, it's often the grit of the driver, not the vehicle itself, that determines whether you'll make it. That's not to say you should be bull-headed and plow through come what may. When you assess the road, just be aware of your level of confidence and your capacity for patience.

No need to check this one with a stick.

• Faced with deeply worn tracks on the sides of the road, and a high ridge in the middle that might scrape your underbelly, drive with one tire on the ridge and the other outside the track.

• When there's a deep rut across the road, don't approach it straight on. You might bottom-out. Instead, slice across at an angle, from one side of the road toward the other. That way your tires drop into the rut one at a time, instead of both at once.

• Before you splash through a big mud hole, get out and check how deep it is. Feel with a stick, or drop a large stone in and see what happens. That's a lot easier than getting stuck.

• In mud or sand, don't slow to a crawl. You need momentum. To avoid getting stuck, it's often best to proceed and hope the road surface improves. If you're not stuck yet, but it appears you will be, reverse out immediately. Trying to turn around can land you in a bigger mess. When fishtailing, straighten your vehicle by turning the front wheels in the direction your rear wheels are sliding.

• Know what you're risking. Ask yourself: "How many vehicles have been on the road today? What's the likelihood of seeing another? How far back is the highway? The last possible telephone? The nearest lived-in-looking house?" Consider your worst-case options before you plunge in. It might sway your decision.

HELP IS ON THE WAY

Concerned about being stranded in the outback? Don't be. Help is probably on the way. Though some roads in this book might seem desolate, they're not. You can usually expect someone to come along within an hour. A few locals and outdoorspeople are always wandering the backcountry. You'll often encounter logging company employees in pickup trucks. If necessary, signal them to stop; you'll find they're friendly and glad to assist. If your vehicle konks out, wave down a logging truck; they all have radios and can call for help.

MEN IN TRUCKS KNOW

Reading *Camp Free* should relieve you of asking anyone for directions. But when you explore backroads other than those described here, you'll probably want to check your bearings with someone. Before you do, a word of caution: assume nothing.

Be very specific when asking for directions. State the names of roads, geographic features, or other landmarks. Be certain you're both talking about the same thing. Rely on your intuition as much as anyone else's opinion—even a local who should know the area. It's alarming how many people are unaware of what's beyond their backyard.

Many rough access roads like this one are passable in a 2WD car, if the driver is careful and patient.

Look for men in trucks. That's not a chauvinistic stereotype, that's reality. Men in trucks usually dispense reliable information. They tend to ply the backroads to earn their living, or at least to hunt and fish. So if you're a man, you're in a truck, and you don't know, you better find out, because here they come.

HOW'S THE ROAD?

Stop four drivers on the same road and you'll get four different impressions of what it's like. Ask "How's the road?" and you'll often hear "It's gravel." Unless you're driving a rugged truck, a 4WD vehicle, or an old beater you don't care about, that's too vague. If you want a detailed road report, ask specific questions. How rough is the road? How steep? How narrow? How muddy? How rocky?

Locals who frequent the backroads are generally quick and direct with their answers. But before you heed anyone's advice, consider the source. Do they seem sensible and mature? Inexperienced and timid? Wild and reckless?

Some four-wheelers are determined to uphold the macho mystique of their off-road rigs. They consider cars an inferior subspecies, little more than go-carts. They would eye ours with disdain and say, "I wouldn't try it in *that*." Then they'd leave us in a cloud of dust, and we'd slowly pick our way through the rocks and potholes until we reached our destination.

Others tried to be open-minded. After scrutinizing our car, one fellow said, "Well, if you go slow, you'll probably make it. But there's a lot of sharp rocks. You better have a good set of spare tires." That sounded like an accurate road-condition summary. And it was. Our car survived, but we hated it and decided you would too, so it's not in the book.

Even when the road looked questionable to us, people were usually encouraging. "Aw, you'll be fine," they said. "Just take 'er easy. Lots of people make it. There's big RVs in there." They were right.

Listen to opinions, then decide for yourself. The power to propel you through a difficult patch is probably in your head, regardless of what's under your hood. Technique and determination will take you surprisingly far. And if the road gets too hairy, just turn around. There's always someplace else to explore.

BEYOND CAMP FREE

This is not a comprehensive guidebook. B.C. has hundreds of free campgrounds not described in *Camp Free*. Some are too far off main highways. We recognize there's a limit to most people's tolerance for dusty, rocky, bouncy backroads. And some final-access roads are forbiddingly rough. If you need 4WD and a kidney belt to get there, it's not in the book.

Few campgrounds listed in *Camp Free Volume I* are more than 30 km (18 mi) from pavement. Central B.C. has a more extensive backroad network and longer chains of remote campgrounds, so *Camp Free Volume II* describes full-day excursions off pavement.

If you have a burly vehicle and a questing mind, call or visit the FS office for the district you'll be exploring. They're listed in the back of this book. Ask if a recreation map is available. If so, it will help you find campgrounds beyond *Camp Free*.

With Camp Free *you'll avoid crowds like this at commercial and provincial-park campgrounds.*

When you see someone sacked out on the roadside, kindly suggest they buy this book.

GUERILLA CAMPING

It's late. You're tired. You're nowhere near an official, free camp-ground. You're also unaware of any commercial campgrounds in the area, but you don't want to pay to camp anyway. And you prefer to avoid hotels.

It's still possible to camp free.

Sniffing out places to free-camp is a skill you can develop. As you become proficient, you'll only pay to camp when you're desperate for a shower. Even then, you can just pay for the shower and camp free elsewhere. Unless the land is all fenced off or way too steep, or you absolutely must stop immediately, you probably don't have to pay to camp.

The free-camping spots you find on your own, however, might not be great places to hang around the next morning. They'll likely be adequate only for a night's sleep, nothing more. And it's much easier if you have a vehicle you can sleep in—at least the back of a truck or the bed of a mini-van. It's hard to find places you can safely, comfortably pitch a tent for free.

So what we're really talking about here is creative parking. We call it guerilla camping. It's the only way to cope with all the NO CAMPING signs that have appeared on public land during the last few years.

Is there a conspiracy to make us all pay to sleep? It's unwarranted. Campers who pull off the road for a night, whether they sleep in their vehicles or bravely pitch their tents, rarely harm the land or other people. They're just sleeping! If they're allowed to park there all day, why not at night? What's the harm?

Beat the system. Be a guerilla camper. The following questions will help you assess where and when. Just don't violate people's property rights. If you know it's private, don't camp without asking permission. And always respect the land. Never trash it. As a thank-you for a night's sleep, leave it cleaner than you found it.

What are the options? Be open-minded. Use your imagination. How far you must stretch your thinking depends on where you've free-camped before, what you consider safe, and how bold you are. Some people are audacious. They'll camp anywhere it's wide enough to pull a vehicle off the road. But you can also be a stealth camper, cautiously choosing tranquil, secretive locations.

What's your sense of the place? Does it feel inviting, or creepy? Trust your instinct. If it looks clean, you know people don't park there to drink and party. If it makes you feel vulnerable, that feeling will only grow with every noise you hear. You'll lie awake in the dark, straining to detect anything suspicious. A passing car will slow down and you'll be on edge until it's gone. That's not a good night's sleep. That's miserable. Find another spot where you can relax.

Is it secluded enough? Before you decide to stay, consider what might awaken you later. Are bright lights shining nearby? What's the noise level? How many cars or pedestrians are passing by? Even if you've pulled off what seems like a little-used road, sit there for ten minutes to gauge the traffic before you settle in for the night; you might be surprised.

Will you harm the land? Guerilla camping isn't crashing your way into places you shouldn't be. It's gliding in at night, then slipping out in the morning, without leaving a trace. Vegetation, even grass, should be left intact. Harm nothing, take nothing, leave nothing. If that's not possible, move on.

Have you tried residential areas? If you can sleep in your vehicle, you might feel safer parked in a town near homes, rather than on a road that's lonely but still close to civilization. Just outside a town, you're within range of malicious teenagers or other suspicious characters, and somewhat defenseless against them. In town, on a quiet, dark, residential street, it's unlikely you'll be hassled, because help is just a horn-honk away.

In a neighbourhood, never intrude on anyone's privacy. Try not to park directly in front of a house. You'll be less obvious beside a field or vacant lot. Ideally you won't be noticed. A resident who peeks out a window should assume you're guests of a neighbour.

Compared to urbanites, people in small towns are generally less jumpy about unfamiliar parked cars. Live and let live seems to be the rural attitude. Plus, small towns have fewer parking restrictions and often no police to enforce them.

Are you arriving late enough so you won't be noticed? At residential streets, university grounds, and hospital or church parking lots, the later you arrive the better your chances of an uninterrupted night. You want to be situated so you're inconspicuous—where it's normal to see a few cars parked overnight, but not many. If you're noticed, it shouldn't occur to anyone that you're sleeping in your vehicle. That means you have to finish cooking and arranging your bed elsewhere, before you park. You'll also have to depart early. By 7:30 a.m. you'll probably attract someone's attention, but at that point it might not matter.

If you're noticed, will anyone care? This is highly subjective. Parked close to anything of obvious importance or value, near any potential object of theft or vandalism, someone will probably care if they notice you. That means they might wake you up and tell you to move, which is always a pain and can be scary. It's better to invest a little more time finding a spot where nobody will care if they suspect you're sacked out.

You don't know B.C. until you've visited its far-flung communities, like Kaslo. Camp Free *will get you there.*

RESPECT OTHER CAMPERS

Most people live cheek-by-jowl with their neighbors back home. They want a little privacy when they go camping. So don't barge in on someone who already occupies the limited space at a small campground. Make sure there's plenty of room for one more. If you can't leave a buffer between your camp and others, and there's still daylight left to look elsewhere, please go. If it's late and you decide to stay, be as quiet as a deer mouse. Speak softly and ready yourself for sleep without commotion.

If you're the captain of a fully-equipped motorhome, please consider the rest of us before firing up your generator. Several times that wicked racket has forced us to pack and move late at night. Recognize that your generator, though a convenience to you, is a nuisance to others. It shatters what many of us cherish most about camping: peace. Make sure your system is fully charged before you arrive at a campground. If you must run your generator, do it midday when fellow-campers are most active. Everyone will appreciate that.

Some Neanderthals don't just go camping, they go wild—bellowing at each other, roaring with laughter, blasting stereos, letting their kids rampage. It's rude and obnoxious—night or day. Then there's the couple, inexperienced at backing their trailer into a campsite, who arrives late. The wife shouts directions for fifteen minutes while the husband rocks and rolls the rig. If any of these descriptions sound like you, please be quieter and more considerate.

Because of rowdy, disrespectful campers, a few campgrounds now charge a "keep the peace" fee to employ live-in attendants during summer. They make sure everyone's quiet after 10 p.m. It solves the late-night noise problem but degrades the camping experience and burdens you with an expense. Help prevent it from happening elsewhere.

CAMPGROUND DIPLOMACY

What should you do when Roseanne and family pull into the campsite next to yours and start screaming? Or worse, when Beavis, Butthead and friends crank up the stereo, intent on partying? (1) Don't assume the noise will stop or the offenders will leave. And don't rely on subtle hints to express your feelings. Be very upfront. Talk to them, or the situation and your anger will escalate. (2) Don't shout at them from your site. Walk over and calmly explain the problem. Maybe they were unaware you were bothered. A simple statement might solve it. (3) Kindly but firmly suggest a specific action. Don't be obnoxious, insulting, or demanding; it will only make them defensive. (4) If it's obvious that diplomacy won't work, move—to another campsite farther away, or to another campground if necessary. Yes, it's unfair. But the misery of enduring a joyless day or sleepless night is worse than the hassle of leaving.

BE REVERENT

Reverence is achingly absent from the world today. And if there's anyplace we can and should feel reverent, it's out in nature. Reverence is simply being aware of and respecting life in all its manifestations, including our forests, meadows, rivers and lakes. What you revere, you care for.

Most FS campgrounds are *User Maintained.* No trash cans. No garbage trucks. No cleaning crews. It's your responsibility to pick up after yourself. That's largely why all these campgrounds are free, and why the annual Camping Pass is modestly priced.

If campgrounds are trashed and abused, the price of the Camping Pass will increase. If maintenance costs mount, you'll eventually be slapped with an entry fee at every campground. Most of us can't imagine leaving garbage at a campsite or damaging the already minimal facilities. Please help spread that ethic.

Always carry a few extra garbage bags. If previous campers left anything behind, you can pick it up. You'll be doing your share of user maintenance. And anyone observing you will see reverence in action.

Always haul out your garbage.

Whenever trash is left, even in a fire pit, it encourages others to assume they can add to the mess. So take a few minutes to fill up your garbage bag. On your way home, drop it in a dumpster, preferably in a city. Small towns have limited garbage capacity and infrequent pickups.

Anything campers leave behind is trash. Orange and banana peels take years to biodegrade, and animals won't eat them. Cigarette butts are even worse. Smokers have been allowed to assume butts don't qualify as litter. It's time to change that. They give campgrounds a dirty, ravaged look that saddens and disgusts most campers. Never leave your cigarette butts at a campground. It's easy to haul them away with the rest of your trash.

In general, leave as little impact as possible. For example, you'll find more fire rings than are necessary at most campgrounds. If you light a campfire, use an existing ring so you don't further scar the land. Burn only small pieces of deadfall. The foliage is part of the scenery; don't destroy it for firewood. Be sure your fire is stone-cold dead before you leave or go to sleep. Also, never wash dishes near a lake or stream. Use a plastic basin, then dump the waste water in thick brush, well away from campsites. Always use biodegradable soap.

Wouldn't it be refreshing to arrive at a campground and find no evidence anyone had camped there before you? Do it for the next campers. Maybe someone will do it for you.

PRACTICAL STUFF

This is a how-to-get-there guidebook, not a how-to-do-it manual. You've probably camped many times and know what you need to take on a camping trip. It's not like backpacking, where you can haul only so much and you're a long way from a road. This is *car* camping. You can take whatever you want, or as much as your vehicle can hold. So, if you're not sure, just bring it. The more you camp, the better you'll get at keeping your load light and compact, without forgetting necessities. Until then, this list of practical stuff might be helpful.

• **Water.** Bring plenty. You'll almost never find a potable water source at a free campground.

• **Toilet paper, trowel, plastic bag.** FS campgrounds are basic, often referred to as primitive or rustic. Most have outhouses, which are usually stocked with toilet paper but not always. Bring a spare roll. Unofficial free campgrounds and overnight pullouts have no facilities whatsoever. There you'll need a trowel to bury your poop, and a plastic bag to hold used toilet paper.

• **Garbage bags.** Bring one for all your trash, and another to pick up after other campers less considerate than you.

• **Stove, fuel, matches.** Firewood might not be available. Besides, cooking over an open fire is difficult, time consuming and wasteful. Keep extra matches or a lighter in your vehicle.

• **Can Opener.** Ever try to open a can with a rock?

• **Flashlight and extra batteries.** You'll never see Tiki torches lining a cement walkway to a "comfort station" at a free campground. If you let your eyes adjust to the dark, it's surprising how well you can see without a flashlight. But there are times you'll need one.

B.C. STANDS FOR BEAR COUNTRY

The moment you leave any of B.C.'s major cities, you're in bear country. You can encounter a bruin anytime, anywhere—not just on remote hiking trails. Black bears are a common sight on backroads, even on some highways. Grizzly sightings are less frequent but always a possibility.

That doesn't mean bears are lurking behind every bush, stalking you, ready to pounce. They usually avoid human contact. They're generally calm, passive, shy. So don't be bearanoid. Just be practical.

Avoid inviting bears into your camp. Their strongest sense is smell, so never leave food untended. After you eat, keep leftovers sealed in plastic bags and containers, locked in your vehicle. At night, don't even leave your cooler out.

When walking, stay alert and make noise so you won't surprise a bear. Given sufficient warning, they'll usually depart before you see them. If startled, their instinctive response could be aggressive.

If you see a bear, don't look it in the eyes; it might think you're challenging it. Never run. Be still. If you must move, do it in

Keep your campsite clean. Food odours attract bears. This one's a grizzly.

slow motion. Bears are more likely to attack if you flee, and they're fast, much faster than humans. A grizzly can outsprint a racehorse. And it's a myth that bears can't run downhill. They're also capable swimmers. Remember: it's highly unlikely you'll provoke an attack as long as you stay calm, retreat slowly, and make soothing sounds to convey a nonthreatening presence.

What if a bear charges you?

Climbing a tree is an escape option. Some people have saved their lives this way, others have been caught in the process. Despite their ungainly appearance, bears are excellent climbers. To be out of reach of an adult bear, you'd have to climb at least 10 meters (33 feet), something few people are capable of. And you'd probably need to be at least two football fields from the bear to beat it up a tree.

Playing dead is debatable. It used to be the recommended response to a charge, but now some scientists, rangers and surviving victims say it might be better to fight back. It's your call. Every encounter involves different bears, people and circumstances, so the results vary. Even bear behaviour experts cannot suggest one all-purpose response technique. Black bears

Black bear looks both ways before crossing a highway in the West Kootenays.

can be intimidated if you fight back. Grizzlies tend to break off their attack if you remain totally passive. But quickly identifying a bear while under threat requires expertise. To learn more, read Dave Smith's *Backcountry Bear Basics*.

Rating System for Campgrounds and Backroads

Scenery and Recreation

You'll enjoy staying longer at campgrounds with better scenery and more recreation. So that's the basis for these ratings. Just keep higher-rated campgrounds in mind for short stays too, because they're not necessarily farther from pavement.

DESTINATION
You could spend your vacation here. If it's a long drive, it's worth it. The scenery and the campground are wonderful. The recreation is excellent and varied.

WEEKEND
A couple days here might be pleasant, but any longer and you'd want a prettier campground or more impressive scenery. Recreation is available but limited.

OVERNIGHT
Stop here for a convenient place to sleep, but that's it. Don't expect anything special. Something's lacking: either the scenery or the site itself is poor to mediocre.

Note: Nearly all FS campgrounds have tables, pit toilets, and fire rings. Our descriptions warn you where these are absent. Unofficial, free campgrounds and overnight pullouts have no facilities whatsoever.

Access

At a glance, these ratings tell you the distance to the campground, the quality of the road surfaces, and the patience needed to follow the directions.

EASY
Right under your nose. Mr. Magoo could find it. The road is smooth and the distance short—usually less than 10 km (6.2 mi) from pavement.

MODERATE
Just around the corner. Probably 10 to 20 km (6.2 to 12.4 mi) from pavement. There could be a few rough stretches.

DIFFICULT
Back of beyond. You must be patient and adventurous. The navigating is difficult, the roads challenging, or the distances longer—up to 30 km (18.6 mi) from pavement.

Maps

In addition to the overview map of camping regions, each chapter begins with a regional map indicating campground locations. Even the regional maps, however, are for general reference only. They were simplified to help you quickly assess campground locations in relation to each other, and to determine which ones are within range. But *Camp Free's* directions are very precise and should provide you with all necessary details.

Tripometer

When you read *Set your tripometer to 0* in the directions, push the button to reset your trip odometer to 0 at that point. Odometer readings on different vehicles vary. Mechanics say this might be the result of road jostling, tires that are not the manufacturer's specified size, or an imprecise odometer. So your distances might differ slightly from those in *Camp Free*. Just be looking for the turns or landmarks near the stated distances. If you encounter a discrepancy of 0.5 km (0.3 mi) or more, we apologize. That might be an error, in which case we welcome your suggested changes.

Recreation Site Numbers

FS campgrounds are officially referred to as Recreation Sites. Each FS district numbers their sites. The numbers are printed on FS recreation maps. *Camp Free* uses these same numbers, enabling you to read FS recreation maps in conjunction with this book. If FS districts issue new recreation maps with revised numbers, then the *Camp Free* numbers will differ. But within the book, that won't matter. The numbers will still be consistent on *Camp Free* maps and route descriptions.

"Got Everything? Okay, let's go."

Directions to the Campgrounds

Confusing but enticing network of backroads, Sunshine Coast

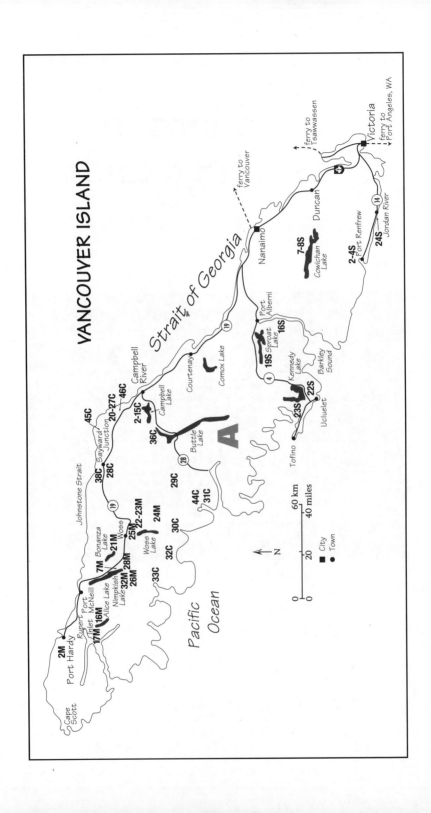

A: Vancouver Island

The letter indicates which FS district the campground is in. **S** stands for South Island FS District. **C** stands for Campbell River FS District. **M** stands for Port McNeill FS District.

2-10 C	Campbell Lake		23 S	Clayoquot Arm Beach
2 M	Georgie Lake		24 C	Pye Lake
2 S	Fairy Lake		24 M	Vernon Lake
3 S	San Juan Bridge		24 S	Jordan River
4 S	Lizard Lake		25 C	McCreight Lake
7 M	Kinman Creek		25 M	Woss Lake
7 S	Pine Point		26 C	Aldergrove
8 S	Maple Grove		26 M	Atluck Lake
11 C	Gray Lake		27 C	Sitka Spruce Beach
12 C	Merrill Lake		28 C	Elk Creek
13 C	Apple Point		28 M	Nimpish Lake
14 C	Brewster Lake		29 C	Muchalat Lake
15 C	Mohun Lake		30 C	Leiner River
16 M	Alice Lake		31 C	Cougar Creek
16 S	Arden Creek		32 C	Resolution Park
17 M	Marble River		32 M	Anutz Lake
19 S	Snow Creek		33 C	Fair Harbour
20 C	Stella Beach		36 C	Strathcona Dam
21 C	Little Bear Bay		38 C	Junction Pool
21 M	Bonanza Lake		42 C	Naka Creek
22 M	Lower Klaklakama Lake		44 C	Conuma River
22 S	Toquart Bay		45 C	Bear Creek
23 M	Upper Klaklakama Lake		46 C	Elk Bay

Vancouver Island

Vancouver Island harbours are certifiably picturesque.

Long, spectacular lakes here provide a wealth of recreation. It's definitely worth a special trip to visit the campgrounds rated Destination. Others don't justify a journey all the way from the Mainland, but they're fine if you're already traveling in the area.

Vancouver Island has been clearcut mercilessly. Witnessing this is valuable. It's an inspiration to conserve the world's few remaining ancient forests. Still, cutblocks are not visible from every campground on the Island. Beauty is still abundant and readily available, though not to the same awesome extent as in the Mainland's numerous, world-class mountain ranges.

VICTORIA TO PORT RENFREW

From downtown Vancouver, including the ferry ride to Schwartz Bay, it's about six hours to Port Renfrew. Victoria to Port Renfrew is an easy two-and-a-half hours. From Victoria, head southwest on Hwy 14. Set your tripometer to 0 in Colwood.

0 km (0 mi)
Starting southwest on Hwy 14 from Colwood, just west of Victoria.

26.1 km (16.2 mi)
Drive through Sooke, at the start of the West Coast Road. Proceed west along the shoreline, enjoying ocean views.

36.7 km (22.8 mi)
Reach Gordon's Beach, a good place to relax in the sun.

39.7 km (24.7 mi)
Cross a bridge and turn left. Pass an **overnight pullout** in a big, gravel lot.

48 km (29.8 mi)
Pass French Beach Provincial Park.

56 km (34.8 mi)
Pass the Sandcut trailhead.

57.8 km (35.9 mi)
Pass Jordan River **overnight pullout** on the left, at a WFP sign.

It's okay for a night's sleep if you arrive late, but it's not pleasant enough for a longer stay.

58.4 km (36.3 mi)
Arrive at Jordan River campground.

> Though little more than a gravel lot, this Western Forest Products campground is very popular. It has a front-row view across Juan de Fuca Strait, to the Olympic Mountains in Washington. You'll be lucky to find a vacant site here in summer. There are water faucets, but you must purify the water for drinking. Sites without tables are beyond the stand of trees, in another big, gravel lot, along the river's mouth.

JORDAN RIVER CAMPGROUND #24
Destination / Easy
10 drive-up tables, 6 tables in trees for tenters, more campsites
Accessible by motorhomes and 5th-wheels

Continuing west on Hwy 14, passing Jordan River campground.

62.8 km (39 mi)
Pass China Beach Provincial Park.

64.7 km (40.2 mi)
Pass Mystic Beach Trail (logged in the 1940's, planted in '46). Views of the Strait and the Olympics are now limited until Port Renfrew.

78.2 km (48.6 mi)
Attain a sweeping view of coastal forest in various logging stages. The bouncy, serpentine, paved road winds higher onto the hillsides. Several one-lane bridges require caution. You can safely average 50 kph (30 mph).

84.5 km (52.5 mi)
Ascend a hairpin turn.

85.5 km (53.1 mi)
Pass an **overnight pullout** on the left. The setting is dull, but there's an excellent view of the Strait and the Olympics.

95.6 km (59.4 mi)
Descend a long hill.

96.6 km (60 mi)
Enter Port Renfrew. Pass a sign for West Coast Trail information.

98.8 km (61.4 mi)
Pass signs for West Coast Trail information and Cowichan Lake. In Port Renfrew, Hwy 14 becomes Parkinson Street. Proceed to the fork and turn right to reach the Trailhead Store, where you can take a shower or do laundry.

PORT RENFREW TO COWICHAN LAKE

Highway 14 ends in Port Renfrew. You'll find more campgrounds northeast, en route to Cowichan Lake. Set your tripometer to 0 in Port Renfrew, at the sign for Cowichan Lake. Directions from Cowichan Lake southwest to Port Renfrew are on page 42.

If you're heading northeast from
Port Renfrew to Cowichan Lake

0 km (0 mi)
Starting on Deering Road, departing Port Renfrew, heading northeast toward Cowichan Lake. Cross a bridge in 300 meters.

0.6 km (0.4 mi)
Continue on the main road for FS campgrounds. Left enters private property owned by the Pacheenaht Band.

1.6 km (1 mi)
Reach a fork. Go right (northeast).

3.2 km (2 mi)
Turn right. Pass a Timber West sign: PUBLIC ROUTE, HARRIS CRK MAINLINE, FAIRY L CAMPSITE 3 KM, LIZARD L CAMPSITE 14 KM, MESACHIE L 52 KM. Mesachie Lake is near the east end of Cowichan Lake, so you can proceed on this road all the way to Hwy 18.

6.5 km (4 mi)
Arrive at Fairy Lake campground.

Although heavily used, the campground is large enough that a vacant site is likely. The lake itself is pleasant, but the scenery is mediocre. Clearcuts are visible. A sign warns that the area can flood during heavy rain.

FAIRY LAKE RECREATION SITE #2
Weekend / Moderate
Elev: 5 m (16 ft) / Lake: 0.8 km (0.5 mi) long, 32 ha
30 campsites, most with tables
Accessible by motorhomes and 5th-wheels

Continuing northeast on the main road, passing Fairy Lake campground.

12 km (7.4 mi)
Go right at the fork, staying on pavement, which soon lapses into rocky, bumpy dirt.

16.3 km (10.1 mi)
Reach a fork. Proceed left (following directions on page 41) for Lizard Lake campground, Mesachie Lake, and Cowichan Lake. Turn right and set your tripometer to 0 for San Juan campground.

0 km (0 mi)
Starting east, heading for San Juan Bridge campground.

0.3 km (0.2 mi)
Pass Lens Creek trailhead.

2.5 km (1.6 mi)
Go right at the fork, staying on the main road. A yellow sign warns this is a dead-end road. Williams Creek Bridge has been dismantled, but you're not going that far.

4 km (2.5 mi)
Descend a hill to the river.

4.5 km (2.8 mi)
Cross the bridge.

4.7 km (2.9 mi)
Arrive at San Juan Bridge campground, on the left.

Lizard Lake

The campsites are above a fine-gravel beach on the river. The shallow, slow water, and smooth, sandy riverbed invite wading. Shade is abundant. A mammoth Sitka Spruce enhances the setting.

SAN JUAN BRIDGE RECREATION SITE #3
Weekend / Moderate
5 well-spaced campsites, no tables
Accessible by motorhomes and 5th-wheels

Proceeding left at the 16.3-km (10.1-mile) junction, heading for Lizard Lake campground, Mesachie Lake, and Cowichan Lake.

17.9 km (11.1 mi)
Arrive at Lizard Lake campground.

The small lake has a sandy beach and deep, clear water. It's ringed by forest, but clearcut hillsides are visible beyond. This is a popular campground in summer.

LIZARD LAKE RECREATION SITE #4
Weekend / Moderate
Elev: 70 m (230 ft) / Lake: 10 ha
21 campsites with tables, 4 walk-in tentsites with tables
4 picnic tables, wharf
Accessible by motorhomes and 5th-wheels

Continuing north, passing Lizard Lake campground, heading for Mesachie Lake, Cowichan Lake, and Hwy 18.

22.7 km (14.1 mi)
Stay right at the fork. A creek is on your right.

33.5 km (20.8 mi)
Pass a sign: COWICHAN LAKE (24 KM) and a blue Fletcher Challenge sign: PORT RENFREW (33 KM).

47 km (29.1 mi)
Go right at the fork.

56.3 km (35 mi)
Reach a stop sign in the community of Mesachie Lake. Pavement resumes. Turn right for the town of Lake Cowichan.

If you're heading southwest from
Lake Cowichan to Port Renfrew

Follow Hwy 18 to the 3-way intersection on the east side of the town of Lake Cowichan. Drive 1.1 km (0.7 mi) into town and set your tripometer to 0 across from Central Park where the South and North Shore roads join. Notice the green highway sign for Mesachie Lake, Honeymoon Bay, and Youbou. Follow the signs straight (southwest) to Mesachie Lake.

0 km (0 mi)
Starting southwest on South Shore Road.

6.5 km (4 mi)
Reach the community of Mesachie Lake.

7 km (4.3 mi)
Pass a sign pointing left: PUBLIC ACCESS TO PORT RENFREW 53.
Turn left in 100 meters at the flashing yellow light.

For details about the route southwest to Port Renfrew, read the
northeast directions in reverse, starting at the 56.3-km (35-mi)
point. But the following summary should suffice. Set your
tripometer to 0 at the flashing yellow light in Mesachie Lake. In
9 km (5.5 mi), turn left at the fork. Reach **Lizard Lake campground** in about 38 km (23.5 mi). About 1.6 km (1 mi) beyond
Lizard Lake, go right at a junction; left leads to **San Juan
Bridge campground**. Stay left at the next junction to reach
Fairy Lake campground. From Fairy Lake it's 6.5 km (4 mi)
to Port Renfrew.

COWICHAN LAKE

East of Cowichan Lake is the scenic Cowichan River. It's worth
a detour to admire Skutz Falls. The area offers excellent hiking,
swimming and fishing. But free-camping was eliminated here
when BC Parks assumed authority over what were previously FS
campgrounds.

Cowichan Lake is one of Vancouver Island's largest. It's 31.5 km
(19.5 mi) long, 3.5 km (2.2 mi) wide, and covers 6214 hectares.
The elevation is 163 m (535 ft). On the north shore are two very
large FS campgrounds: Pine Point and Maple Grove. They're
close to one another and therefore similar, but Maple Grove is
more heavily treed and has a fine-gravel beach. Both have
charged per-night fees in the past.

Pine Point should be open May 1 through Thanksgiving. Maple
Grove is probably open May 1 only through September 30.
Keep in mind that these dates can change from year to year,
and the entrances to both campgrounds are gated.

It's possible to reach Cowichan Lake by driving northeast on
backroads from Port Renfrew, following directions on page 39.
Most people drive west on Hwy 18 from near Duncan, as
described here.

Cowichan Lake at sunset

If you're heading northwest or southeast on Hwy 1

From the junction of Hwys 1 and 18, northwest of Duncan, drive Hwy 18 west 26.2 km (16.2 mi) to the 3-way junction and map sign on the east side of Lake Cowichan community. Set your tripometer to 0.

0 km (0 mi)
Starting west on Hwy 18, heading toward Youbou, from the 3-way junction on the east side of Lake Cowichan community.

4.9 km (3 mi)
Cross a bridge over Meades Creek.

6.4 km (4 mi)
For Pine Point and Maple Grove campgrounds, stay straight (west) on Hwy 18. Proceed through Youbou and beyond the lumber mill. For **Spring Beach day-use area** on Cowichan Lake, turn left onto Meades Creek Road.

12.8 km (7.9 mi)
Turn left to enter Pine Point campground on Cowichan Lake. Stay straight for Maple Grove campground.

PINE POINT RECREATION SITE #7
Weekend / Easy
35 campsites with tables, boat launch
Accessible by motorhomes and 5th-wheels

Continuing west, passing the turnoff to Pine Point campground.

14.7 km (9.1 mi)
Turn left to enter Maple Grove campground on Cowichan Lake.

MAPLE GROVE RECREATION SITE #8
Weekend / Easy
35 campsites with tables, boat launch, fine-gravel beach
Accessible by motorhomes and 5th-wheels

SOUTH OF PORT ALBERNI

South of Port Alberni, the only reasonably accessible FS campground is Arden Creek, on Alberni Inlet. Even it requires you to travel a jittery road through grim country. The hills were never impressive, but logging has left them looking abused. Reaching the campground is a relief. It's a lovely haven, across the inlet from China Creek Provincial Park.

Arden Creek campground is small, accommodating only very modest RVs. Launching a cartop boat here is easy. And the inlet is often windy—ideal for boardsailing. When the winds die, be prepared for mosquitoes. Shade is plentiful, so this is a comfortable place to relax on a hot summer day. A short trail leads to a picnic site with a panoramic view of the inlet. As for noise, the campsites are well off the logging road, so industrial traffic is not annoying.

If you're heading west on Hwy 4 from Parksville

0 km (0 mi)
Starting west on Hwy 4, departing Hwy 19 southeast of Parksville.

47 km (29.2 mi)
Proceed west, passing the first turnoff to Port Alberni.

51.1 km (31.8 mi)
Turn into Port Alberni and head generally west through the city. At its west edge, pass a marina on the left and cross a cement bridge.

53.8 km (33.4 mi)
Cross a metal bridge over Somass River.

54 km (33.5 mi)
Turn left (south) onto paved Mission Road.

If you're heading east on Hwy 4 from Sproat Lake

Approaching the west side of Port Alberni, turn right (south) onto paved Mission Road. It's 200 meters before Hwy 4 crosses the metal bridge over Somass River. If you miss the turn and cross the bridge, you might have to continue 2.8 km (1.7 mi) east before you can safely turn around at the marina on the right.

For either approach above, now follow the directions below

0 km (0 mi)
Starting south on Mission Road. Immediately bear left.

0.5 km (0.3 mi)
Stay left on pavement. Ignore the right fork signed for Sproat Lake Woodlands Division.

2.1 km (1.3 mi)
Pavement ends.

2.4 km (1.5 mi)
Reach a fork. Go right and ascend. Follow the sign for Maktush and Nahmint lakes.

2.9 km (1.8 mi)
Go left at the fork. Pass more signs for Maktush Lake and Sproat Lake Woodlands.

Alberni Inlet, from Arden Creek campground

6 km (3.7 mi)
Turn left. Summit Road is right. The road improves, with fewer big, sharp rocks.

10.3 km (6.4 mi)
Go left at the junction. On the other side of the bridge, bear left again.

16.9 km (10.5 mi)
The road now parallels Alberni Inlet.

20.8 km (12.9 mi)
The road veers left. Turn left to enter Arden Creek campground.

ARDEN CREEK RECREATION SITE #16
Weekend / Difficult
4 tables, cartop boat launch
Accessible by small motorhomes but not trailers

WEST OF PORT ALBERNI

West of Port Alberni, Hwy 4 parallels the north side of Sproat Lake, then briefly follows the north bank of Taylor River. There used to be several unofficial campsites on the lake's northwest shore and along the river, but the access roads are now blocked for good reason. The gravel riverbank and lakeshore are prime spawning habitat for Coho and Sockeye salmon. Please do not camp there. Sproat Lake's FS campground is at Snow Creek, near the lake's west end, on the south shore.

After crossing the Taylor River bridge, Hwy 4 turns southwest. It winds through the MacKenzie Range and eventually passes Kennedy Lake. Southeast of the lake is a huge FS campground on Toquart Bay. On the lake's northwest shore is Clayoquot Arm Beach campground.

Beyond Kennedy Lake, Hwy 4 reaches a T-junction near the coast: turn right (northwest) for Pacific Rim National Park and Tofino, left (south) for Ucluelet or Port Albion. There are no FS campgrounds in either direction. That's unfortunate, because the Park and Tofino are very popular destinations.

Directions for driving Hwy 4 from the coast to Port Alberni are on page 53.

If you're heading west on Hwy 4 from Port Alberni

0 km (0 mi)
Starting west on Hwy 4, from the west edge of Port Alberni. Set your tripometer to 0 on the low cement bridge just past the marina. Follow signs for Sproat Lake.

40.6 km (25.2 mi)
After crossing the Taylor River bridge, proceed straight (west) on Hwy 4 (following directions on page 50) to reach Toquart Bay or Clayoquot Arm Beach campgrounds. For Snow Creek campground on Sproat Lake, turn left onto South Taylor Main FS road and set your tripometer to 0.

0 km (0 mi)
Starting east on South Taylor Main FS road, departing Hwy 4 just south of the Taylor River bridge.

Snow Creek campground on Sproat Lake

0.6 km (0.4 mi)
Bear left at the junction.

5 km (3.1 mi)
Reach a junction. Bear right (east) before the bridge and continue on South Taylor Main FS road.

9.7 km (6 mi)
Turn left to enter Snow Creek campground on Sproat Lake. A few campsites are in the open. Others are less appealing, off the lake, in scrubby trees.

SNOW CREEK RECREATION SITE #19
Weekend / Easy
Elev: 29 m (95 ft) / Lake: 23.3 km (14.5 mi) long
1.2 km (0.8 mi) average width, 4233 ha
2 tables, 7 campsites, rocky beach, rough boat launch
Accessible by small motorhomes and trailers

~

Continuing west on Hwy 4, passing the 40.6-km (25.2-mi) turnoff to Snow Creek campground and winding through the MacKenzie Range.

79.7 km (49.5 mi)
Proceed straight on Hwy 4 to reach Clayoquot Arm Beach campground; directions continue on page 51. Turn left and set your tripometer to 0 for Toquart Bay campground.

0 km (0 mi)
Starting east on Toquart Bay Road, departing Hwy 4.

4.2 km (2.6 mi)
Pass a brown signpost indicating Toquart Bay is straight ahead.

6.3 km (3.9 mi)
Stay straight, passing a right fork.

8 km (5 mi)
Pass Maggie Lake on the right.

16.1 km (10 mi)
Pass an **overnight pullout** on the right. It's treed and secluded, with a boat launch, log wharf, and room for three vehicles. Just beyond, Toquart Bay Road crosses a bridge.

16.3 km (10.1 mi)
Arrive at Toquart Bay campground.

Ocean kayaking and fishing are popular here. Expect a crowd. The campground is a huge, level clearing with room for 100 vehicles. A few campsites are treed, most are exposed, about 15 are on the waterfront.

TOQUART BAY RECREATION SITE #22
Destination / Moderate
28 tables, log pier, cement boat launch
Accessible by motorhomes and 5th-wheels

Toquart Bay campground

Continuing southwest on Hwy 4, passing the 79.7-km (49.5-mi) turnoff to Toquart Bay campground.

81.8 km (50.8 mi)
Pass a pullout on the right, just after a bridge.

83.7 km (52 mi)
Pass a boat launch on the right.

90.6 km (56.3 mi)
Proceed straight on Hwy 4 to reach Pacific Rim National Park, Tofino, Ucluelet, or Port Albion. Turn right onto West Main FS road and set your tripometer to 0 for Clayoquot Arm Beach campground. This major logging road is well after Hwy 4 leaves the shore of Kennedy Lake.

0 km (0 mi)
Starting north on West Main FS road, departing Hwy 4, heading for Clayoquot Arm Beach campground.

2.3 km (1.4 mi)
Bear right at a one-way sign.

6 km (3.7 mi)
Stay right at the junction.

9 km (5.6 mi)
Bear right where Grice Bay Road forks left.

12 km (7.4 mi)
Cross a big bridge over Kennedy River. Ignore Lost Lake Road. Immediately turn right, onto Clayoquot Arm Road.

12.5 km (7.8 mi)
Pass Clayoquot Arm Beach Provincial Forest Recreation Site. There's a parking lot on the left, a nature trail on the right.

13 km (8.1 mi)
Arrive at Clayoquot Arm Beach campground, at the end of the cove, just before the long bridge over Clayoquot Arm.

The campsites string along a treeless, sandy beach. Expect a crowd. Canoeing is popular here. Nearby, conservationists and loggers fought a protracted, publicized battle. Preserving the world's few remaining great forests is vital. This one has been marred forever by clearcutting.

CLAYOQUOT ARM BEACH RECREATION SITE #23
Weekend / Moderate
Lake: 29 km (18 mi) long, 6542 ha
10 campsites, no tables
Accessible by motorhomes and 5th-wheels

If you're heading northeast on Hwy 4 from the coast

0 km (0 mi)
Starting northeast on Hwy 4, from Tofino - Ucluelet Junction, heading for Clayoquot Arm Beach campground, Toquart Bay campground, Snow Creek campground on Sproat Lake, or Port Alberni.

Kennedy Lake's Clayoquot Arm

1.6 km (1 mi)
Turn left onto West Main FS road (following directions on page 52) for **Clayoquot Arm Beach campground**.

10.5 km (6.5 mi)
Pass a pullout on the left, just before a bridge.

12.5 km (7.8 mi)
Turn right (following directions on page 50) for **Toquart Bay campground.**

51.6 km (32.1 mi)
After winding through the MacKenzie Range, Hwy 4 crosses the Taylor River bridge and proceeds west to Port Alberni. Just before the Taylor River bridge, turn right onto South Taylor Main FS road (following directions on page 48) for **Snow Creek campground** on Sproat Lake.

92.2 km (57.3 mi)
Arrive in Port Alberni, near the marina.

WEST OF CAMPBELL RIVER

The hills just west of the town of Campbell River are splashed with lakes. Cozied up to their shores are a couple dozen FS campgrounds. Of the dozen or so described here, nearly half are on Campbell Lake. It's sprawling: 18 km (11.2 mi) long, up to 7.5 km (4.7 mi) wide, covering 2147 hectares, at 178 m (585 ft) elevation. But you don't need a boat or even a fishing rod to enjoy it. Just dive in. The clear, comfortably-cool water is a swimmer's delight. Other campgrounds described here are on smaller lakes just west and north of Campbell Lake. The entire area is popular, so solitude is elusive, but there seems to be enough campgrounds to comfortably absorb all the campers.

You have a choice of access routes. This one is the most direct. It starts on the west edge of Campbell River, heads generally west along the north shore of Campbell Lake, then loops back east to intersect Hwy 19 about 14.8 km (9.2 mi) northwest of town. Excluded from the loop route description, however, is Strathcona Dam campground. Though it's near the loop, the easiest access is directly off Hwy 28, farther west from Campbell River. So Strathcona Dam campground is described separately, on page 59.

If you're heading north or south on Hwy 19

Set your tripometer to 0 at the junction of Hwys 19 and 28. Drive west on Hwy 28. After crossing the river, enter Elk Falls Park at 1.6 km (1 mi).

At 4.4 km (2.7 mi) turn right, following the sign for Loveland Bay Park, and reset your tripometer to 0. Hwy 28 proceeds left (southwest) to Strathcona Park, Gold River, and the coast. Page 60 describes remote campgrounds in that direction.

0 km (0 mi)
Starting northwest toward Loveland Bay Park, departing Hwy 28.

0.5 km (0.3 mi)
Cross above the Campbell River at John Hart Dam. Curve left around John Hart Lake. Follow the paved road until the next junction.

Campbell Lake

2 km (1.2 mi)
Turn left onto gravel at the brown sign: LOVELAND BAY PROVINCIAL PARK 10.5 KM.

3 km (1.8 mi)
Go left at the fork signed for Snowden Forest and Campbell Lake. Continue on well-graded gravel.

9.8 km (6.1 mi)
Proceed straight (west) for most of the area's campgrounds. Turn left (south) for Big Bay campground on Campbell Lake.

BIG BAY RECREATION SITE #1
Weekend / Easy
10 tables, gravel beach
Accessible by small motorhomes and trailers

12.7 km (7.9 mi)
Pass Loveland Bay Provincial Park.

13.1 km (8.1 mi)
Turn sharply left (south) onto Sayward FS road. Pass a sign for Snowden Demonstration Forest. (What a laughable concept. How about a Demonstration Ancient Forest? That wouldn't need a sign. The awesome giants themselves would stop everyone in their tracks.)

15.6 km (9.7 mi)
Proceed on the main road for most of the area's campgrounds. Right soon leads to Gosling Lake campground, on the left.

GOSLING LAKE RECREATION SITE #3
Weekend / Easy
Elev: 225 m (738 ft) / Lake: 3 km (1.9 mi) long, 69.5 ha
4 tables, small float
Accessible by small motorhomes and trailers

18.4 km (11.4 mi)
Proceed on the main road for most of the area's campgrounds. Turn left to reach Gosling Bay campground in 0.5 km (0.3 mi). It has a beautiful, rocky beach, and a grand view across the widest part of Campbell Lake.

GOSLING BAY RECREATION SITE #2
Destination / Easy
7 tables, rough boat launch
Accessible by motorhomes and 5th-wheels

19.3 km (12 mi)
Proceed on the main road for most of the area's campgrounds. Left descends to fully-treed Fir Grove campground on Campbell Lake.

FIR GROVE RECREATION SITE #4
Weekend / Moderate
3 tables, rocky beach
Accessible by small motorhomes and trailers

22.2 km (13.8 mi)
Proceed on the main road for more campgrounds. Turn left for Campbell Lake campground. It has grassy areas, plentiful shade, and a view of the mainland Coast Mountains.

CAMPBELL LAKE RECREATION SITE #6
Destination / Moderate
20 tables, rocky beach
Accessible by motorhomes and 5th-wheels

~

23 km (14.3 mi)
Proceed on the main road for more campgrounds. Turn left for Dogwood Bay campground. It's less appealing than others on Campbell Lake, because the campsites are grouped closely at a circular pullout.

DOGWOOD BAY RECREATION SITE #7
Weekend / Moderate
3 tables, 4 campsites, boat launch, sand/gravel beach
Accessible by motorhomes and 5th-wheels

~

24 km (14.9 mi)
Proceed on the main road for more campgrounds. Turn left for Loon Bay campground on Campbell Lake.

LOON BAY RECREATION SITE #9
Weekend / Moderate
10 campsites, sandy beach at low water
Accessible by motorhomes and 5th-wheels

~

26.5 (16.4 mi)
Proceed on the main road for more campgrounds. Turn left for Fry Lake campground.

FRY LAKE RECREATION SITE #9b
Weekend / Moderate
Elev: 170 m (558 ft) / Lake: 68 ha
5 tables, beach, rough boat launch
Inaccessible by motorhomes and trailers

~

27 km (16.8 mi)
Proceed on the main road for more campgrounds. Turn left for Orchard Meadow campground on Fry Lake. After descending, go right to find intimate campsites on a narrow arm.

ORCHARD MEADOW RECREATION SITE #10
Weekend / Moderate
6 tables, many more campsites, boat launch
Accessible by motorhomes and 5th-wheels

28.3 km (17.5 mi)
Reach a junction. Proceed straight (north) on the main road.

30.3 km (18.8 mi)
Proceed on the main road for more campgrounds. Turn left to reach Gray Lake campground in 300 meters. The sites are cramped.

GRAY LAKE RECREATION SITE #11
Weekend / Difficult (due only to distance)
Elev: 170 m (558 ft) / Lake: 4 km (2.5 mi) long, 55 ha
5 tables, boat launch
Not suitable for motorhomes and 5th-wheels

31 km (19.2 mi) to **33 km (20.5 mi)**
Watch left for two new campgrounds. **Brittany Bay Recreation Site**, on Gray Lake, has three tables. **Brewster Camp Recreation Site**, on the channel between Gray and Brewster Lakes, has seven tables.

33.6 km (20.9 mi)
Reach a junction. Go straight onto a wide main road, staying on the east side of Brewster Lake. Apple Point campground is on the shore, beside the road.

APPLE POINT RECREATION SITE #13
Weekend / Difficult (due only to distance)
Elev: 213 m (700 ft) / Lake: 5.3 km (3.3 mi) long, 480 ha
6 tables, boat launch
Accessible by motorhomes and 5th-wheels

39.4 km (24.5 mi)
Proceed east on the main road for Hwy 19. Turn left to enter Mohun Lake campground.

MOHUN LAKE RECREATION SITE #15
Weekend / Difficult (due only to distance)
Elev: 198 m (650 ft) / Lake: 9.5 km (6 mi) long, 612 ha
2 tables, cement boat launch
Accessible by motorhomes and 5th-wheels

41 km (25.5 mi)
Proceed east on the main road for Hwy 19. Left leads north to Morton Lake Provincial Park.

51 km (31.5 mi)
Reach Hwy 19, at the Mac Blo Menzies Bay Division. Campbell River is right (southeast). Turn left for campgrounds northwest of Campbell River.

For Strathcona Dam, now follow the directions below

From the junction of Hwys 19 and 28, drive Hwy 28 west, then southwest. In about 29 km (18 mi) turn right (north) onto Strathcona Dam Road to reach the BC-Hydro-managed campground in about 4 km (2.5 mi). It's below the dam retaining Upper Campbell Lake, at the southwest tip of Lower Campbell Lake.

STRATHCONA DAM CAMPGROUND #36
Weekend / Easy
11 tables, small beach, boat launch, garbage cans
Accessible by motorhomes and 5th-wheels

WEST OF STRATHCONA PARK

From the junction of Hwys 19 and 28, on the west edge of the town of Campbell River, Hwy 28 heads generally southwest all the way to the coast. It reaches Strathcona Provincial Park in about 50 km (31 mi), the village of Gold River in about 90 km (56 mi), and finally the west end of Muchalat Inlet in about 105 km (65 mi).

Past Gold River and beyond the scope of this book are four FS campgrounds reached via remote logging roads. If the following brief descriptions intrigue you, and you're willing to drive the entire width of Vancouver Island for an adventurous camping experience, ask if a recreation map is available for Campbell River Forest District. The phone number and address is in the back of this book. These campgrounds are 2WD accessible and able to accommodate big RVs.

Near the north end of Tahsis Inlet, about 60 km (37 mi) beyond Gold River, is the farthest of these campgrounds: **Leiner River Recreation Site #30**. It's treed, near a swimming hole, and has room for up to 10 vehicles.

Conuma River Recreation Site #44 is a small campground on the riverbank near the north end of Tlupana Inlet. You can watch black bears feeding on salmon here each fall.

The biggest of these campgrounds is **Cougar Creek Recreation Site #31**, on the east side of Tlupana Inlet. It has a float, gravel boat launch, extensive docks, and room for up to 50 vehicles. On a map, the location looks lonely. It's not. Expect to see a fleet of RVs here in summer.

On the east end of Muchalat Lake, about 16 km (10 mi) north-west of Gold River, is the nearest of these campgrounds: **Muchalat Lake Recreation Site #29**. It has a float, boat launch, gravel and sand beaches, and room for up to 20 vehicles. The lake is 6.5 km (4 mi) long and covers 531 hectares, at 200 m (656 ft) elevation.

Rock Bay on Johnstone Strait, near Little Bear Bay campground

NORTHWEST OF CAMPBELL RIVER

The country northwest of Campbell River is exciting. More mountainous than the area around Campbell Lake, it looks wilder, despite all the second-growth forest. Many campgrounds here feel secluded yet are easily and quickly reached.

McCreight Lake is rated Destination. The well-spaced campsites are in lush forest, on a bench above the rocky shore. Scramble down to the clear water for a refreshing swim. The lake is just the right size, and the setting beautiful enough, that canoeists can enjoy exploring it all. McCreight is 5 km (3 mi) long, 0.8 km (0.5 mi) wide, and covers 275 hectares.

Past McCreight is another Destination campground: Little Bear Bay. Though small and usually crowded, the location is idyllic. From here, boaters can venture into Johnstone Strait and numerous channels.

South of Little Bear Bay is Elk Bay campground, also on Johnstone Strait. It's described separately, on page 65, because the direct access is different than for campgrounds en route to Little Bear Bay.

If you're heading northwest
on Hwy 19 from Campbell River

From the junction of Hwys 19 and 28, drive Hwy 19 northwest 41 km (25.5 mi). Turn right (north) onto Rock Bay Road and set your tripometer to 0. (It's 3.4 km / 2.1 mi past Pye Lake West FS road, and 200 meters before the bridge over Amor De Cosmos Creek.)

If you're heading southeast
on Hwy 19 from Sayward Junction

From Sayward Junction, drive Hwy 19 southeast 24 km (15 mi). Turn left (north) onto Rock Bay Road and set your tripometer to 0. (It's 200 meters past the bridge over Amor De Cosmos Creek.)

For either approach above, now follow the directions below

0 km (0 mi)
Starting north on Rock Bay Road, departing Hwy 19. Expect potholes all the way to Rock Bay on Johnstone Strait.

3 km (1.8 mi)
Reach a pullout on the left. A short path leads to Sitka Spruce Beach campground.

> For tenters only, this small campground is on a beach at the south end of McCreight Lake. The view north is stirring. Behind the beach is a lovely hemlock-and-cedar forest.

SITKA SPRUCE BEACH RECREATION SITE #27
Destination / Easy
Several campsites for tenters only, sandy beach, no tables
Footpath accessible by all vehicles

Continuing north on the main road, passing the pullout for Sitka Spruce Beach campground.

3.3 km (2 mi)
Proceed straight (north) for campgrounds at McCreight Lake, Bear Creek, Pye Lake, Stella Lake, Little Bear Bay, and for Rock Bay. Turn left for Aldergrove campground.

Near the south end of McCreight Lake, this tiny, treed campground is on an old, logging railroad grade. The lake is not visible from the campsites, but a trail leads to a sandy beach.

ALDERGROVE RECREATION SITE #26
Weekend / Easy
2 tables, trail to sandy beach
Accessible by small motorhomes and trailers

~~

Continuing north on the main road, passing the turnoff to Aldergrove campground.

4 km (2.4 mi)
Proceed straight (northeast) for campgrounds at Bear Creek, Pye Lake, Stella Lake, Little Bear Bay, and for Rock Bay. Turn left to enter McCreight Lake campground.

McCREIGHT LAKE RECREATION SITE #25
Destination / Easy
2 tables, 3 well-spaced campsites, rough boat launch
Accessible by small motorhomes and trailers

~~

Continuing northeast on the main road, passing the turnoff to McCreight Lake campground.

7.8 km (4.8 mi)
Proceed right (northeast) for campgrounds at Pye Lake, Stella Lake, Little Bear Bay, and for Rock Bay. Turn left (north) onto Bear Bite Road to reach Bear Creek campground, on the left, in about 5 km (3.1 mi).

BEAR CREEK RECREATION SITE #45
Weekend / Moderate
5 tables
Inaccessible by motorhomes and trailers

~~

Continuing northeast on the main road, passing the turnoff to Bear Creek campground.

9 km (5.6 mi)

Proceed straight (east) for campgrounds at Stella Lake and Little Bear Bay, and for Rock Bay. Right (south) leads to Pye Lake campground in a couple kilometers. It's also accessible from Hwy 19, via Pye Lake West FS road, 3.4 km (2.1 mi) east of Rock Bay Road. Both approaches are rough.

PYE LAKE RECREATION SITE #24
Weekend / Moderate
Elev: 150 m (492 ft) / Lake: 4 km (2.5 mi) long, 370 ha
4 tables, small beach
Inaccessible by motorhomes and 5th-wheels

Continuing east on the main road, passing the turnoff to Pye Lake campground.

11.3 km (7 mi) and 13 km (8.1 mi)

Proceed straight.

14.1 km (8.7 mi)

Proceed straight (northeast) for Little Bear Bay campground and Rock Bay. Turn right (southeast) to reach Stella Beach campground in about 5 km (3.1 mi), and Stella Bay campground just beyond.

Both campgrounds are on Stella Lake, at 150 m (392 ft) elevation. The lake is 6 km (3.7 mi) long and covers 422 hectares. These campgrounds are also accessible en route to Elk Bay campground (page 65).

STELLA BEACH RECREATION SITE #20a
Weekend / Moderate
10 tables, sandy beach, boat launch
Accessible by small motorhomes and trailers

STELLA BAY RECREATION SITE #20b
Weekend / Moderate
2 tables, small sandy beach, boat launch
Too small for motorhomes and trailers

Continuing northeast on the main road, passing the turnoff to the Stella Lake campgrounds.

16.7 km (10.4 mi)
Reach a junction. Turn left and descend toward the fish hatchery for Little Bear Bay campground. (Right, then left at 18.2 km / 11.3 mi, quickly leads to a commercial campground and small marina on Rock Bay.)

17.5 km (10.9 mi)
Go right to enter Little Bear Bay campground. A river flows into Johnstone Strait here. The setting is beautiful. The campground is often full.

LITTLE BEAR BAY RECREATION SITE #21
Destination / Moderate
10 tables, grassy area, rough boat launch, short trail to waterfall
Accessible by small motorhomes and trailers

For ELK BAY, now follow the directions below

From the junction of Hwys 19 and 28, drive Hwy 19 northwest 32.8 km (20.3 mi). Or, from Sayward Junction, drive Hwy 19 southeast 32.2 km (20 mi). From either approach turn northeast onto Elk Bay Road and set your tripometer to 0. At 11.3 km (7 mi) reach a T-junction. Left (northwest) soon passes the Stella Lake campgrounds (described on page 64) and later intersects Rock Bay Road. Turn right (southeast). At 14.5 km (9 mi) reach the Elk Bay log dump and turn right (south). At 15.2 km (9.4 mi) reach the main Elk Bay campground. A smaller, second camping area is 400 meters farther, across the creek.

ELK BAY RECREATION SITE #46
Weekend / Moderate
7 tables, rough boat launch
Accessible by small motorhomes and trailers

NORTHWEST OF SAYWARD JUNCTION

Sayward Junction is on Hwy 19, about midway between Campbell River and Woss. A road leads north from here to the village of Sayward, on Johnstone Strait, but it accesses no FS campgrounds. Sayward Junction is just an easily identified waypoint for directional purposes.

A couple minutes northwest of Sayward Junction, just off Hwy 19, is Elk Creek campground. It's very handy for a night's sleep but has little appeal in daylight.

Near where Hwy 19 veers southwest toward Woss, you can head north on a logging road to two more campgrounds. The first, Junction Pool, is by the confluence of Adam and Eve rivers. Beyond is Naka Creek, on Johnstone Strait.

If you're heading northwest
on Hwy 19 from Sayward Junction

0 km (0 mi)
Starting northwest on Hwy 19 from Sayward Junction. You'll see signs here for camping and whale watching at Robson Bight.

0.5 km (0.3 mi)
Proceed northwest on Hwy 19 for Woss, or Junction Pool and Naka Creek campgrounds. Turn left (south) for Elk Creek campground. It's directly across from a white sign: Aircraft Patrolled. It's also 200 meters before Lower Elk Creek bridge.

Just 0.3 km (0.2 mi) off pavement, the campsites are deep in trees, without views. The creek is often just a dribble.

ELK CREEK RECREATION SITE #28
Overnight / Easy
10 tables
Accessible by small motorhomes and trailers

Continuing northwest on Hwy 19, passing the turnoff to Elk Creek campground. Cross the Adam River bridge, proceed beneath the underpass and descend the 3-lane hill.

32 km (19.8 mi)
Proceed southwest on Hwy 19 for Woss. For Junction Pool and Naka Creek campgrounds, turn right (north) onto South Main road and set your tripometer to 0 at the huge log sign: EVE RIVER DIVISION.

0 km (0 mi)
Starting north on South Main, heading for Junction Pool and Naka Creek campgrounds. Cross two small bridged creeks, pass fish farm tanks on the right, and reach a fork. There's a bridge to the left. Go right here on East Main road. Follow it to a stop sign, where you turn left and descend. Cross a bridge over Eve River. Junction Pool campground is a few minutes farther, on the right, near the confluence of Adam and Eve rivers, about 15 km (9.3 mi) from Hwy 19.

JUNCTION POOL RECREATION SITE #38
Weekend / Moderate
10 tables
Accessible by motorhomes and 5th-wheels

Continuing north on the main road, passing Junction Pool campground.

Soon skirt the Mac Blo mechanical shop. A few minutes farther, turn onto Naka Main road. Follow it generally northwest to reach Naka Creek campground in about 20 minutes. It's on Johnstone Strait, near Naka Creek logging camp.

NAKA CREEK RECREATION SITE #42
Weekend / Difficult (due only to distance)
7 tables
Accessible by small motorhomes and trailers

If you're heading east on Hwy 19 from Woss

0 km (0 mi)
Starting east on Hwy 19 from the Woss turnoff. Set your tripometer to 0.

35 km (21.7 mi)
Proceed east on Hwy 19 for Elk Creek campground near Sayward Junction. For **Junction Pool and Naka Creek campgrounds**, turn left (north) onto South Main road and set your tripometer to 0 at the huge log sign: EVE RIVER DIVISION; directions continue on page 67.

66.6 km (41.3 mi)
Turn right (south) for **Elk Creek campground.** It's 200 meters past Lower Elk Creek bridge. It's also directly across from a white sign: Aircraft Patrolled. The campground is just 0.3 km (0.2 mi) off pavement. Read pages 66-67 for details.

67.1 km (41.6 mi)
Reach Sayward Junction. Proceed southeast on Hwy 19 (following directions on page 62) for campgrounds northwest of Campbell River.

SOUTH OF WOSS

To be precise, only Woss Lake campground is directly south of the community of Woss. The other three campgrounds described here are slightly east, but all are in the same area, south of Hwy 19.

Woss Lake campground is big, on a sheltered cove with a sandy beach and a float. Swimmers love it. Pleasant enough to be rated Weekend, it's also close enough to the highway to be convenient for overnight use.

Woss Lake

Two small campgrounds are on Klaklakama Lake—one at the north (lower) end, the other at the south (upper) end. Both are quickly and easily reached from the highway, and neither is special, so they're rated Overnight. But they could be enjoyable for a weekend.

Well south of Klaklakama Lake is another, much larger campground at the north end of Vernon Lake, where you might not be so pressed by other campers.

If you're heading west on Hwy 19 from Sayward Junction

For Klaklakama Lake, turn left (south) off Hwy 19 about 55.7 km (34.6 mi) west of Sayward Junction. This is also the signed west access for Schoen Lake Provincial Park.

For Woss Lake, turn left (south) off Hwy 19 about 66.7 km (41.4 mi) west of Sayward Junction. The turn is signed for the community of Woss.

The distance on Hwy 19 between the turnoffs for Klaklakama and Woss lakes is about 11 km (6.8 mi).

If you're heading southeast on Hwy 19
from Port McNeill

For Woss Lake, turn right (south) off Hwy 19 about 64.7 km (40 mi) southeast of Port McNeill. The turn is signed for the community of Woss.

For Klaklakama Lake, turn right (south) off Hwy 19 about 75.7 km (47 mi) southeast of Port McNeill. This is also the signed west access for Schoen Lake Provincial Park.

The distance on Hwy 19 between the turnoffs for Woss and Klaklakama lakes is about 11 km (6.8 mi).

For KLAKLAKAMA LAKE, now follow the directions below

0 km (0 mi)
Starting south, departing Hwy 19. Set your tripometer to 0.

0.3 km (0.2 mi)
Go right at the wide Y-junction. Left leads to Schoen Lake Park. Soon cross a bridge and curve right.

1 km (0.6 mi)
Reach a fork. Stay left on the main road.

2.6 km (1.6 mi)
Bear right (south) for Upper Klaklakama Lake campground. Turn left (east) to reach Lower Klaklakama Lake campground in about 1.1 km (0.7 mi), on the right.

Scruffy, second-growth forest offers little shade here. You can swim from the rocky beach. The lake itself is pleasant, but the clearcut hills are unsightly. Two campsites are on the shore.

LOWER KLAKLAKAMA LAKE RECREATION SITE #22
Overnight / Easy
Elev: 293 m (535 ft) / Lake: 4.3 km (2.6 mi) long, 255 ha
5 tables, rocky beach
Accessible by small motorhomes and trailers

Continuing south from the 2.6-km (1.6-mi) junction, passing the turnoff to Lower Klaklakama Lake campground.

7 km (4.3 mi)
Reach Upper Klaklakama Lake campground.

Views of clearcuts are worse here than at the lower campground, but the campsites are more private. Three are on the shore. Also, several huge trees are still standing—a reminder that Vancouver Island was once covered by glorious, ancient monarchs.

UPPER KLAKLAKAMA LAKE RECREATION SITE #23
Overnight / Easy
Elev: 293 m (535 ft) / Lake: 4.3 km (2.6 mi) long, 255 ha
4 tables, sandy beach, boat launch
Accessible by small motorhomes and trailers

~

Continuing south from Upper Klaklakama Lake campground.

About 16 km (9.9 mi) beyond Upper Klaklakama Lake campground is a much larger campground at the north end of Vernon Lake. Get there by proceeding generally south on the main road. Immediately after crossing a bridge over Nimpkish River, reach a junction. Turn right (northwest). After the road curves south again, bear left at the next major junction and continue south, soon reaching the lake.

VERNON LAKE RECREATION SITE #24
Weekend / Moderate
Elev: 221 m (725 ft) / Lake: 7 km (4.3 mi) long, 802 ha
20 tables, boat launch
Accessible by motorhomes and 5th-wheels

~

For WOSS LAKE, now follow the directions below

0 km (0 mi)
Starting south, departing Hwy 19. Set your tripometer to 0.

0.7 km (0.4 mi)
Cross railroad tracks.

1.1 km (0.7 mi)
Cross railroad tracks again and immediately curve right. Turn left on S. Railway Avenue. Cross the bridge and go right. (Just after the bridge, left follows the Nimpkish River Valley about 22 km / 13.6 mi to Vernon Lake campground—described on page 71.)

4.3 km (2.7 mi)
Fork left.

4.6 km (2.9 mi)
Fork right to enter Woss Lake campground.

> A sheltered cove, a float, and a sandy beach make this a great place to swim. The campsites are close together, near the north end of the lake. Clearcuts glare at you across the cove.

WOSS LAKE RECREATION SITE #25
Weekend / Easy
Elev: 150 m (492 ft) / Lake: 16.2 km (10 mi) long
1 km (0.6 mi) wide, 1378 ha
20 tables, sandy beach, boat launch
Accessible by motorhomes and 5th-wheels

WOSS TO PORT MCNEILL

Several superior campgrounds are located on inviting lakes very close to Hwy 19 between Woss and Port McNeill.

Bonanza Lake (10.5 km / 6.5 mi long) is longer than McCreight Lake, but shorter than Woss Lake or giant Nimpkish Lake (25.5 km / 15.8 mi long). The large, pleasant campground on Bonanza Lake's south shore is rated Destination. It has a spacious, sandy beach where you can swim and enjoy a grand view. The campsites are in cedar-and-hemlock forest. There are two ways to access Bonanza Lake. The south approach, described here, takes only about 15 minutes on good road. The north approach, from Telegraph Cove, passes two small FS campgrounds (Ida Lake and Bonanza North), but it's longer and the road rougher.

Nimpkish Lake

Just south of Nimpkish Lake is small Anutz Lake. On its south shore is a large, open, grassy campground provided by Canadian Forest Products. Atluck Lake (5.8 km / 3.6 mi long), south of Anutz, is about the same size as Klaklakama Lake. The campground at its north end is small and partially treed. Beyond Atluck, a logging road continues way south to two campgrounds (described on page 76) near isolated settlements on West Coast inlets.

Nimpkish Lake, beneath sweeping mountainsides, is stunning. It has two Destination-rated campgrounds a short way off the highway. Both are ideal for a convenient overnight stop or a multi-day retreat. Strong, dependable winds make this a fine boardsailing lake. You can also just sit on the beach and lose yourself in the exciting scenery.

Kinman Creek campground is in forest, high above Nimpkish Lake. You can reach the shore by walking about a kilometer down a wide gravel path. A benefit of the campground's distance from the lake is that the stony beach feels wild. The campground itself is provincial-park quality. It was thoughtfully planned and is well maintained. Campsites are comfortably spaced among tall trees.

Nimpkish Lake campground, as the name suggests, is right on the lake. Most of the campsites are along the shore and have lakeviews. It's grassy here, with a treed hillside behind. The sites offer less privacy than those at Kinman, and they're exposed to the lake's frequently strong winds, but the scenery compensates.

If you're heading northwest on Hwy 19 from Woss

For Bonanza Lake, turn right (east) off Hwy 19 just south of the Steele Creek bridge, about 21.5 km (13.3 mi) northwest of Woss.

For Anutz and Atluck lakes, turn left (west) off Hwy 19 just north of the Steele Creek bridge, about 21.7 km (13.5 mi) northwest of Woss. The turnoff is signed for Zeballos.

For Kinman Creek and Nimpkish Lake, turn left (west) off Hwy 19 about 30.5 km (18.9 mi) northwest of Woss.

If you're heading southeast on Hwy 19 from Port McNeill

For Kinman Creek and Nimpkish Lake, turn right (west) off Hwy 19 about 34.2 km (21.2 mi) southeast of Port McNeill.

For Anutz and Atluck lakes, turn right (west) off Hwy 19 just north of the Steele Creek bridge, about 43 km (26.7 mi) southeast of Port McNeill. The turnoff is signed for Zeballos.

For Bonanza Lake, turn left (east) off Hwy 19 just south of the Steele Creek bridge, about 43.2 km (26.8 mi) southeast of Port McNeill.

For BONANZA LAKE, now follow the directions below

0 km (0 mi)
Starting east, departing Hwy 19. Set your tripometer to 0. Cross railroad tracks and curve right. Do not drive left over the railroad trestle bridge. Ignore the right fork.

1.5 km (0.9 mi)
Bear left. At subsequent minor forks, stay straight on the main road. The trees here are about 30 years old—mere infants. The lower half of the mountain slopes have been logged and replanted the entire length of the valley.

13.7 km (8.5 mi)
Bonanza Lake is visible.

15.3 km (9.5 mi)
Bear left and cross the Bonanza River bridge.

16 km (9.9 mi)
Just before a Forest Fire Hazard sign, turn left and descend for Bonanza Lake campground. The main road continues north along Bonanza Lake's east shore, passing tiny **Bonanza Lake North Recreation Site #20** and small **Ida Lake Recreation Site #19** en route to Telegraph Cove.

16.3 km (10.1 mi)
Arrive at Bonanza Lake campground.

BONANZA LAKE SOUTH RECREATION SITE #21
Destination / Moderate
Elev: 267 m (876 ft) / Lake: 10.5 km (6.5 mi) long
1.3 km (0.8 mi) wide, 896 ha
10 tables, sandy beach, rough boat launch
Accessible by small motorhomes and trailers

**For ANUTZ and ATLUCK LAKES,
now follow the directions below**

0 km (0 mi)
Starting west, departing Hwy 19. Set your tripometer to 0. The road immediately bends northwest, paralleling the highway.

1.3 km (0.8 mi)
Bear left on the main road. Proceed straight at the next two minor forks.

2 km (1.2 mi)
Cross a high bridge over Nimpkish River.

2.4 km (1.5 mi)
Stay straight.

2.8 km (1.7 mi)
Go right.

3.1 km (1.9 mi)
Reach a junction. Turn right (north) for Anutz Lake campground; directions continue on page 77. Turn left (south) for Atluck Lake campground or to continue way south to remote campgrounds on two West Coast inlets.

Atluck Lake campground is about 10 km (6.2 mi) beyond the 3.1-km (1.9-mi) junction. Stay on the main road, then turn right (west) just north of Wolfe Lake, where the main road proceeds south to Zeballos. Shortly after crossing Atluck Creek, stay straight where right returns north to Anutz Lake. Soon reach the campground on Atluck Lake's north shore.

ATLUCK LAKE RECREATION SITE #26
Weekend / Moderate
Elev: 134 m (440 ft) / Lake: 5.8 km (3.6 mi) long, 278 ha
5 tables, gravel beach
Accessible by small motorhomes and trailers

Continuing south on the main road to Zeballos, passing the turnoff to Atluck Lake campground.

After crossing the boundary between the Port McNeill and Campbell River FS districts, the main road eventually reaches Zeballos. From there you can proceed northwest to Fair Harbour. Both are isolated settlements on West Coast inlets, and both have FS campgrounds nearby: **Resolution Park Recreation Site #32**, and **Fair Harbour Recreation Site #33**. If you're up for a long drive through remote country (2WD cars and big RVs should be able to make it), ask if a recreation map is available for Campbell River Forest District. The phone number and address is in the back of this book. Resolution Park has 12 tables, a cobble beach, a boat launch, a float, and a fresh-water source. Fair Harbour has 15 tables, a boat launch, and a nearby government dock.

Turning right (north) at the 3.1-km (1.9-mi) junction, heading for Anutz Lake campground.

Camping Builds Confident, Caring Kids

Introducing children to the great outdoors can have a significant, long-lasting impact on their lives. Helping kids see, understand and appreciate nature encourages them to learn skills that will bolster their personal confidence and make them more competent at navigating the human and physical environments. Also, most adolescent love affairs with the outdoors continue into adulthood. In one study, 73% of Canadians said their passion for outdoor recreation is the direct result of fun times they had outdoors while growing up. 50% of those said their conservation ethic, their active concern for the earth, was sparked before the age of eight.

5.8 km (3.6 mi)
Fork right.

6.4 km (4 mi)
Fork left.

6.6 km (4.1 mi)
Go right and descend.

6.8 km (4.2 mi)
Arrive at Anutz Lake campground.

ANUTZ LAKE CAMPGROUND #32
Overnight / Easy
Elev: 300 m (984 ft) / Lake: 1.5 km (0.9 mi) long, 87 ha
14 tables around a large field
Accessible by motorhomes and 5th-wheels

For KINMAN CREEK and NIMPKISH LAKE,
now follow the directions below

0 km (0 mi)
Starting west, departing Hwy 19. Set your tripometer to 0. There's an old gas station here.

100 meters
Proceed straight for Nimpkish Lake campground. Turn right across from the gas station, immediately cross railroad tracks, then descend to reach Kinman Creek campground at 1.3 km (0.8 mi). A map sign indicates all the campsites.

KINMAN CREEK RECREATION SITE #7
Destination / Easy
Elev: 70 m (230 ft) / Lake: 25.5 km (15.8 mi) long, 3680 ha
24 tables, 6 walk-in tent sites, trail to lake
Accessible by motorhomes and 5th-wheels

Proceeding straight at the gas station, passing the turnoff to Kinman Creek campground.

0.3 km (0.2 mi)
Turn left at the T-junction.

0.8 km (0.5 mi)
Go right, then immediately stay left at another fork.

1 km (0.6 mi)
Ignore the left fork. Stay straight, proceeding downhill.

1.5 km (0.9 mi)
Arrive at Nimpkish Lake campground.

NIMPKISH LAKE RECREATION SITE #28
Destination / Easy
Elev: 20 m (65 ft) / Lake: 25.5 km (15.8 mi) long
2 km (1.2 mi) wide, 3680 ha
20 tables, short trail to a point
Accessible by motorhomes and 5th-wheels

SOUTHWEST OF PORT MCNEILL

Most of the campgrounds southwest of Port McNeill are small and remote. The two described here are big. The first is very convenient, the second is reasonably so.

Marble River campground is provincial-park quality. Reached via paved road, it's on a playful, spirited river, at the north end of Alice Lake, in a wonderful, forested setting. Several campsites line the riverbank. Others are well away from the campground road, with privacy created by trees and bushes. The river is audible at most sites, even if it's not visible. Shade is abundant. Large, grassy areas at many sites are great for pitching your tent on, or curling your toes in. This is as attractive as any campground in B.C. Expect mosquitoes in summer.

Alice Lake campground has a rough, wild atmosphere—totally unlike the intimate, manicured Marble River campground. It's not a long drive off pavement, but the claustrophobic access road feels like Alice in Wonderland's rabbit hole. The final approach has light branches arching overhead that might scrape the tops of big rigs. This is an open strip-camp, where RVs line up close together on the stone beach. Drift-logs have blown ashore and piled up here. The strong winds that often whip across this exciting lake keep the bugs down.

If you're heading northwest on Hwy 19 from Port McNeill

Set your tripometer to 0 at the turnoff to Port McNeill. Drive 20 km (12.5 mi) northwest, then turn left (south) onto Port Alice Road and reset your tripometer to 0. There's a map sign here.

If you're heading southeast on Hwy 19 from Port Hardy

Set your tripometer to 0 at the Welcome to Port Hardy sign with the cavorting bears on it. This is also the turnoff for the ferry terminal. Drive 16.4 km (10.2 mi) southeast, then turn right (south) onto Port Alice Road and reset your tripometer to 0. There's a map sign here.

For either approach above, now follow the directions below

0 km (0 mi)
Starting south on paved Port Alice Road, departing Hwy 19. Stay left on the main road.

10.6 km (6.6 mi)
For Marble River campground, proceed straight (southwest) where a logging road crosses the highway. Turn right (northwest) for commercial campgrounds on Rupert Inlet. Turn left

(south) and reset your tripometer to 0 for Alice Lake campground; directions continue below on this page.

14.6 km (9.1 mi)
Cross Marble River bridge. You'll see picnic tables for day use on the right, in grass beside the bridge. Immediately after the bridge, turn right and follow the dirt road past the big WFP sign.

15.3 km (9.5 mi)
Reach a fork. Right descends to forested riverside campsites in 100 meters. Left leads to grassy campsites.

MARBLE RIVER RECREATION SITE #17
Destination / Easy
30 campsites, most with tables
Accessible by motorhomes and 5th-wheels

Turning left (south), departing Port Alice Road at the 10.6-km (6.6 mi) junction described above, heading for Alice Lake campground.

0 km (0 mi)
Starting south on Alice Lake Main FS road.

1.2 km (0.7 mi)
Stay right at the fork.

8.2 km (5.1 mi)
Stay right. In 100 meters, go right again onto a narrower road. Trees arch overhead.

12 km (7.4 mi)
Reach Alice Lake.

13.2 km (8.2 mi)
Arrive at Alice Lake campground.

ALICE LAKE RECREATION SITES #16
Weekend / Moderate
Elev: 56 m (185 ft) / Lake: 14.3 km (8.8 mi) long, 1074 ha
12 campsites, no tables
Accessible by motorhomes and 5th-wheels

NORTH OF PORT HARDY

The FS campground closest to Port Hardy, and the only one north of it, is on the east end of Georgie Lake, about a 20-minute drive from the ferry terminal. The area has been violently logged. Thankfully, no clearcuts are visible from the lake. Boaters might enjoy it here, but the campground lacks appeal. A 3-km (1.9-mi) hiking trail leads to Songhees Lake.

Bound for Cape Scott, at the northwest tip of Vancouver Island? Georgie Lake is a possible overnight refuge, but it's out of the way. Helper Creek campground, near the southwest shore of Nahwitti Lake, is beside the road to Cape Scott.

0 km (0 mi)
Set your tripometer to 0 at the Welcome to Port Hardy sign with the cavorting bears on it. This is also the turnoff for the ferry terminal.

1.3 km (0.8 mi)
Pass the turnoff to Coal Harbour.

2.1 km (1.3 mi)
Turn left (west) toward Cape Scott.

4.7 km (2.9 mi)
Pavement ends.

9.2 km (5.7 mi)
Reach a junction. Bear right (north) for Georgie Lake campground and cross a small, narrow bridge. Left (west) proceeds across the island, passing **Helper Creek Recreation Site #1** (10 campsites with tables) near the southwest shore of Nahwitti Lake, grazing Holberg Inlet, and eventually reaching Cape Scott Provincial Park on the west coast.

14.8 km (9.2 mi)
Fork right to quickly reach Georgie Lake campground.

GEORGIE LAKE RECREATION SITE #2
Overnight / Moderate
Elev: 218 m (715 ft) / Lake: 8.8 km (5.4 mi) long, 486 ha
4 tables, sandy beach, boat launch, short hiking trail
Accessible by small motorhomes and trailers

Premier Hikes in BC *and* Don't Waste Your Time in the BC Coast Mountains, *described on pages 394-5, lead you to exceptional alpine vistas like this.*

B: Sunshine Coast

All these campgrounds are in the Sunshine Coast FS District.

3	Klein Lake
4	Khartoum Lake
5	Lois Lake
8	Nanton Lake
12	Dodd Lake
29	Dinner Rock

Sunshine Coast

LANGDALE TO EARLS COVE, page 85
SALTERY BAY TO POWELL RIVER, page 86
NORTH OF POWELL RIVER, page 90

Klein Lake campground

The Sunshine Coast has high, rugged mountains and luxuriant forests, ocean inlets and long, mysterious lakes. The continental clash of rock and water is dramatic, often soul-stirring.

This stretch of coast north of Vancouver seems a long way from civilization, yet the journey is short: two brief ferry rides and a couple hours of driving will bring you to Lund, the northern terminus of Hwy 101.

Between Langdale and Earls Cove, the only convenient FS campground is at Klein Lake, near Earls Cove. But there are many more inland from Powell River, which is about midway between Saltery Bay and Lund.

LANGDALE TO EARLS COVE

Klein Lake campground, though handy, is not scenic. If it's your only stop between Langdale and Earls Cove, you won't fully appreciate this section of the Sunshine Coast. So visit some of the many regional and provincial parks along the way. Smugglers Cove, for example, has a small network of short trails allowing you to easily wander around an idyllic coastal nook. It's reached via Brooks Road, just northwest of Halfmoon Bay, or about 19.8 km (12.3 mi) northwest of Sechelt.

For more excitement, drive 3.8 km (2.4 mi) beyond the Klein Lake turnoff, toward Egmont, then walk the 4-km (2.5-mi) trail to Skookumchuck Narrows. You'll witness the sea surging through an impressive tidal bore. The constantly energized water is also a good place to observe seastars.

If you're heading northwest on Hwy 101 from Langdale

From Langdale ferry terminal, drive Hwy 101 generally northwest about 83 km (51.5 mi) to a junction 1 km (0.6 mi) before Earls Cove ferry terminal. Turn right (northeast) toward Egmont and reset your tripometer to 0.

If you're heading southeast on Hwy 101 from Earls Cove

From Earls Cove ferry terminal, drive Hwy 101 southeast 1 km (0.6 mi), then turn left (northeast) toward Egmont and reset your tripometer to 0.

For either approach above, now follow the directions below

0 km (0 mi)
Starting northeast toward Egmont, departing Hwy 101.

1.7 km (1.1 mi)
Turn right (southeast) onto North Lake FS road.

3 km (1.9 mi)
After passing cottages and nearing the end of North Lake, bear right for Klein Lake.

4.9 km (3 mi)
Arrive at Klein Lake campground. Go right or left to campsites. The road circles the lake.

KLEIN LAKE RECREATION SITE #3
Overnight / Easy
Elev: almost sea level / Lake: 1.5 km (0.9 mi) long, 35 ha
19 tables, cartop boat launch (electric motors only)
Accessible by small motorhomes and trailers

SALTERY BAY TO POWELL RIVER

Midway between Saltery Bay and Powell River, if you turn north off Hwy 101 you can quickly reach Lois Lake campground or continue to campgrounds at Khartoum, Nanton and Dodd lakes. All have a wild, lonely atmosphere that campers find relaxing yet revitalizing. These long lakes are part of the Powell Forest Canoe Route (PFCR)—a good alternative to the much busier Bowron Lakes circuit farther north in B.C. For a grand view of the area, including the Strait of Georgia, hike the short but rigorous trail to the summit of Tin Hat Mountain. The trailhead is near Nanton Lake. Directions are on page 90.

The access described below, via Stillwater Main FS road, is restricted due to logging operations. It's open to public travel on weekends, holidays, and between 8 p.m. and 5 a.m. weekdays.

For direct, unrestricted access to Lois Lake campground, turn north off Hwy 101 onto Canoe Main FS road. It's a few minutes east of Stillwater Main FS road and the steel bridge over Lois River. Canoe Main is also a better road than Branch 41 described below.

If you're heading west on Hwy 101 from Saltery Bay

From Saltery Bay ferry terminal, drive Hwy 101 west 11.5 km (7.1 mi). Turn right (north) just before the steel bridge over Lois River and reset your tripometer to 0.

Lois Lake campground

If you're heading southeast on Hwy 101 from Powell River

From the east edge of the town of Powell River, drive Hwy 101 generally southeast 14.5 km (9 mi). Turn left (north) just after the steel bridge over Lois River and reset your tripometer to 0.

For either approach above, now follow the directions below

0 km (0 mi)
Starting north on Stillwater Main FS road, departing Hwy 101.

1.1 km (0.7 mi)
Reach a junction. Continue left for campgrounds at Khartoum, Nanton and Dodd lakes. Turn right onto Branch 41 and reset your tripometer to 0 for Lois Lake campground.

0 km (0 mi)
Turning right onto Branch 41, heading for Lois Lake campground. The road is rough but passable in a 2WD car.

3.6 km (2.2 mi)
Reach a junction. Turn left and descend.

4.5 km (2.8 mi)
Curve right.

4.7 km (2.9 mi)
Arrive at Lois Lake campground.

LOIS LAKE RECREATION SITE #5
Destination / Easy
Elev: 131 m (430 ft) / Lake: 14 km (8.7 mi) long, 2252 ha
8 tables, 3 walk-in tent sites, cartop boat launch
Accessible by small motorhomes and trailers

Continuing left at the 1.1-km (0.7-mi) junction, heading for Khartoum, Nanton and Dodd lakes, passing the turnoff to Lois Lake campground.

1.7 km (1.1 mi)
Stay right.

3.9 km (2.4 mi) and **5.2 km (3.2 mi)**
Proceed straight on the main road.

6.7 km (4.1 mi) and **8.5 km (5.3 mi)**
Pass overnight pullouts on Lois Lake.

12.3 km (7.6 mi)
Reach a fork. Continue left for campgrounds on Nanton and Dodd lakes. Turn right and set your tripometer to 0 for Khartoum Lake campground.

0 km (0 mi)
Turning right, heading for Khartoum Lake campground.

7.4 km (4.6 mi)
Proceed through a fish farm on Lois Lake.

10 km (6.2 mi)
The road is narrow, steep, rocky, but passable in a 2WD car.

Khartoum Lake

15.1 km (9.4 mi)

Turn right for the sharp descent to Khartoum Lake campground. If you're high on a cliff with a clear view of the lake way below, you've gone about 2.3 km (1.4 mi) too far; turn back. This viewpoint, however, is worth walking or driving to from the campground. It enables you to appreciate the lake's dramatic, mountain-valley setting. As for the campsites, several are in the open, along the shore; others are among beautiful trees; one is next to a loud creek.

KHARTOUM LAKE RECREATION SITE #4
Destination / Moderate
Elev: 131 m (430 ft) / Lake: 6.8 km (4.2 mi) long, 436 ha
6 tables, boat launch
Accessible by small motorhomes and trailers

Continuing left at the 12.3-km (7.6-mi) fork, heading for Nanton and Dodd lakes, passing the turnoff to Khartoum Lake campground.

13.1 km (8.1 mi)
Stay right on Goat Lake Main FS road.

17.5 km (10.9 mi)
Tin Hat Mountain is visible ahead.

18.8 km (11.7 mi)
Reach a junction. Go right, onto the wider road, for Nanton and Dodd lakes. (Left ascends to the Tin Hat Mountain trailhead. It's about 450 meters past tiny Spring Lake. Start hiking on the old logging road that forks right. In about two hours, follow a faint trail left to the rocky summit.)

20 km (12.4 mi)
Proceed straight (north) for Dodd Lake campground. Turn right and descend to reach Nanton Lake campground in 200 meters. Mountains are visible across the lake. A couple campsites are on the shore; most are in trees.

NANTON LAKE RECREATION SITE #8
Weekend / Moderate
Elev: 175 m (575 ft) / Lake: 1.3 km (0.8 mi) long, 129 ha
13 tables, boat launch
Accessible by small motorhomes and trailers

Continuing north, passing the turnoff to Nanton Lake campground.

25.2 km (15.6 mi)
Turn right for Dodd Lake campground. It's a pretty lake among beautiful mountains.

DODD LAKE RECREATION SITE #12
Weekend / Moderate
Elev: 210 m (670 ft) / Lake: 6.4 km (4 mi) long, 704 ha
12 tables, boat launch
Accessible by small motorhomes and trailers

NORTH OF POWELL RIVER

The Sunshine Coast ends north of Powell River. Paved road extends only as far as Lund and Okeover Inlet. Free camping is limited to Dinner Rock campground, on the Strait of Georgia, just southeast of Lund.

On the entire Sunshine Coast, Dinner Rock is the only drive-in FS campground that's actually on the coast. It's well manicured, with several campsites directly above the sea. You can launch a cartop boat here. Dinner Rock is closed October 15 through April 15, when a locked gate prevents vehicle access.

From the Petro Canada station on the north edge of the town of Powell River, drive Hwy 101 northwest 15.8 km (9.8 mi). Or, from the turnoff to Okeover Inlet, drive Hwy 101 southeast 1.3 km (0.8 mi). From either approach, turn west onto the rough, steeply descending access road. The campground is 1.6 km (1 mi) off pavement. Don't try it in a big RV; others have required tow-truck rescue.

DINNER ROCK RECREATION SITE #29
Destination / Easy
12 tables, cartop boat launch, picnic sites
Inaccessible by motorhomes and trailers

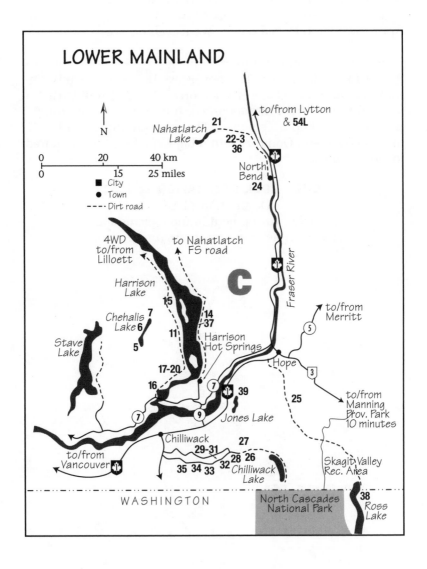

LOWER MAINLAND

N

to/from Lytton
& **54L**

Nahatlatch **21**
Lake

22-3
36

North
Bend
24

0   20   40 km
0   15   25 miles
■ City
● Town
--- Dirt road

4WD
to/from
Lilloett

to Nahatlatch
FS road

Harrison
Lake

Chehalis **7**
Lake **6**

15

14
37

Harrison
Hot Springs

Stave
Lake

5

11

17-20

16

Fraser River

to/from
Merritt

⑤

•Hope

③

25

to/from
Manning
Prov. Park
10 minutes

⑦

⑦   **39**

⑨   *Jones Lake*

⑦

to/from
Vancouver

•Chilliwack

27

29-31

28 26

35 34 33 **32** *Chilliwack*
Lake

Skagit Valley
Rec. Area

WASHINGTON

North Cascades
National Park

38
Ross
Lake

C: Lower Mainland

All but one of these campgrounds are in the Chilliwack FS District. **L** stands for Lillooet FS District.

5	Chehalis Lake South	26	Riverside
6	Skwellepil Creek	27	Foley Lake
7	Chehalis Lake North	28	Camp Foley
11	Wood Lake	29	Chipmunk Peninsula
14	Cogburn Beach	30	Rapids
15	Twenty Mile Bay	31	Eagles Roost
16	Chehalis River	32	Pierce Creek
17	Grace Lake	33	Thurston Meadows
18	Wolf Lake	34	Allison Pool
19	Weaver Lake	35	Tamihi Creek
20	Francis Lake	36	Nahatlatch River
21	Log Creek	37	Bear Creek
22	Fir Flat	38	Hozomeen
23	Apocynum	39	Jones Lake
24	Scuzzy Creek	54L	Botanie Lake
25	Eaton Creek		

Lower Mainland

Harrison Lake and the Coast Mountains

B.C.'s lower left-hand corner is called the Lower Mainland. It's vast, with a great diversity of campgrounds. Many are clustered around Harrison Lake and its outlet, Chehalis River. Another group is sprinkled along Chilliwack River, upstream toward Chilliwack Lake. What they all have in common is proximity to the metropolitan sprawl of Vancouver and its pressure valve —Trans-Canada Hwy 1—which vents a burst of urban steam every weekend, when all the wage slaves flee the city in search of sanity. The result is a lot of frequently full campgrounds, sometimes the insanity of a wild, beer-drenched party, and once in a while the perversion of a torched outhouse or chopped-up campsite table. The Forest Service does a commendable job of coping despite limited means. Thanks to them, your camping experience here is likely to be safe and enjoyable. Just be aware that most of these campgrounds are not remote. Even those with access discouraging to family vans are relished by men seeking to burnish their machismo in 4WD vehicles. The campgrounds near Lytton (along Nahatlatch River and at Botanie Lake) are farther from Vancouver and therefore less popular and more tranquil. But strictly speaking, they're outside the Lower Mainland, though *Camp Free* includes them here for reasons explained below.

STAVE LAKE

Though Stave Lake is a big, impressive body of water (24 km / 15 mi long, 5687 hectares), camping in the area is discouraging for several reasons. Access is long and rough. Cypress Point is the only campground on Stave Lake. There are just two others nearby. All are small, none is appealing. Massive clearcuts dominate the scenery. And gun lovers come here to target practice. Does anything in that description encourage you to risk camping, or even driving, where bullets might be whizzing around? That's why directions to Salsbury Lake Recreation Site #1, Cypress Point Recreation Site #2, and Kenyon Lake Recreation Site #3 were deleted from this edition of *Camp Free*.

CHEHALIS LAKE

Chehalis Lake is in a valley between Harrison and Stave lakes. Access is long and can be rough depending on the current level of industrial traffic. Motorhomes, 5th-wheels and trailers might suffer here. Public travel is prohibited weekdays 6 a.m. to 6 p.m. due to logging. But if you're driving a rugged vehicle, and you're indifferent to clearcuts, maybe you'll enjoy one of the three substantial campgrounds on Chehalis Lake. The following brief directions should be adequate for experienced explorers.

If you're heading east or west on Hwy 7

Drive to Harrison Mills. Turn north onto Morris Valley Road. In 0.5 km (0.3 mi) turn left onto Chehalis FS road and follow it generally north. Above and west of Chehalis River, the road angles northwest. After crossing the bridge over Statlu Creek, proceed generally north to reach the south end of Chehalis Lake, about 21 km (13 mi) from Harrison Mills. The road continues north, following the lake's west shore. Turnoffs to the other campgrounds are about 31 km (19 mi) and 34 km (21 mi) from Harrison Mills.

Chehalis South Recreation Site #5 is on the lake's south shore. It's a medium-size, forested campground: 13 campsites without tables.

Skwellepil Creek Recreation Site #6 is about two-thirds of the way up the lake's west shore. The final approach is a steep, rugged descent, possibly requiring 4WD. It's a large, forested campground with a gravel beach. It has only 15 tables, but room for about 40 vehicles. You can launch a cartop boat here. There's also an upland overflow camping area—handy if the main campground is full or too noisy for you.

Chehalis Lake North Recreation Site #7 is on the lake's north shore. It's a large, forested campground with 30 tables. The beach has no vehicle access, but there is a gravel boat launch.

CHEHALIS RIVER & HARRISON LAKE

Harrison Lake is 60 km (37 mi) long and up to 7.5 km (4.7 mi) wide. Backroads head north, up the west and east shores. The driving is tedious. Most visitors don't venture beyond the tourist town of Harrison Hot Springs—on the south shore, reached via paved Hwy 9. That's far enough to appreciate the lake's magnitude and beauty.

Chehalis River campground, en route to Harrison Lake's west shore, is the most attractive and easily accessible in the area. The only drive-in campground actually on the west shore of Harrison Lake is halfway up the lake, at Twenty Mile Bay.

Within easier reach are both of Harrison Lake's east-shore campgrounds: Bear Creek and Cogburn Beach. They're about 18 km (11.2 mi) beyond where pavement ends. Bear Creek is popular with boardsailors. The Cogburn Beach campsites are for tenters only, in a stand of ancient trees.

Even if you're not camping, Chehalis River and Harrison Lake are good destinations for a scenic drive. En route, Hwy 7 plies the lush, pastoral Fraser Valley and grants views of monstrous Mt. Cheam and the Border Peaks. Come here in early October, and you'll also see salmon in Weaver Creek and the spawning channel near the lake's southwest arm.

If you're heading east on Hwy 7 from Vancouver

Drive Hwy 7 to Harrison Mills. Turn left (north) onto Morris Valley Road and set your tripometer to 0.

If you're heading east or west on Trans-Canada Hwy 1

Between Chilliwack and Hope (36 km / 22.3 mi southwest of Hope), take Exit 135 signed for Bridal Falls, Agassiz, and Harrison Hot Springs. Head north and cross the Fraser River. Turn left (west) on Hwy 7. Proceed straight (west) where Hwy 9 goes right (north) to Harrison Hot Springs. Cross a huge metal bridge over Harrison River (good salmon viewing here in October). About 21 km (13 mi) from Hwy 1, reach Harrison Mills. Turn right (north) onto Morris Valley Road and set your tripometer to 0.

For either approach above, now follow the directions below

0 km (0 mi)
Starting north on Morris Valley Road, departing Hwy 7 at Harrison Mills. You'll see signs for Hemlock Valley Recreation Area, Chehalis River Hatchery (6 km), and Weaver Creek Spawning Channel (12 km).

0.5 km (0.3 mi)
Proceed straight, on pavement, toward Hemlock Valley and Harrison Lake. Left is Chehalis FS road leading to Chehalis Lake; directions continue on page 96.

5.8 km (3.6 mi)
Stay straight for Harrison Lake and campgrounds at Weaver, Wolf, Grace and Wood lakes. Turn right to reach the first and largest Chehalis River campground in 0.3 km (0.2 mi). The campsites are well-spaced in forest, near the wide, shallow river.

CHEHALIS RIVER RECREATION SITE #16
Weekend / Easy
40 tables, sandy beach
Accessible by motorhomes and 5th-wheels

Continuing north on Morris Valley Road, passing the turnoff to Chehalis River campground.

6 km (3.7 mi)
Proceed over the steel bridge for Harrison Lake and campgrounds at Weaver, Wolf, Grace and Wood lakes. Before the bridge, turn left to reach the second **Chehalis River campground**. Smaller and less attractive than the first one, it has five tables.

6.1 km (3.8 mi)
Cross the steel bridge and stay straight for Harrison Lake and campgrounds at Weaver, Wolf, Grace and Wood lakes. Immediately after the bridge, turn left for the third **Chehalis River campground**. This one's the smallest and least appealing, but if the others are full you'll find three tables here.

6.8 km (4.2 mi)
Reach a junction. Stay straight on Morris Valley Road.

7.9 km (4.9 mi)
Go straight through the junction, toward Weaver Creek Spawning Channel. Left leads to Hemlock Ski Area.

10.9 km (6.8 mi)
Pavement ends.

11.4 km (7.1 mi)
Cross a bridge and arrive at the spawning channel. If the salmon are running, check out the action in Weaver Creek. The road begins ascending.

House Hold

If you own a house, it can hold you to it. Maintenance and improvements sap your time and energy. No wonder people try to justify it all by staying home and enjoying the place. If you own a house, but still yearn for adventure, be strong. Break the hold. Go camping. Each time you return, you'll appreciate your house more for what it really is: shelter from the elements.

13 km (8.1 mi)

Proceed on Harrison West FS road for Harrison Lake and campgrounds at Wolf, Grace and Wood lakes. Left is a rough, steep road leading about 5 km (3.1 mi) to Weaver Lake campground. It's passable but challenging in a 2WD car. High clearance is helpful; 4WD is preferable. A 6.2-km (3.8-mi) hiking trail circles the small lake.

WEAVER LAKE RECREATION SITE #19
Weekend / Difficult
Elev: 255 m (836 ft) / Lake: 1.7 km (1.1 mi) long, 78 ha
16 tables, hiking trail
Inaccessible by motorhomes and trailers

Continuing east on Harrison West FS road, passing the turnoff to Weaver Lake campground.

13.2 km (8.2 mi)

Arrive at Wolf Lake campground. Proceed on Harrison West FS road for Harrison Lake and campgrounds at Grace and Wood lakes.

Wolf Lake is tiny, surrounded by forest. Power boats are prohibited. Campsites are near the road. One has a lakeview.

WOLF LAKE RECREATION SITE #18
Overnight / Easy
Elev: 91 m (298 ft) / Lake: 2 ha
3 tables, short trail to lake
Accessible by small motorhomes and trailers

Continuing north on Harrison West FS road, passing Wolf Lake campground.

13.4 km (8.3 mi)
Reach the turnoff for Grace Lake campground. Proceed on Harrison West FS road for Wood Lake campground and Harrison Lake.

> The Grace Lake access road is narrow, with insufficient room for big rigs to turn around. In 150 meters fork right. Arrive at the campground in another 300 meters. The lake is in a steep-sided, forested bowl that feels secluded. The campsites are too high above the shore for lakeviews. Yet the campground is superior to the one at Wolf Lake and should be quieter. Power boats are prohibited.

GRACE LAKE RECREATION SITE #17
Overnight / Easy
Elev: 100 m (328 ft) / Lake: 4.5 ha
2 tables, steep trail to lake
Inaccessible by motorhomes and trailers

Continuing north on Harrison West FS road, passing the turnoff to Grace Lake campground.

17 km (10.5 mi)
Reach a high viewpoint above Harrison Lake. Having ascended, the road now levels as it continues north.

19.6 km (12.2 mi)
Proceed on Harrison West FS road for Wood Lake campground. Sharp left ascends to **Francis Lake Recreation Site #20**. It's a small campground on a tiny lake, accessible only by 4WD.

25.4 km (15.7 mi)
Cross a bridged creek.

28.7 km (17.8 mi)
Pass Harrison West - Simms Cr FS road on the left.

30.3 km (18.8 mi)
Cross a bridged creek. Pass Harrison West - Walian Cr FS road on the left.

32.4 km (20.1 mi)
Reach a junction. Go right, then bear left at the fork to arrive at Wood Lake campground. (Continue on the main road another 150 meters for the turnoff to more campsites on the other side of Wood Lake.)

A view of the distant, glacier-clad Pemberton Mountains is insufficient reward for driving this far. Consider camping at Wood Lake only if you're exploring much farther north.

WOOD LAKE RECREATION SITE #11
Weekend / Difficult (due only to distance)
Elev: 152 m (500 ft) / Lake: 5 ha
8 tables, 10 campsites
Not recommended for motorhomes and trailers

Harrison West FS road continues north, following the west shore of Harrison Lake. At about the lake's midpoint is **Twenty Mile Bay Recreation Site #15**. *It's a medium-size, forested campground with a cartop boat launch. Nearby is a rough emergency airstrip for light aircraft.*

HARRISON LAKE EAST SHORE

It's a beautiful drive from Harrison Hot Springs up the east shore of Harrison Lake. Unlike the west shore road, this one initially hugs the water's edge. A massive glacier is visible far north. Opportunities to camp free are limited to Bear Creek, and a small, tenters-only campground at Cogburn Beach. The alternative is to pay to camp at Sasquatch Provincial Park, above the lake's southeast corner.

If you're heading east or west on Trans-Canada Hwy 1

Between Chilliwack and Hope (36 km / 22.3 mi southwest of Hope), take Exit 135 signed for Bridal Falls, Agassiz, and Harrison Hot Springs. Head north and cross the Fraser River. Turn left (west) on Hwy 7. Soon turn right (north) onto Hwy 9. Follow it to Harrison Hot Springs, on Harrison Lake's south shore, about 16 km (9.9 mi) from Hwy 1. At the T-junction in town, set your tripometer 0 and turn right onto the road following the lake's east shore, heading for Sasquatch Provincial Park.

0 km (0 mi)
Starting northeast from the T-junction in Harrison Hot Springs. The roller-coaster road is paved until Sasquatch Park.

6.3 km (3.9 mi)
Reach a junction. Go right, toward Sasquatch Park and Hicks Lake. Left leads to a day-use area.

7.4 km (4.6 mi)
Reach a junction. Go left onto Harrison East FS road for Bear Creek and Cogburn Beach campgrounds.

22 km (13.6 mi)
Reach Bear Creek campground on Harrison Lake. Proceed north for Cogburn Beach campground.

BEAR CREEK RECREATION SITE #37
Weekend / Difficult (due only to distance)
10 tables, gravel beach
Accessible by small motorhomes and trailers

Continuing north on Harrison East FS road, passing Bear Creek campground.

25 km (15.5 mi)
Reach Cogburn Beach campground on Harrison Lake.

For tenters only, the campsites are in a stand of ancient trees beside the lake. They're reached via short trail (about a 6-minute walk) descending from the road. Vehicles are prohibited on the beach. A small mill and booming-ground are nearby.

COGBURN BEACH RECREATION SITE #14
Weekend / Difficult (due only to distance)
4 tentsites with tables, gravel beach
Parking accessible by all vehicles

CHILLIWACK RIVER

On Trans-Canada Hwy 1, about 105 km (65 mi) east of downtown Vancouver, is the town of Chilliwack. South of town is the Chilliwack River, flowing from Chilliwack Lake farther east. The North Cascade mountains rise abruptly along the U.S. border here, creating an impressive backdrop. It's an inviting area, well worth a weekend or more. Recreation opportunities—hiking, kayaking, boating, fishing—are abundant. FS campgrounds are numerous and easy to access. Proximity to Vancouver, however, ensures a constant flow of campers. Don't come here seeking solitude.

If you're heading east or west on Trans-Canada Hwy 1

Take Exit 119A signed for Sardis and Cultus Lake. Drive south on Vedder Road, past fast-food restaurants and gas stations in the town of Chilliwack. About 5.5 km (3.4 mi) from Hwy 1, reach a three-way junction at the metal bridge over Chilliwack River. Set your tripometer to 0 and turn left (southeast) just before the bridge. Follow the sign for Chilliwack Lake Provincial Park (42 km).

0 km (0 mi)
Starting southeast along the north side of Chilliwack River, from the three-way junction at the metal bridge.

9.7 km (6 mi)
Proceed straight on the main road where Slesse Park Road forks left.

10 km (6.2 mi)
Pass a treed pullout near the river.

10.5 km (6.5 mi)
After crossing a bridge to the south side of Chilliwack River, proceed east on the main road for more campgrounds. Turn right (south) onto Chilliwack - Liumchen Creek FS road to reach Tamihi Creek campground in 0.4 km (0.2 mi). Bear right and cross Tamihi Creek bridge; don't fork left up Chilliwack - Tamihi Cr FS road.

This is a large, provincial-park quality campground, in a healthy, deciduous forest. Many campsites are beside the lovely creek. A city-park atmosphere can prevail here when it's crowded, which is often.

TAMIHI CREEK RECREATION SITE #35
Weekend / Easy
30 tables, day-use area
Accessible by small motorhomes and trailers

Continuing east on the main road, passing the turnoff to Tamihi Creek campground, following the south side of Chilliwack River.

14 km (8.7 mi)
Proceed east on the main road for more campgrounds. Turn left for the short descent to Allison Pool campground on Chilliwack River.

ALLISON POOL RECREATION SITE #34
Weekend / Easy
4 well-spaced tables
Too small for motorhomes and trailers

Continuing east on the main road, passing the turnoff to Allison Pool campground, following the south side of Chilliwack River.

15.8 km (9.8 mi)
Pass a large pullout on the left. Footpaths access the river.

17.4 km (10.8 mi)
Proceed east on the main road for more campgrounds. Turn left to enter Thurston Meadows campground on Chilliwack River.

The campsites ring a clearing. The road is nearby, but noise is minimal at the riverbank sites.

Thurston Meadows campground on Chilliwack River

THURSTON MEADOWS RECREATION SITE #33
Weekend / Easy
14 tables
Accessible by motorhomes and 5th-wheels

Continuing east on the main road, passing the turnoff to Thurston Meadow campground, following the south side of Chilliwack River.

23.2 km (14.4 mi)
Proceed northeast on the main road for more campgrounds. Turn right to reach Pierce Creek campground in 0.3 km (0.2 mi).

PIERCE CREEK RECREATION SITE #32
Overnight / Easy
2 tables
Accessible by small motorhomes and trailers

Continuing northeast on the main road, passing the turnoff to Pierce Creek campground, following the south side of Chilliwack River.

27.2 km (16.9 mi)
Cross a bridge to Chilliwack River's north side. Proceed east on the main road for Riverside campground and Chilliwack Lake. Turn left (between the bridge and Foley Creek FS road) for Camp Foley. After turning, double back toward the river.

Camp Foley is a big pullout with lush trees on two sides. It's next to Chilliwack River but also beside the road. Passing vehicles are audible.

CAMP FOLEY RECREATION SITE #28
Overnight / Easy
3 tables
Accessible by small motorhomes and trailers

Continuing east on the main road, passing the turnoff to Camp Foley.

27.4 km (17 mi)
Proceed east on the main road for Riverside campground and Chilliwack Lake. For more campgrounds on the north side of Chilliwack River, turn left (north) onto Foley Creek FS road (just past Camp Foley) and set your tripometer to 0; directions continue on the next page.

28.8 km (17.9 mi)
Pavement ends.

30.1 km (19 mi)
Proceed east on the main road for Chilliwack Lake. Turn right
to enter Riverside campground on Chilliwack River.

The campsites are well-spaced among Douglas firs. Little
sunlight penetrates the forest. The road is nearby, but the
river helps muffle noise.

RIVERSIDE RECREATION SITE #26
Weekend / Easy
2 tables
Accessible by small motorhomes and trailers

*Continuing east on the main road, passing the turnoff to Riverside camp-
ground.*

40.4 km (25.1 mi)
Stay straight for Chilliwack Lake. Left quickly reaches the
Lindeman, Greendrop and Flora lakes trailhead.

41 km (25.4 mi)
Arrive at Chilliwack Lake Provincial Park.

*Turning left (north) onto Foley Creek FS road, departing paved Chilliwack
River road at 27.4 km (17 mi). Set your tripometer to 0.*

0 km (0 mi)
Starting north on Foley Creek FS road, heading for Chipmunk
Peninsula, Rapids and Eagles Roost campgrounds. All are on
Chilliwack River's north bank.

2.1 km (1.3 mi)
Cross a bridge over Foley Creek and turn left (southwest). Right
follows Foley Creek upstream (northeast) about 13 km (8 mi) to
Foley Lake Recreation Site #27. Access is rough but passable in a 2WD car. The lake and campground are tiny.

4 km (2.5 mi)
Proceed straight (southwest) where Chipmunk Creek FS road
forks right (north).

4.5 km (2.8 mi)
Proceed southwest on the main road for Rapids and Eagles
Roost campgrounds. Turn left to enter Chipmunk Peninsula
campground on Chilliwack River.

The sites at this provincial-park-quality campground are
well-spaced among ancient evergreens. The atmosphere is
enhanced by the revitalizing sound of river rapids.
Motorcyclists frequently camp here because nearby trails
are open to off-road riding.

CHIPMUNK PENINSULA RECREATION SITE #29
Destination / Easy
14 tables, nearby motorcycle trails
Accessible by motorhomes and 5th-wheels

~~

*Continuing southwest on the main road, passing the turnoff to Chipmunk
Peninsula campground, following the north side of Chilliwack River.*

6.8 km (4.2 mi)
Pass Mt. Thurston FS road.

7.3 km (4.5 mi)
Proceed southwest on the main road for Eagles Roost camp-
ground. Turn left to enter Rapids campground on Chilliwack
River.

As the name suggests, roaring rapids are the entertainment
here. A big, sloping rock serves as grandstand. The river is
too swift for swimming or even wading.

RAPIDS RECREATION SITE #30
Weekend / Easy
1 table, 3 campsites
Too small for motorhomes and trailers

~~

Continuing southwest on the main road, passing the turnoff to Rapids campground, following the north side of Chilliwack River.

8.1 km (5 mi)
Turn left to enter Eagles Roost campground near deep pools and roaring whitewater along Chilliwack River. See photo on page 3.

EAGLES ROOST RECREATION SITE #31
Weekend / Easy
1 table, 2 campsites
Too small for motorhomes and trailers

NEAR HOPE

The North Cascade Mountains loom south of Hope and Trans-Canada Hwy 1. Free campgrounds await you in two of the valleys that pierce this mighty range.

BC Hydro manages a large campground at the north end of Jones Lake. It's only 10 km (6.2 mi) off the highway but is rated moderate because the road is steep with sharp switchbacks. It's challenging for even small motorhomes and trailers, but 2WD cars can make it easily if slowly. Dramatic peaks rise south of the lake. In fall, brilliantly-coloured deciduous trees compensate for unsightly low water-levels that time of year.

The small FS campground at Eaton Creek is en route to huge Ross Lake. The campsites are on a bench above the road, allowing you to appreciate Silverhope Creek valley's fine scenery and exuberant fall colours. The entry road is short, but steep and rough. When dry, it's passable in a 2WD car. Even the smallest motorhomes and trailers will struggle. This is a good basecamp for hikers. Several trails climb into the surrounding mountains. The Eaton Lake trail begins near the campground. It gains 880 m (2886 ft) in 6.5 km (4 mi), ending at the alpine lake that feeds Eaton Creek.

About 47 km (29 mi) south of Eaton Creek campground is Ross Lake. It sounds like a long way to drive on dirt, but the road's good, and the destination is compelling: Hozomeen campground, just across the U.S. border, at the north end of Ross

Silverhope Creek valley, en route to Eaton Creek campground

Lake. The lake extends south 32.3 km (20 mi) into Washington State. The campground is monstrous, and there's currently (1999) no fee. Recreation opportunities are rife. Boaters, anglers and hikers will easily entertain themselves. Plop-and-admire-the-scenery campers will be smiling too.

In Washington, Ross Lake is visible from Hwy 20, but the shore is roadless. The only way to reach it is by hiking, or portaging a canoe. So vehicle access to Ross Lake is a B.C. exclusive. As for the border crossing—no worries. It's very relaxed. You're unlikely to be questioned.

Hozomeen campground is in cool, dense forest, but some campsites have lakeviews. A choice of boat launches will please the weekend admiral. "Winnebago Flats," just before Hozomeen, is an open area where RV pilots can land even the biggest rigs. Ross Lake, fed by mountain streams, is not "full pool" until about July 1. In spring, the water level is kept low to allow for snowmelt.

A 6-km (3.7-mi) trail climbs 350 m (1150 ft) from near Ross Lake to much smaller Hozomeen Lake beneath the sky-spearing twin pinnacles of Hozomeen Mountain. It's an excellent dayhike. For details, read *Don't Waste Your Time in the North Cascades*, described on page 395.

If you're heading east or west on Trans-Canada Hwy 1

For Jones Lake, take Exit 153 signed for Laidlaw and Jones Lake. The exit is 18.7 km (11.6 mi) northeast of Harrison Hot Springs Exit 135, or 17.3 km (10.7 mi) west of Hope. Set your tripometer to 0.

For Eaton Creek and Ross Lake, take Exit 168 signed for Flood - Hope Rd and Silverhope Creek. The exit is 32.7 km (20.3 mi) northeast of Harrison Hot Springs Exit 135, or 3.2 km (2 mi) west of Hope. Set your tripometer to 0. (Coming from the west, the 0 point is 0.5 km / 0.3 mi off the highway.)

For JONES LAKE, now follow the directions below

0 km (0 mi)
Starting on Laidlaw Road, departing Hwy 1.

0.8 km (0.5 mi)
Cross a bridge over Jones Creek and immediately veer right. Ascend steeply. Proceed south on Jones Lake FS road, ignoring forks.

4 km (2.5 mi)
The road levels. The grade is easy the rest of the way.

8.5 km (5.3 mi)
Reach a junction. Stay straight on Jones Lake FS road, or fork right on Jones Lake West FS road; both quickly lead to campsites.

10 km (6.2 mi)
Arrive at Jones Lake campground. Sites are on the east and west sides of the dam, near the lake's north end.

East of the dam are 22 campsites between the lakeshore and Boulder Creek. Just south of the creek are 3 more sites, a small beach and a grassy landing. West of the dam are 11 campsites.

JONES LAKE CAMPGROUND #39
Weekend / Moderate
Lake: 5 km (3.1 mi) long, 1 km (0.6 mi) wide, 133 ha
36 tables, cartop boat launch
Accessible by small motorhomes and trailers

For EATON CREEK AND ROSS LAKE,
now follow the directions below
0 km (0 mi)
Starting on Flood - Hope Road, departing Hwy 1.

0.3 km (0.2 mi)
Turn south onto Silver Skagit Road. Pass a sign for Silver Lake and Hozomeen campground.

2.6 km (1.6 mi)
Pavement ends.

6.6 km (4.1 mi)
Reach a junction. Bear left and continue south toward Skagit Valley and Ross Lake. Right leads to Silver Lake's west shore in 1 km (0.6 mi).

Hozomeen campground on Ross Lake

8.4 km (5.2 mi)
Watch for possible **overnight pullouts** for the next 6.4 km (4 mi), on the right, beside Silverhope Creek.

17.2 km (10.7 mi)
Turn left and ascend to enter Eaton Creek campground. Proceed on the main road to reach Ross Lake, the U.S. border, and Hozomeen Campground.

EATON CREEK RECREATION SITE #25
Weekend / Easy
3 tables, hiking trail to Eaton Lake
Not suitable for motorhomes and trailers

Continuing generally southeast on the main road, passing the turnoff to Eaton Creek campground.

64.5 km (40 mi)
Nearing road's end, pass the B.C. Parks Ross Lake Campground. Fork left where right leads to the International Point day-use area. Pass the Canadian warden office, cross the border, enter Ross Lake National Recreation Area, and pass the American ranger station (an A-frame cabin). Rangers are on duty May through late October.

65.5 km (40.6 mi)
Reach "Winnebago Flats" camping area for RVs just before Hozomeen campground on Ross Lake. A sign directs you left to the Hozomeen Lake trail near an old cabin, 3 km (1.8 mi) from the ranger station. You'll find faucets with potable water there.

HOZOMEEN CAMPGROUND #38
Destination / Difficult (due only to distance)
Elev: 518 m (1700 ft) / Lake: 34 km (21 mi) long
120 campsites, many with tables
3 boat launches (2 cement, 1 gravel)
Accessible by motorhomes and 5th-wheels

NEAR LYTTON

Several FS campgrounds are on the Nahatlatch River, south of Lytton. Another is at Botanie Lake, just north of Lytton. All are outside what is generally understood as the Lower Mainland. But the Nahatlatch River is in Chilliwack Forest District, which covers the Lower Mainland. And most campers reach Botanie Lake via Hwy 1 from the Lower Mainland. So *Camp Free* groups these campgrounds with others in the southwest corner of B.C.

The Nahatlatch is a fast, glorious, whitewater river, in a sunny valley, at about 305 m (1000 ft) elevation. Kayakers and rafters love it. The river's fury makes swimming dangerous, but just watching all that water rush past seems to have a cooling effect. Farther up valley is a string of lakes fed by streams tumbling down from the wild, remote Upper Stein Wilderness. All four Nahatlatch campgrounds are small. The road is passable by most vehicles, but only Fir Flat and Log Creek campgrounds can accommodate motorhomes and trailers. Apocynum and Nahatlatch River campgrounds are not big enough. If you find the Nahatlatch campgrounds too crowded, try the one at Scuzzy Creek. Though nearby, it's less popular. Small motorhomes and trailers can get there but must be adequately powered, because the road is steep.

The slopes of Botanie Mountain are a dazzling wildflower garden in spring. Hiking to the lookout site on the mountain's minor summit is a rewarding challenge, but the trail climbs 1425 m (4674 ft) in 8.8 km (5.5 mi), and this is a heat-stroke

Nahatlatch River

zone in summer. East of the mountain is tiny Botanie Lake, on a Native reserve. The small campground near its shore is accessible by all vehicles.

For **Nahatlatch River and Scuzzy Creek**, turn west off Trans-Canada Hwy 1 at the village of Boston Bar and set your tripometer to 0 midway across the Fraser River bridge. Boston Bar is about 45 km (30 mi) south of Lytton, or about 65 km (40 mi) north of the Fraser River bridge in Hope.

For **Botanie Lake**, drive to Lytton, where Hwys 1 and 12 intersect. Follow Hwy 12 across the Thompson River bridge just north of town. About 0.5 km (0.3 mi) north of the bridge, turn right (northeast) onto Botanie Valley Road and set your tripometer to 0.

For NAHATLATCH RIVER, now follow the directions below

0 km (0 mi)
Midway across the Fraser River bridge. On the west bank, cross railroad tracks and follow the paved West Side Road north through the village of North Bend.

7.7 km (4.8 mi)
Pavement ends.

10.7 km (6.6 mi)
Bear left at the fork. Soon rejoin the main road after skirting
a ranch.

13.7 km (8.5 mi)
Bear right on the main road for campgrounds on the north
bank of Nahatlatch River. Fork left onto Powderpuff Main FS
road for the south bank Nahatlatch River campground.

> About 2.5 km (1.6 mi) up the Powderpuff Main, fork right.
> Proceed upstream, generally northwest, another 10 minutes
> to the campground at road's end, where a bridge used to
> span the river.

NAHATLATCH RIVER RECREATION SITE #36
Weekend / Moderate
6 tables
Too small for motorhomes and trailers

*Bearing right on the main road at the 13.7-km (8.5-mi) fork, passing the
turnoff to the south bank Nahatlatch River campground.*

15.4 km (9.5 mi)
Cross a narrow bridge over Nahatlatch River, which roars
through a chasm here.

16.7 km (10.3 mi)
After passing a spur on the left, pass a sharp fork ascending
right. Proceed northwest on the main road, following
Nahatlatch River upstream.

16.8 km (10.4 mi)
Bear left on the main road where Nahatlatch Lookout Road
ascends right.

18.4 km (11.4 mi)
Proceed west on the main road for Fir Flat and Log Creek campgrounds. Turn left to enter Apocynum campground on

Nahatlatch River. The access road ends abruptly at the river-bank in 0.4 km (0.2 mi), so approach slowly.

APOCYNUM RECREATION SITE #23
Weekend / Moderate
7 tables
Too small for motorhomes and trailers

~

Continuing west on the main road, passing the turnoff to Apocynum campground.

19.9 km (12.3 mi)
Proceed west on the main road for Log Creek campground. Left is Fir Flat campground on Nahatlatch River. There's just enough shade here to create a welcome refuge in this hot, dry valley.

FIR FLAT RECREATION SITE #22
Weekend / Moderate
3 tables
Accessible by small motorhomes and trailers

~

Continuing west on the main road, passing Fir Flat campground.

20.8 km (12.9 mi)
Pass an **overnight pullout** on the left, near the river.

25.3 km (15.7 mi)
Proceed west on the main road, passing a right fork near Log Creek.

25.4 km (15.8 mi)
Turn left to enter Log Creek campground on Nahatlatch River.

LOG CREEK RECREATION SITE #21
Weekend / Difficult
4 tables
Accessible by small motorhomes and trailers

~

Upper Nahatlatch Valley

Continuing west on the main road, passing Log Creek campground.

26 km (16.1 mi)
Reach a junction. Proceed west (staying on the north side of the river) for the upper Nahatlatch valley lakes. Left crosses a bridge over Nahatlatch River and follows Kookipi Creek south.

36 km (22.3 mi)
Reach the road's high point, and a view of truly wild country.

For SCUZZY CREEK, now follow the directions below

From midway across the Fraser River bridge, it's about 13 km (8 mi) to Scuzzy Creek campground. After crossing railroad tracks on the river's west bank, turn left (south) where right (north) enters the village of North Bend. Proceed straight (south) on Scuzzy Creek FS road, following the Fraser River. The road soon veers northwest, away from the river. It climbs steeply, staying north of Scuzzy Creek. After the terrain levels, cross the bridge to the creek's south bank, then bear right (southwest). The camp-ground is about 8 minutes farther, on the right.

SCUZZY CREEK RECREATION SITE #24
Weekend / Moderate
6 tables
Accessible by small motorhomes & trailers

For BOTANIE LAKE, now follow the directions below

0 km (0 mi)
Starting northeast on Botanie Valley Road, departing Hwy 12.
Ascend gradually.

6.8 km (4.2 mi)
Proceed north on Botanie Valley Road for Botanie Lake campground. Fork left onto Botanie Mountain Lookout Road for the
trailhead.

17 km (10.5 mi)
Arrive at Botanie Lake campground, 300 meters from the south
shore.

BOTANIE LAKE RECREATION SITE #54
Weekend / Moderate (due only to distance)
Elev: 1115 m (3657 ft) / Lake: 12.5 ha
3 tables
Accessible by motorhomes and 5th-wheels

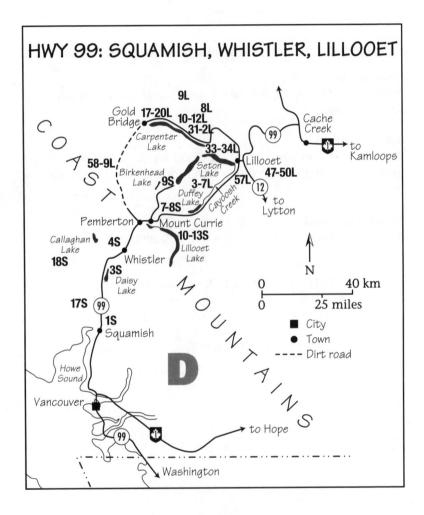

HWY 99: SQUAMISH, WHISTLER, LILLOOET

9L
8L
Gold **17-20L**
Bridge
10-12L
31-2L
Carpenter
Lake
33-34L
Cache
Creek
99
COAST
58-9L
Seton
Lake
Lilloet
47-50L
to
Kamloops
Birkenhead
Lake
9S
3-7L
57L
12
Duffey
Lake
Cayoosh Creek
to
Lytton
7-8S
Pemberton
Mount Currie
10-13S
Callaghan
Lake
4S
Lillooet
Lake
N
18S
Whistler
3S
Daisy
Lake
0   40 km
17S 99
0   25 miles
1S
Squamish
■ City
● Town
--- Dirt road
Howe
Sound
M O U N T A I N S
D
Vancouver
to Hope
99
Washington

D: Hwy 99: Squamish, Whistler, Lillooet

The letter indicates which FS district the campground is in.
S stands for Squamish FS District. **L** stands for Lillooet FS District.

1S	Cat Lake	11S	Twin One Creek
3S	Cal-Cheak Confluence	12S	Lizzie Bay
3L	Cayoosh Creek	13S	Driftwood Bay
4S	Alexander Falls	17L	Gun Lake South
4L	Roger Creek	17S	Lower Squamish River
5L	Gott Creek	18L	Gun Creek
6L	Cottonwood	18S	Upper Squamish River
7L	Cinnamon	19L	Mowson Pond
7S	Owl Creek	20L	Tyaughton Lake
8L	Yalakom	31L	Bighorn Creek
8S	Spetch Creek	32L	Jones Creek
9L	Beaverdam	33L	Mission Dam
9S	Blackwater Lake	34L	Carpenter Lake
10L	Carol Lake	47-50L	Kwotlenemo Lake
10S	Strawberry Point	57L	Seton Dam
11L	Marshall Creek	58L	Donelly Creek
12L	Marshall Lake North	59L	Hope Creek

Hwy 99: Squamish, Whistler, Lillooet

National-park quality scenery in the Tantalus Range, en route to Squamish River campgrounds

SQUAMISH TO WHISTLER

Looking for the nearest free campgrounds north of Vancouver? Exploring the massive mountains and fierce rivers of B.C.'s southern Coast Range? Want to enjoy Whistler on the cheap? The campgrounds described here will serve you well. They're listed from south to north, according to their turnoff points from Hwy 99.

On the **Squamish River** are a couple small, primitive campgrounds without tables. They're up the scenic Squamish Valley Road, north-northwest of Squamish. The first is only 1.3 km (0.8 mi) off pavement, about 25 minutes from Hwy 99. The second is 27 km (16.7 mi) beyond where pavement ends and takes about an hour to reach from Hwy 99.

If you don't mind walking the 1-km (0.6-mi) access trail, the tenters-only campground at tiny **Cat Lake** (page 125) is conveniently located for an easy, overnight stop. The turnoff, just north of Alice Lake Provincial Park, is a mere 15-minute drive north of Squamish. The parking area is only 3 km (1.9 mi) east of Hwy 99.

Callaghan Creek flows into Cheakamus River about 5.5 km (3.4 mi) southwest of Whistler. You'll find three **Cal-Cheak Confluence campgrounds** here (page 126). The first is just 200 meters east of Hwy 99. The others are only a few minutes farther. Lush forest, roaring water, and a hiking trail to Brandywine Falls are the attractions.

A tenters-only campground is perched above thundering **Alexander Falls** (page 128). It's west of Whistler but is reached by turning off Hwy 99 about 5 km (3.1 mi) southwest of Whistler. The turnoff is nearly across the highway from the turnoff for Cal-Cheak Confluence. The road to Alexander Falls grants views of mountains that most people, speeding between Vancouver and Whistler, never see. Continue driving past the falls to reach photogenic Callaghan Lake, ringed by rugged peaks, a glacier, and a waterfall. Bring your canoe, or scramble around the lakeshore. Driving back to the highway, you'll see the Black Tusk east across the valley.

SQUAMISH RIVER

If you're heading north on Hwy 99 from Vancouver

From the Horseshoe Bay exit just north of Vancouver, drive Hwy 99 north 54.4 km (33.7 mi), then turn left (west) onto Squamish Valley Road (across from the Alice Lake Provincial Park turnoff). Set your tripometer to 0.

If you're heading south on Hwy 99 from Whistler

From Brandywine Falls Provincial Park, drive Hwy 99 south 31.6 km (19.6 mi), then turn right (west) onto Squamish Valley Road (across from the Alice Lake Provincial Park turnoff). Set your tripometer to 0.

For either approach above, now follow the directions below

0 km (0 mi)
Starting west on Squamish Valley Road, departing Hwy 99.

2 km (1.3 mi)
Stay straight (north). Left leads back to Squamish.

3.7 km (2.3 mi)
Cross a bridge over Cheakamus River. At the junction 100 meters beyond, stay left (northwest) on Squamish Valley Road. Proceed through Native reserve.

23 km (14.3 mi)
Pavement ends.

24.2 km (15 mi)
Proceed straight (north) for upper Squamish River campground. Quickly reach the first Squamish River campground by turning left (west) here, crossing the Squamish River bridge, then immediately turning right. It's on the west bank.

SQUAMISH RIVER CAMPGROUND #17
Weekend / Easy
3 campsites without tables, beneath cottonwoods
Accessible by small motorhomes and trailers

Continuing north on Squamish River Road, passing the turnoff to the first Squamish River campground.

26.5 km (16.4 mi)
Pass a powerhouse and cross a bridged creek.

27.3 km (16.9 mi)
Pass High Falls Creek trailhead on the right. It begins 100 meters past the creek and should be signed. The trail stays left / northwest of the creek and soon climbs a rocky bluff. For details about this premier hike, and others in the area, read *Don't Waste Your Time in the BC Coast Mountains*, described on page 395.

31.5 km (19.5 mi)
Stay straight and cross a bridge.

43 km (26.7 mi)
Bear left on the main road.

50 km (31 mi)
Reach upper Squamish River campground on the left. It's on the east bank, near the confluence of the Squamish and Elaho rivers, just past a Mile 37 sign, about 0.4 km (0.25 mi) before Elaho River FS road forks left (west).

UPPER SQUAMISH RIVER CAMPGROUND #18
Weekend / Difficult (due only to distance)
3 campsites without tables
Accessible by small motorhomes and trailers

CAT LAKE

If you're heading north on Hwy 99 from Vancouver

From the Horseshoe Bay exit just north of Vancouver, drive Hwy 99 north about 61 km (37.8 mi), then turn right (east) onto Brohm FS road (the first right after Alice Lake Provincial Park). Set your tripometer to 0.

If you're heading south on Hwy 99 from Whistler

From Brandywine Falls Provincial Park, drive Hwy 99 south about 25 km (15.5 mi), then turn left (east) onto Brohm FS road. Set your tripometer to 0.

For either approach above, now follow the directions below

Follow Brohm FS road. Stay right. Reach a gate at about 3 km (1.9 mi). Park there and walk about 1 km (0.6 mi) to the tenters-only campground on the shore of Cat Lake.

CAT LAKE RECREATION SITE #1
Weekend / Easy
Elev: 330 m (1082 ft) / Lake: 6 ha
10 walk-in tentsites with tables
Parking accessible by all vehicles

CAL-CHEAK CONFLUENCE

If you're heading north on Hwy 99 from Vancouver

From the Horseshoe Bay exit just north of Vancouver, drive Hwy 99 north about 90 km (55.8 mi), then turn right (southeast) onto Daisy Lake FS road (4 km / 2.5 mi past Brandywine Falls Provincial Park, and just past Callaghan Creek bridge). Set your tripometer to 0.

If you're heading south on Hwy 99 from Whistler

From Whistler, at Village Gate Blvd. (where there's a traffic light and WELCOME TO WHISTLER sign), drive Hwy 99 south 5.5 km (3.4 mi), then turn left (southeast) onto Daisy Lake FS road just before Callaghan Creek bridge. Set your tripometer to 0.

For either approach above, now follow the directions below

0 km (0 mi)
Starting southeast on Daisy Lake FS road, departing Hwy 99.

200 meters
Turn right for the first Cal-Cheak camping area. The campsites ring a cleared cul de sac near the highway.

CAL-CHEAK CONFLUENCE RECREATION SITE #3
First Camping Area
Overnight / Easy
5 tables near Callaghan Creek
Accessible by motorhomes and 5th-wheels

Settled in at Cal Cheak Confluence campground

Continuing southeast on Daisy Lake FS road, passing the first Cal-Cheak camping area.

0.5 km (0.3 mi)
Proceed right (south) for the third Cal-Cheak camping area and the day-use site. Turn left to reach the second Cal-Cheak camping area in 0.3 km (0.2 mi).

CAL-CHEAK CONFLUENCE RECREATION SITE #3
Second Camping Area
Weekend / Easy
9 tables near Cheakamus River
Accessible by small motorhomes and trailers

Continuing south on Daisy Lake FS road, passing the turnoff to the second Cal-Cheak camping area.

0.8 km (0.5 mi)
Proceed straight (south) for the Cal-Cheak day-use site. Turn right for the third Cal-Cheak camping area.

CAL-CHEAK CONFLUENCE RECREATION SITE #3
Third Camping Area
Weekend / Easy
8 tables near Callaghan Creek
Accessible by small motorhomes and trailers

~~

Continuing south on Daisy Lake FS road, passing the third Cal-Cheak camping area.

0.9 km (0.6 mi)
Reach the Cal-Cheak day-use site, near the powerline structure and the confluence of Callaghan Creek and Cheakamus River. Walk across the suspension bridge to begin the 4-km (2.5-mi) hike to Brandywine Falls.

~~

ALEXANDER FALLS

If you're heading north on Hwy 99 from Vancouver

From the Horseshoe Bay exit just north of Vancouver, drive Hwy 99 north about 90.5 km (56 mi), then turn left (northwest) onto Callaghan Lake FS road (300 meters past Callaghan Creek bridge). Set your tripometer to 0.

If you're heading south on Hwy 99 from Whistler

From Whistler, at Village Gate Blvd. (where there's a traffic light and WELCOME TO WHISTLER sign), drive Hwy 99 south 5 km (3 mi), then turn right (northwest) onto Callaghan Lake FS road (300 meters before Callaghan Creek bridge). Set your tripometer to 0.

For either approach above, now follow the directions below

0 km (0 mi)
Starting northwest on Callaghan Lake FS road, departing Hwy 99. The road is stony and rough. Drive through a recovery area and see a clearcut hillside to the west.

9 km (5.5 mi)
Reach a junction. Less than 200 meters beyond, on the left, is Alexander Falls campground. It's for tenters only.

ALEXANDER FALLS RECREATION SITE #4
Overnight / Moderate
5 tentsites with tables
Parking accessible by all vehicles.

Continuing north on Callaghan Lake FS road, passing Alexander Falls campground, heading for Callaghan Lake.

9.2 km (5.7 mi)
Cross a bridged creek, pass a huge pullout / viewpoint, and ascend.

9.5 km (5.9 mi)
Proceed northwest on Callaghan Lake FS road for Callaghan Lake. The right fork leads to Madely Lake.

17.7 km (11 mi)
Reach Callaghan Lake at 1204 m (3950 ft) elevation. BC Parks now has authority over the old FS campground here.

NORTHEAST OF PEMBERTON

The crowd stops at Whistler. But the B.C. Coast Mountains keep marching north. So do the campgrounds. Turn off Hwy 99 at the town of Mount Currie. The road is paved nearly to its end at Birkenhead Lake Provincial Park. The lake is a beauty: 6 km (3.7 mi) long, boldly guarded by Birkenhead Peak and its sentinel siblings along the ridge. A short trail allows you to appreciate the ancient forest gracing the lake's north shore.

En route to Birkenhead Lake are three FS campgrounds. The first is on Owl Creek, where it flows into Birkenhead River, not far from Hwy 99 and Mount Currie. A choice of campsites (creekside, riverside, clearing, forest) and a variety of hiking trails nearby (read *Don't Waste Your Time in the B.C. Coast Mountains,* described on page 395) earn Owl a Destination rating. It has room for all but behemoth RVs.

The second campground is just up the road, at Spetch Creek. Rated Weekend, Spetch is smaller and less scenic than Owl, but it feels more secluded, which some people prefer. The entry road and campsites accommodate nothing larger than trucks with campers.

Just outside Birkenhead Park is an Overnight campground on tiny, lackluster Blackwater Lake. It's next to the road, so small motorhomes and trailers can squeeze in, but the only attraction here is avoiding the cost of provincial-park camping.

If you're heading east on Hwy 99 from Pemberton

From the edge of Pemberton (at the junction by the Petro Canada gas station) drive Hwy 99 east 7.1 km (4.4 mi) to Mount Currie, then reset your tripometer to 0.

If you're heading southwest on Hwy 99 from Lillooet

From Joffre Lakes Recreation Area parking lot, drive Hwy 99 southwest 23.5 km (14.6 mi) to Mount Currie, then reset your tripometer to 0.

Owl Creek campground

For either approach above, now follow the directions below

0 km (0 mi)
Starting north, from the 3-way intersection in Mount Currie, heading toward D'Arcy and Birkenhead Lake Provincial Park.

4.6 km (2.8 mi)
Cross a bridge over Owl Creek. Proceed straight (north) for campgrounds at Spetch Creek and Blackwater Lake. Turn right (under the lines from a small power station) for Owl Creek campground.

In 0.3 km (0.2 mi) cross railroad tracks. Fork right for campsites on Owl Creek, left for camping areas near Birkenhead River. Big RVs should go left, where there's room to turn around. The mixed forest provides plentiful shade. The Cayoosh Range rises abruptly to the east. The confluence of two romping streams keeps campers entertained.

OWL CREEK RECREATION SITE #7
Destination / Easy
13 tables
Accessible by motorhomes and trailers

Continuing north, passing the turnoff to Owl Creek campground.

6.6 km (4.1 mi)
Look for possible **overnight pullouts** after crossing the bridge over Birkenhead River.

12.2 km (7.6 mi)
Turn right to arrive at Spetch Creek campground in 0.3 km (0.2 mi). It's not as open or spacious as Owl Creek campground.

SPETCH CREEK RECREATION SITE #8
Weekend / Easy
6 secluded campsites with tables, near the creek
Inaccessible by motorhomes and trailers

Continuing north, passing the turnoff to Spetch Creek campground.

34.6 km (21.5 mi)
Reach a junction. Turn left (northwest) for Blackwater campground and Birkenhead Lake Provincial Park. Straight (northeast) soon reaches D'Arcy, at the southwest end of Anderson Lake.

36 km (22.3 mi)
Pavement ends. Cross a bridge over Blackwater Creek.

43 km (26.7 mi)
Proceed straight (west) for Birkenhead Lake Provincial Park. Turn left to enter Blackwater Lake campground.

Because this campground lacks charm, few campers stop here and none stay long, so it's usually quiet. The lake is tiny. The campsites are private, huddled in a horseshoe of brush and trees. The convenient location allows you to enjoy the grandeur of Birkenhead Lake without paying to stay at the huge provincial park campground.

BLACKWATER LAKE RECREATION SITE #9
Overnight / Easy
Elev: 770 m (2525 ft) / Lake: 15 ha
3 tables, 6 campsites
Accessible by small motorhomes and trailers

Continuing west, passing Blackwater Lake campground.

50.2 km (31.1 mi)
Arrive at Birkenhead Lake Provincial Park. In addition to a sprawling campground, it has a day-use area, sandy beach, large expanse of grass, and lakeshore hiking trail among ancient trees.

LILLOOET LAKE

Hikers bound for the Upper Stein Wilderness have the convenient option of a pre- or post-trip refuge at any of four campgrounds on Lillooet Lake. For details about the superb alpine

Lillooet Lake, from Driftwood Bay campground

hiking nearby, read *Don't Waste Your Time in the BC Coast Mountains*, described on page 395. But you don't have to go beyond Lillooet Lake to find enjoyment. The campgrounds on its east shore, south of Hwy 99, are themselves worthy goals. Two are rated Destination: Strawberry Point (walk-in tentsites only) and Lizzie Bay. At 195 m (640 ft) elevation, Lillooet Lake is 24 km (15 mi) long and covers 3220 hectares.

If you're heading east on Hwy 99 from Pemberton

From the 3-way junction in Mount Currie, drive Hwy 99 east 10.3 km (6.4 mi), then turn right (southeast) onto In-SHUCK-ch FS road (where the highway begins climbing, before the winter closure gate and sign for Lillooet). Reset your tripometer to 0.

If you're heading southwest on Hwy 99 from Lillooet

From Joffre Lakes Recreation Area parking lot, drive Hwy 99 southwest 13.2 km (8.2 mi), then turn left (southeast) onto In-SHUCK-ch FS road (just after the winter closure gate, at the bottom of the steep hill). Reset your tripometer to 0.

For either approach above, now follow the directions below

0 km (0 mi)
Starting southeast on In-SHUCK-ch FS road, following the northeast shore of Lillooet Lake.

6.8 km (4.2 mi)
Reach the parking area for Strawberry Point tenters-only campground, on the right.

It's a five-minute walk down to this peaceful little campground on Lillooet Lake. The scenery across the lake includes a glacier. An abundance of driftwood encourages playful creativity. If you have a campfire, use an existing fire ring; don't further mar the beach.

STRAWBERRY POINT RECREATION SITE #10
Destination / Easy
2 walk-in tentsites with tables, gravel beach
Parking accessible by all vehicles

Continuing southeast on the main road, passing Strawberry Point campground.

9.4 km (5.8 mi)
Proceed straight (southeast) on the main road for more campgrounds on Lillooet Lake. Twin One Creek Haul Road forks left and ascends.

10 km (6.2 mi)
Proceed straight (southeast) on the main road for more campgrounds on Lillooet Lake. Turn right to descend to Twin One Creek campground on Lillooet Lake. A couple campsites are in the open, beside the lake. Others are in trees.

TWIN ONE CREEK RECREATION SITE #11
Overnight / Moderate
5 tables, boat launch
Accessible by small motorhomes and trailers

Continuing southeast on the main road, passing the turnoff to Twin One Creek campground.

11.6 km (7.2 mi)
Pass a lodge and commercial campground.

15.8 km (9.8 mi)
Pass a KM 16 sign. Look for a campsite on the right, in trees, at the end of Lizzie Bay. It has one table, a beach and a boat launch.

16 km (9.9 mi)
Proceed straight (south) on the main road for Driftwood Bay campground. Turn right and descend to reach Lizzie Bay campground in 300 meters.

> This is Lillooet Lake's best campground. The campsites are well spaced, surrounded by trees, on the waterfront, with views north up the lake. Only one campsite has a sandy beach on this rocky shore.

LIZZIE BAY RECREATION SITE #12
Destination / Moderate
9 tables, level tentsites
Accessible by small motorhomes and trailers

Continuing south on the main road, passing the turnoff to Lizzie Bay campground.

16.6 km (10.3 mi)
Proceed straight (south) on the main road for Driftwood Bay campground. Turn left (southeast) onto Douglas-Lizzie Cr Branch FS road to reach **Lizzie Lake Recreation Site #14** and the Stein Divide trailhead in 11 km (6.8 mi). About 8 km (5 mi) up, the steep, rough ascent demands 4WD. The small campground is at the lake's north end.

17.7 km (11 mi)
Turn right and descend to reach Driftwood Bay campground in 200 meters.

DRIFTWOOD BAY RECREATION SITE #13
Weekend / Moderate
3 tables
Accessible by small motorhomes and trailers

LILLOOET LAKE TO LILLOOET

Between Lillooet Lake and the town of Lillooet, Hwy 99 plies the valley that cradles Duffey Lake. Most people blast through here. There are two good reasons not to: (1) a surprising number of free campgrounds, all just off the pavement; and (2) engaging scenery.

At the valley's southwest end are glacier-capped peaks. After passing Duffey Lake, the highway meanders along delightful Cayoosh Creek and crosses several one-lane wooden bridges built when a slower pace of travel allowed greater appreciation of the land. Farther northeast, the highway works through a deep, rugged canyon, hugging the cliffsides then careening into the town of Lillooet, on the Fraser River.

Beautiful year-round, this stretch of Hwy 99 is especially pleasing in October, when fall colours are intense. But it can be chilly here then, even when sunny.

If you're heading east on Hwy 99 from Pemberton

From the edge of Pemberton (at the junction by the Petro Canada gas station) drive Hwy 99 east 17.3 km (10.7 mi). You'll pass through Mount Currie, then cross the narrow, north arm of Lillooet Lake. Just before the winter closure gate and sign for Lillooet (where In-SHUCK-ch FS road forks right / southeast along Lillooet Lake, and the highway begins climbing) reset your tripometer to 0.

0 km (0 mi)
Proceeding northeast on Hwy 99, from the north end of Lillooet Lake.

13.2 km (8.2 mi)
Pass Joffre Lakes Recreation Area on the right. The two-hour hike to Upper Joffre Lake, beneath Matier Glacier and Joffre

Campsite view of Cayoosh Creek

Peak, is spectacular. For details read *Don't Waste Your Time in the B.C. Coast Mountains*, described on page 395.

32.8 km (20.4 mi)
Pass **Duffey Lake Provincial Park campground** on the left. It was still fee-free in 1999. Set in trees, at the marshy, frog-happy, northeast end of the lake, it has a stupendous mountain view. But the highway is so close that you'll hear every passing vehicle.

The four tables are best left to picnickers. For even a brief overnight stay, the FS campgrounds farther northeast are superior.

35.1 km (21.8 mi)
Watch for possible **overnight pullouts** along Cayoosh Creek.

45.2 km (28.1 mi)
Turn left, just before the bridge, to enter Cayoosh Creek campground. Treed campsites line the creek.

CAYOOSH CREEK RECREATION SITE #3
Weekend / Easy
6 tables
Accessible by small motorhomes and trailers

49.4 km (30.7 mi)
Turn right to enter Roger Creek campground.

Roger Creek campground is on Cayoosh Creek. The namesake creek flows into Cayoosh farther northeast. This is the first of two Roger Creek camping areas. The sites here face dense forest and feel private, but by October they're shaded until 11:30 a.m.

ROGER CREEK RECREATION SITE #4a
Weekend / Easy
4 tables
Accessible by small motorhomes and trailers

49.9 km (30.9 mi)
Turn right to enter Roger Creek campground.

This is the second Roger Creek camping area. It's more open, so it's sunnier and easier for big rigs to enter and turn around in.

Cottonwood campground

ROGER CREEK RECREATION SITE #4b
Weekend / Easy
4 tables, 5 campsites
Accessible by motorhomes and 5th-wheels

51.5 km (32 mi)
Turn left to enter Gott Creek campground, at the confluence of Cayoosh and Gott Creeks.

GOTT CREEK RECREATION SITE #5
Overnight / Easy
2 tables
Too small for motorhomes and trailers

58.9 km (36.6 mi)
Turn left to enter Cottonwood campground, just before Downton Creek FS road forks left.

The campsites are well spaced, beneath thin pines and tall cottonwoods, near the creek but not on it. Big RVs should camp only in the first clearing, where there are no tables.

COTTONWOOD RECREATION SITE #6
Weekend / Easy
7 tables
Accessible by motorhomes and 5th-wheels

~

62.5 km (38.8 mi)
Turn left to enter Cinnamon campground.

This is the most developed of the Cayoosh Creek campgrounds. It's a pretty spot, with a view of a dry, rugged
mountainside. A couple campsites are on the creek.

CINNAMON RECREATION SITE #7
Weekend / Easy
12 tables
Accessible by motorhomes and 5th-wheels

~

77.8 km (48.3 mi)
Turn right to enter Seton Dam campground, near Lillooet.

This huge, well-maintained campground is provided by BC
Hydro. Across the highway is Seton Reservoir (22 km / 13.6
mi long, covering 2475 hectares) where you'll find a beach,
boat launch, and day-use area. Compared to Cayoosh
Creek valley, it's much warmer here due to lower elevation
(236 m / 774 ft) and greater sun exposure. Watch for
mountain goats performing anti-gravity stunts on the
sheer cliffs across the valley.

SETON DAM CAMPGROUND #57
Weekend / Easy
47 campsites, 32 tables, garbage cans, firewood
Accessible by motorhomes and 5th-wheels

~

82.1 km (51 mi)
Arrive at the junction of Hwys 99 and 12 in Lillooet, on the
Fraser River's west bank.

~

If you're heading southwest on Hwy 99 from Lillooet

0 km (0 mi)
Starting southwest on Hwy 99 from the junction of Hwys 99 and 12 in Lillooet, on the Fraser River's west bank.

4.3 km (2.7 mi)
Turn left to enter **Seton Dam campground**, described on page 140. The highway begins ascending steeply through the canyon, toward Duffey Lake.

19.6 km (12.2 mi)
Turn right to enter **Cinnamon campground**, described on page 140.

23.2 km (14.4 mi)
Turn right to enter **Cottonwood campground**, described on page 140.

30.6 km (19 mi)
Turn right to enter **Gott Creek campground**, described on page 139.

32.7 km (20.3 mi)
Turn left to enter **Roger Creek campground**, described on page 138.

37 km (22.9 mi)
Turn right, just after the bridge, to enter **Cayoosh Creek campground**, described on page 138.

49.3 km (30.6 mi)
Pass **Duffey Lake Provincial Park campground** on the right, described on page 137.

68.9 km (42.7 mi)
Pass Joffre Lakes Recreation Area on the left.

82.1 km (51 mi)
Proceed straight (west) on Hwy 99 for Mount Currie, Pemberton, Whistler, Squamish and Vancouver. Turn left (southeast) onto In-SHUCK-ch FS road for campgrounds on Lillooet Lake; directions continue on page 134.

Firewood artist creates masterpiece at Seton Dam campground.

EAST OF LILLOOET

Fountain Ridge forms the east wall of Fraser River canyon near Lillooet. Just over the ridge is Kwotlenemo Lake (also called Fountain Lake) in Fountain Valley. Clustered around the lake are four FS campgrounds. Two accommodate big RVs. You can launch a cartop boat on the lake, but only electric motors are allowed.

A gravel road runs north-south about 28 km (17.4 mi) through Fountain Valley, providing reasonable access even for motorhomes. The lake is 10.5 km (6.5 mi) south of Hwy 99, or 16 km (9.9 mi) north of Hwy 12.

Blue skies prevail here, so Fountain Valley is a good spring camping destination for Lower Mainlanders seeking to escape West Coast drizzle. If you're travelling through Fraser River canyon in summer, where soaring temperatures can be oppressive, you'll find Fountain Valley slightly cooler because it's 500 m (1640 ft) higher. The lake is roughly at the valley's highest point and is surrounded by rugged, dry mountains.

Kwotlenemo Lake South campground is large and very open. It has 20 tables and accommodates motorhomes and 5th-wheels.

Kwotlenemo Lake West campground is small and quiet. It has only 2 tables and is accessible by nothing bigger than trucks with campers.

Kwotlenemo Lake East campground is small (just 2 tables) but not quiet. It's on the main road, near private cabins. It's also on a hillside, so access is limited to vehicles no larger than trucks with campers.

Kwotlenemo Lake North campground has 10 tables, is very open and therefore accessible by all vehicles. Camping is allowed, but this is primarily a day-use area.

The southern approach, from Hwy 12

From Trans-Canada Hwy 1 at Lytton, drive Hwy 12 north 39.5 km (24.5 mi). Or, from the Fraser River bridge in Lillooet, drive Hwy 12 southeast 22.4 km (13.9 mi). From either approach, turn north onto Fountain Valley Road and reset your tripometer to 0. At 16 km (9.9 mi) reach the south end of Kwotlenemo Lake. At 17.5 km (10.9 mi) reach the lake's north end. At 28 km (17.4 mi) intersect Hwy 99.

The northern approach, from Hwy 99

From the junction of Hwys 99 and 97 (11 km / 6.8 mi northwest of Cache Creek), drive Hwy 99 west 61.3 km (38 mi). Or, from the Fraser River bridge in Lillooet, drive Hwy 99 northeast 14 km (8.7 mi). From either approach, turn south onto Fountain Valley Road and reset your tripometer to 0. At 10.5 km (6.5 mi) reach the north end of Kwotlenemo Lake. At 12 km (7.4 mi) reach the lake's south end. At 28 km (17.4 mi) intersect Hwy 12.

KWOTLENEMO (FOUNTAIN) LAKE RECREATION SITES #47-50
Weekend / Easy
Elev: 910 m (2985 ft) / Lake: 35 ha
34 tables, cartop boat launch (electric motors only)
Accessible by motorhomes and 5th-wheels

CARPENTER LAKE

Carpenter Lake is a sinuous blue swath about a 45-minute drive west-northwest of Lillooet. You can choose from more than a dozen free campgrounds here. Two are big, well-maintained, BC Hydro campgrounds, on the lake's north shore. The rest are smaller FS campgrounds, mostly on tiny satellite lakes just north of Carpenter.

At 654 m (2145 ft) elevation, Carpenter Lake is 57 km (35 mi) long and covers 4625 hectares. The surrounding mountains are dry, scattered with pines and firs. The sun seems to be a constant fixture in the perpetually blue sky. In summer, prepare to broil. But Carpenter Lake is a springtime haven for anyone seeking to escape the gray and damp that clings to areas farther west.

Northwest of Carpenter Lake is the Southern Chilcotin—premier backpacking country distinguished by wondrous red-and-mauve soil and vast meadowed slopes. For details about an exquisite alpine circuit, read *Don't Waste Your Time in the B.C. Coast Mountains,* described on page 395.

Overlooking Cinnabar Basin, in the Southern Chilcotin mountains

0 km (0 mi)
Starting north into Lillooet, from the junction of Hwys 99 and 12, on the Fraser River's west bank. Follow signs for Gold Bridge.

0.8 km (0.5 mi)
After crossing railroad tracks, turn right onto Main Street. Drive north through Lillooet. Fill up with gas before leaving town.

2.9 km (1.8 mi)
Turn left at Old Mill Mall, following the green highway sign: SHALATH (69 KM), GOLD BRIDGE (101 KM).

9 km (5.6 mi)
Cross a bridge over Bridge River, at a deep, narrow chasm.

9.4 km (5.8 mi)
Stay straight on the main road. It's paved for a while, then well-graded gravel, and later alternates. Pass Slok FS road on the right.

33.8 km (21 mi)
Reach a signed junction. For Carpenter Lake and Gold Bridge, bear left and descend to the Yalakom River bridge. For Yalakom and Beaverdam campgrounds, bear right, reset your tripometer to 0, and proceed northwest on Yalakom FS road.

> **0 km (0 mi)**
> Proceeding northwest on Yalakom FS road, from the 33.8-km (21-mi) junction.

> **8.5 km (5.3 mi)**
> Reach Yalakom campground, on Yalakom River's east bank, just before the next bridge over the river. The tight valley limits sun exposure.

YALAKOM RECREATION SITE #8
Weekend / Moderate
3 tables
Accessible by motorhomes and 5th-wheels

~

Continuing northwest on Yalakom FS road, passing Yalakom campground.

22.5 km (14 mi)
Reach Beaverdam campground, on the left. It's just before the bridge over Beaverdam Creek, near its confluence with Yalakom River. There's another camping area across the bridge. The valley is broader and sunnier here than at Yalakom campground.

BEAVERDAM RECREATION SITE #9
Weekend / Difficult (due only to distance)
6 tables
Accessible by motorhomes and 5th-wheels

~~

Continuing left at the 33.8-km (21-mi) junction, heading for Carpenter Lake and Gold Bridge.

35.4 km (22 mi)
Cross the Yalakom River bridge. You're now in a deep, narrow canyon. Pavement ends in 10 km (6 mi).

50 km (31 mi)
Proceed straight (west) for Carpenter Lake. Turn left and descend to reach Mission Dam campground in 400 meters.

Though it's beneath the dam, where scenery is nil, this campground is big and open, ideal for large groups.

MISSION DAM RECREATION SITE #33
Overnight / Difficult (due only to distance)
3 tables
Accessible by motorhomes and 5th-wheels

~~

Bighorn Creek campground on Carpenter Lake

Continuing west on the main road, passing the turnoff to Mission Dam campground.

50.9 km (31.6 mi)
Reach a junction at the dam. Proceed right (west) for most Carpenter Lake area campgrounds. Turn left onto Mission Mtn. road, cross the dam and go through the tunnel to reach **Carpenter Lake Recreation Site #34** in 1.6 km (1 mi). It's tiny (2 tables), across the road from the lake, not recommended.

69.6 km (43.2 mi)
Proceed straight (northwest) on the main road for most Carpenter Lake area campgrounds. Turn left and descend to quickly reach BC Hydro's Bighorn Creek campground on Carpenter Lake.

BIGHORN CREEK CAMPGROUND #31
Destination / Difficult (due only to distance)
15 tables, 12 campsites, garbage cans, rough boat launch
day-use area
Accessible by motorhomes and 5th-wheels

〰

Continuing northwest on the main road, passing the turnoff to Bighorn Creek campground.

72 km (44.6 mi)
Proceed straight (west) on the main road for more Carpenter Lake area campgrounds. Turn left (just after crossing the bridge) and descend (bearing left) to reach Jones Creek campground in about 0.7 km (0.4 mi).

Big RVs can proceed as far as the gravel pit, after which they should scout the final, narrow access, where bushes and trees encroach. Because it's well off the main road, this is a special campground on Carpenter Lake. The forest is pretty, with lots of aspen. A couple more campsites, including one on the creek, are beyond those with tables.

JONES CREEK RECREATION SITE #32
Destination / Difficult (due only to distance)
3 tables, more campsites
Accessible by small motorhomes and trailers

Continuing west on the main road, passing the turnoff to Jones Creek campground.

72.2 km (44.8 mi)
Reach a junction. For more Carpenter Lake area campgrounds and Gold Bridge, bear left (west) on the main road. For campgrounds on Carol Lake, Marshall Creek and Marshall Lake, turn right, reset your tripometer to 0, and ascend northwest.

0 km (0 mi)
Starting northwest from the 72.2-km (44.8-mi) junction.

3 km (1.9 mi)
Proceed straight (northwest) for campgrounds on Marshall Creek and Lake. Turn right (northeast) to reach the campground on tiny Carol Lake in 0.7 km (0.4 mi).

CAROL LAKE RECREATION SITE #10
Weekend / Difficult (due only to distance)
8 tables
Accessible by motorhomes and 5th-wheels

~

Continuing straight (northwest) passing the turnoff to Carol Lake campground.

11.7 km (7.3 mi)
Proceed straight (northwest) for Marshall Lake North campground. Turn left to enter Marshall Creek campground, near the lake outlet.

MARSHALL CREEK RECREATION SITE #11
Weekend / Difficult (due only to distance)
3 tables
Inaccessible by motorhomes and trailers

~

Continuing straight (northwest), passing the turnoff to Marshall Creek campground.

12 km (7.4 mi)
Reach a fork. Turn left onto rougher Marshall Lake Road. The main road continues right.

16.5 km (10.2 mi)
Arrive at Marshall Lake North campground on the west side of the lake's north end, near private cabins. It's larger and more open than Marshall Creek campground.

MARSHALL LAKE NORTH RECREATION SITE #12
Weekend / Difficult (due only to distance)
Lake: 65 ha
7 tables, beach, cartop boat launch
Accessible by small motorhomes and trailers

~

Continuing west on the main road along Carpenter Lake, from the 72.2-km (44.8-mi) junction.

95.7 km (59.3 mi)
Reach **Tyax Junction Recreation Site #60,** on the left, below the main road. It's small (2 tables), inaccessible by big RVs, near a busy crossroads, not recommended for camping. A rough boat launch is an incentive for day use.

95.8 km (59.4 mi)
Reach Tyax Junction. For Gun Creek campground on Carpenter Lake, Gold Bridge, and Gun Lake South campground, bear left and follow the main road southwest along Carpenter Lake. For campgrounds on Mowson Pond, Pearson Pond and Tyaughton Lake, turn right, reset your tripometer to 0, and ascend steeply northwest.

0 km (0 mi)
Starting northwest from the 95.8-km (59.4-mi) junction.

2 km (1.2 mi)
Reach Mowson Pond campground, at the top of the rise, on the left. The surrounding mountains are visible.

MOWSON POND RECREATION SITE #19
Weekend / Difficult (due only to distance)
Elev: 796 m (2611 ft) / Lake: 23 ha
8 well-spaced campsites with tables
Accessible by small motorhomes and trailers

Continuing northwest, passing Mowson Pond campground.

3.5 km (2.2 mi)
Reach a junction. For Friburg campground on Tyaughton Lake, proceed northwest, following signs for Tyax Lodge. To quickly reach the small campground on swampy Pearson Pond, turn left (east) onto Gun Creek FS road; take the first left, then the first right.

Getting Acquainted with Doug Fir

The outdoor activities you can enjoy with your child are limitless. This one develops empathy and perception. Blindfold your child, then lead him to a tree. Introduce them to one another. Urge your child to get acquainted with the tree. Suggest touching it, hugging it, talking to it, listening to it, smelling it. Nudge your child's curiosity by posing questions about the tree's life and history. Then lead your child back to camp, take off the blindfold and ask, "Where's your friend?" Let him find the tree. During your stay, occasionally ask "How's your friend doing?" After he visits it, question him about the experience. "Has the tree changed? Does it have a family nearby? Who are the tree's friends? Bugs? Birds? Chipmunks? If you'll ever return to this campground, tell your child he can visit his friend again. Before you leave, let him say goodbye.

PEARSON POND RECREATION SITE #62
Weekend / Difficult
Elev: 807 m (2647 ft) / Lake: 9 ha
3 tables
Inaccessible by motorhomes and trailers

Continuing northwest, passing the turnoff to Pearson Pond campground.

6 km (3.6 mi)
Pass a road veering left, then reach a fork. Curve left and descend on the main road, passing Hornal Road on the right.

8.2 km (5.1 mi)
Turn right to enter Friburg campground on beautiful Tyaughton Lake.

FRIBURG RECREATION SITE #20
Destination / Difficult (due only to distance)
Elev: 1036 m (3400 ft) / Lake: 90 ha
4 tables, boat launch
Accessible by small motorhomes and trailers

Continuing southwest on the main road along Carpenter Lake, from Tyax Junction at 95.8 km (59.4 mi).

99.5 km (61.8 mi)
Proceed straight (southwest) on the main road for Gold Bridge and Gun Lake South campground. Turn left to enter BC Hydro's Gun Creek campground on Carpenter Lake.

GUN CREEK CAMPGROUND #18
Weekend / Difficult (due only to distance)
13 tables, garbage cans
Accessible by motorhomes and 5th-wheels

Continuing southwest on the main road along Carpenter Lake, passing the turnoff to Gun Creek campground.

107.5 km (66.7 mi)
Reach a junction near the southwest end of Carpenter Lake. Left, across Bridge River, is the community of Gold Bridge. Straight (toward Gun Lake), then left in 250 meters onto Gwyneth Lake Road (signed for Pemberton) leads southwest onto Hurley River FS road. Rough but passable in a 2WD car, it accesses FS campgrounds at Hope and Donelly creeks (page 155) before descending into Pemberton Valley. Set your tripometer to 0 and follow the directions below to quickly reach the FS campground on cottage-crowded Gun Lake.

0 km (0 mi)
Proceeding straight at the 107.5-km (66.7-mi) junction (near the southwest end of Carpenter Lake), heading for Gun Lake. In 250 meters stay straight on pavement.

1.3 km (0.8 mi)
Go left on Gun Lake Road West.

2 km (1.2 mi)
Pass Downton Lake. Mt. Sloan is visible southwest.

5.7 km (3.5 mi) and 6.8 km (4.2 mi)
Bear left.

10.2 km (6.3 mi)

Reach Gun Lake South campground, in trees on a bench above the lake. About 200 cottages ring the shore, so don't expect a wilderness experience. There's a cement boat launch at the lake's south end.

GUN LAKE SOUTH RECREATION SITE #17
Weekend / Difficult (due only to distance)
Elev: 888 m (2913 ft) / Lake: 572 ha
6 tables
Accessible by small motorhomes and trailers

CARPENTER LAKE TO PEMBERTON

Hurley River FS road offers a 60-km (37.2-mi) shortcut between Carpenter Lake and the paved Pemberton Valley Road. Though rough, 2WD cars can handle it. Just go slowly—which you'll want to do anyway, especially at the south end, where the road is worst and the scenery best.

On both sides of Pemberton Valley, peaks rise 2010 m (6600 ft). While coaxing your vehicle up the switchbacks, you can stare at the Pemberton Icefield and the peaks marching northwest along the Upper Lillooet River toward Meager Mountain. You'll also pass the turnoff for Tenquille Lake trailhead. It's an outstanding hike over a meadowy, flower-garden pass. For details, read *Don't Waste Your Time in the BC Coast Mountains*, described on page 395.

Two creekside FS campgrounds are just off the Hurley Road, about midway. Both are small and rarely used. Stop for a pleasant overnight stay, or a brief refuge from the rigours of the Hurley Road.

If you're heading south from Carpenter Lake

From the junction at the southwest end of Carpenter Lake (where the community of Gold Bridge is left across Bridge River), go straight toward Gun Lake. In 250 meters, turn left (south) onto Gwyneth Lake Road (signed for Pemberton) and set your tripometer to 0. It leads southwest onto Hurley River FS road (rough but passable in a 2WD car).

0 km (0 mi)
Starting south on Gwyneth Lake Road, from near Gold Bridge and the southwest end of Carpenter Lake. Proceed southwest on Hurley River FS road.

25 km (15.5 mi)
Turn left, just before Hope Creek bridge, to quickly reach **Hope Creek campground**. Read page 155 for details.

29 km (18 mi)
Turn right to quickly reach **Donelly Creek campground**. Read page 155 for details.

60 km (37.2 mi)
Intersect Pemberton Valley Road after crossing the bridge over Lillooet River. Turn left (southeast) to reach Hwy 99 at Pemberton in about 25 km (15.5 mi)

If you're heading northwest from Pemberton

From the Petro Canada gas station on Hwy 99 near Pemberton, drive north into town. At 1 km (0.6 mi), after crossing railroad tracks, reach a T-junction and turn right. At 2.8 km (1.7 mi) turn left (northwest) on Pemberton Valley Road. At 25 km (15.5 mi) turn right (north) onto Hurley River / Upper Lillooet River FS road (signed for Meager Creek, Gold Bridge and Lillooet). Set your tripometer to 0.

0 km (0 mi)
Starting north on Hurley River / Upper Lillooet River FS road.

1.5 km (0.9 mi)
Cross the bridge over Lillooet River. Turn left (northwest), now following the north bank. Pavement ends.

9.1 km (5.6 mi)
Reach a junction. Left (northwest) on Upper Lillooet River FS road leads to Meager Creek Hot Springs in about 40 km (25 mi). Turn right onto Hurley River FS road for Donelly and Hope Creek campgrounds en route to Gold Bridge and Carpenter Lake. The road is rough but passable in a 2WD car. It switchbacks, heading generally north.

31 km (19.2 mi)
Turn left to quickly reach Donelly Creek campground.

DONELLY CREEK RECREATION SITE #58
Weekend / Difficult
3 tables
Accessible by motorhomes and trailers

Continuing northeast on Hurley River FS road, passing the turnoff to Donelly Creek campground.

35 km (21.7 mi)
Turn right, just after crossing Hope Creek bridge, to quickly reach Hope Creek campground.

HOPE CREEK RECREATION SITE #59
Weekend / Difficult
3 tables
Accessible by motorhomes and trailers

60 km (37.2 mi)
Arrive at Gold Bridge and the southwest end of Carpenter Lake.

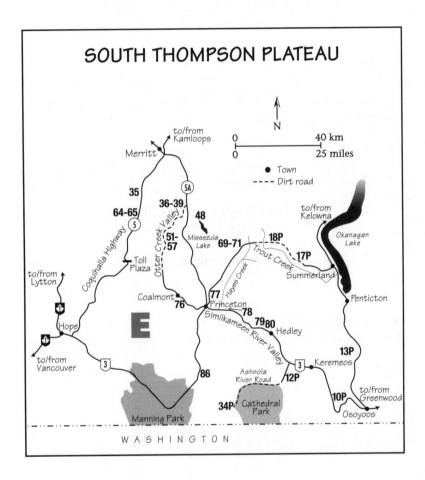

E: South Thompson Plateau

Most of these campgrounds are in the Merritt FS District.
P stands for Penticton FS District.

10P	Mt. Kobau
12P	Red Bridge
13P	Burnell Lake
17P	Trout Creek Crossing
18P	Thirsk Lake
34P	Ashnola River
35	Gillis Lake
36	Shea Lake
37	Tahla Lake
38	Boss Lake
39	Davis Lake
48	Missezula Lake
51-57	Plateau Lakes
64	Murray Lake North
65	Murray Lake South
69	Chain Lake West
70	Link Lake
71	Osprey Lake
76	Granite Creek
77	Martin's Lake
78	Dewdney
79	Old Hedley Road West
80	Old Hedley Road East
86	Copper Creek

South Thompson Plateau

Canoeing the Similkameen River

Most people living elsewhere in the province have just three vague images of the South Thompson Plateau. Cement. Fruit. Forest. The cement is in the form of two recently built, monster highways: the Coquihalla and the Okanagan Connector. The fruit comes from orchards around Keremeos. The forest would be Manning Provincial Park. What else is here? Much more. You'll find it's best appreciated not by aiming for a particular destination, but by roaming with a broad goal in mind: to sample B.C.'s marvelous multiplicity.

Work-stressed, caffeine-buzzed Vancouverites needing a couple day's decompression usually look no farther than the nearby and obvious. That includes Manning Park, which is why it gets frenetic there on summer weekends and offers little respite unless you hike one of the more challenging trails. So drive another hour east, into the Tulameen River valley, northwest of Princeton. Pitch your tent at spacious **Granite Creek campground** (page 162), far from the annoying whine of highway traffic, yet just off pavement.

Up for more adventure? Explore the **Plateau Lakes** (page 164). About midway between Princeton and Merritt, the plateau is splattered with lakes and campgrounds. Bring your mountain bike and cruise the spiderweb of roads. Or come simply for tranquillity. Listen to loons calling and aspen leaves fluttering, instead of boom boxes shattering the peace as often happens at highway-side commercial and provincial campgrounds.

Or, if quiet doesn't relax you, head to Keremeos, drive south toward Cathedral Provincial Park, and settle in at one of the **Ashnola River campgrounds** (page 180). The roaring white-water can be like audio-therapy, drowning out the superficial chatter of your conscious mind, soothing you into a state of deep serenity, allowing the wellspring of your subconscious to bubble-up new insight and understanding.

MANNING PARK TO PRINCETON

Well south of Princeton, just northeast of Manning Provincial Park, Copper Creek flows into the Similkameen River. Near the confluence is an FS campground—the only one on this stretch of Hwy 3. Though small and within earshot of the highway, it's very convenient, barely off pavement. The approach, however, is tricky, because the access road departs the highway at a hairpin turn. Be careful.

If you're heading northeast on Hwy 3
from Manning Park

Set your tripometer to 0 at Manning Park Lodge. Drive Hwy 3 northeast 24 km (15 mi) then turn right, off the highway, just after it descends into a hairpin turn and crosses Copper Creek. There's a dirt pullout here. Descend to quickly reach Copper Creek campground on the right. If you're still on the highway at Sunday Summit, you've gone too far. Turn around and drive back 6.7 km (4.2 mi).

If you're heading south on Hwy 3 from Princeton

Set your tripometer to 0 in Princeton, at the Petro Canada station by the blue bridge over the Similkameen River. Drive Hwy 3 south. At 35 km (21.7 mi) reach 1232-m (4041-ft) Sunday Summit. At 41.7 km (25.8 mi) turn left, off the highway, just before it crosses Copper Creek and ascends out of a hairpin turn. There's a dirt pullout here. Descend to quickly reach Copper Creek campground on the right.

COPPER CREEK RECREATION SITE #86
Overnight / Easy
4 tables
Accessible by small motorhomes and trailers

PRINCETON TO TULAMEEN

The Tulameen River flows into the Similkameen River at Princeton. A paved road follows the Tulameen west, then northwest through a pretty valley to the village of Coalmont. Just beyond is the village of Tulameen, near Otter Lake. There used to be another, much larger settlement here: Granite Creek. In the 1880's, during its prime as a gold-mining town, it comprised more than 200 buildings. You can mingle with the ghosts of Granite Creek at the FS campground that today bears its name. Ponderosa pines and a big, grassy clearing create an inviting atmosphere. It's on the Tulameen River, next to Granite Creek, just outside Coalmont.

Thalia Lake

0 km (0 mi)

Starting northwest on Bridge Street in Princeton, departing Hwy 3 at the Petro Canada station by the blue bridge over the Similkameen River. Set your tripometer to 0 and follow the sign for Hwy 5A. Proceed through the historic downtown, cross a bridge over the Tulameen River, and reach a T-intersection. Turn left, following the sign for Coalmont (18 km) and Tulameen (25 km). The small, curvy road parallels the river, then ascends through a canyon.

20 km (12.4 mi)

Reach Coalmont and the historic hotel established in 1912. For Tulameen (9 km / 5.6 mi farther), Otter Lake, and the Plateau

Lakes, proceed straight (northwest); directions continue on page 163. For Granite Creek campground turn left (south) and cross a bridge over the Tulameen River.

21.6 km (13.4 mi)
Go left for Granite Creek campground. Right eventually leads to **Lodestone Lake Recreation Site #75** and **Wells Lake Recreation Site #84**. Both lakes are tiny. So are the campgrounds. Access requires 4WD.

21.7 km (13.5 mi)
Cross a bridge over Granite Creek, then turn left to reach the campground.

GRANITE CREEK RECREATION SITE #76
Weekend / Easy
20 tables
Accessible by motorhomes and 5th-wheels

TULAMEEN TO PLATEAU LAKES

The Plateau Lakes are about midway between Princeton and Merritt. The shortest, easiest access is via Hwy 5A. That description begins on page 164 and includes more details about the plateau, campgrounds, and driving conditions. If you're an explorer, you might prefer the backroad access described here. It's longer, and the final approach is a rough, steep, 275-m (900-ft) ascent—too much for big RVs. But it's more interesting and adventurous.

With about 16 tiny lakes, 11 small campgrounds, and a snarly network of roads, driving the plateau is potentially confusing. You're unlikely to get lost, but you might have to backtrack. Don't go unless you have the patience and curiosity to be a happy wanderer. This route description is general, follows only the main road (obvious once you're on top of the 1050-m / 3444-ft plateau), and includes only easy-to-find campgrounds. The map on page 167 will help you find the rest.

From Princeton, drive 20 km (12.4 mi) to Coalmont and pass the turnoff to Granite Creek campground (page 161). Continue northwest on the main, paved road, following the directions below.

29 km (18 mi)
Reach the village of Tulameen. Just beyond is Otter Lake Provincial Park. Proceed north, along the west shore of Otter Lake.

40.1 km (24.9 mi)
Pavement ends.

58.6 km (36.3 mi)
Straight (north) soon passes beneath a Kettle Valley Railway trestle, then heads northeast, eventually intersecting Hwy 5A south of Aspen Grove. For the Plateau Lakes, turn right (east) onto narrow Youngsberg Road, near a small wooden bridge, just before the KM 22 sign. The road is rough, steep and rutted as it ascends through an old clearcut. But it should be passable in a 2WD car. Stay on the main road.

65.6 km (40.7 mi)
Pass an **overnight pullout** near the top of the plateau.

67.8 km (42 mi)
Fork left.

68.4 km (42.4 mi)
Reach **Rickey Lake Recreation Site #51**, described on page 166.

68.6 km (42.5 mi)
Straight continues across the plateau. Right leads to **Goose Lake South campground #55** in just over 1 km (0.6 mi). It's described on page 166.

69.2 km (42.9 mi)
Right continues across the plateau. Turn left to enter **Thalia Lake South Recreation Site #54**, described on page 166.

71.2 km (44.1 mi)
Straight continues across the plateau. Turn right to quickly reach **Lodwick Lake North Recreation Site #56**, described on page 165.

74.1 km (45.9 mi)
Pass an **overnight pullout** next to a meadowy hill.

81.8 km (50.7 mi)
Intersect Hwy 5A. Turn left (north) to reach Hwy 5 at Merritt in about 44 km (27.3 mi). Turn right (south) to reach Hwy 3 at Princeton in about 39 km (24.2 mi).

PLATEAU LAKES VIA HWY 5A

The Plateau Lakes are about midway between Princeton and Merritt. The shortest, easiest access, via Hwy 5A, is described here. If you're an explorer, you might prefer the longer, rougher, but more interesting and adventurous backroad access (page 162).

With about 16 tiny lakes, 11 small campgrounds, and a snarly network of roads, driving the plateau is potentially confusing. You're unlikely to get lost, but you might have to backtrack. Don't go unless you have the patience and curiosity to be a happy wanderer. This route description follows only the main road (obvious once you're on top of the plateau) and includes only easy-to-find campgrounds. The map on page 167 will help you find the rest.

Unless recent, heavy rains have turned the roads to slop, a low-clearance 2WD car will get you to most Plateau Lakes, but not all. Even the main road is too narrow for big RVs. Some spurs are little more than a pair of tracks. Before venturing off the main road, consider how your vehicle will fare if conditions deteriorate.

Enough warnings. Now for some encouragement. The plateau, at 1050 m (3444 ft) elevation, is scenic. Aspen lighten the ever-green forest. Meadows welcome in the sunshine. The small campgrounds are intimate. You might end up with one all to yourself. And driving on the plateau can be a joy. During dry weather, wheeling along the soft, gracefully winding roads might remind you of those miniature cars on set tracks at amusement parks that thrilled you as a child. Go slowly. Stay lighthearted. You'll love it.

If you're heading north on Hwy 5A from Princeton

Drive Hwy 5A about 39 km (24.2 mi) north of Hwy 3 at Princeton, then turn left (west). Set your tripometer to 0.

If you're heading south on Hwy 5A from Merritt

Drive Hwy 5A about 44 km (27.3 mi) south of Hwy 5 at Merritt, then turn right (west). Set your tripometer to 0.

For either approach above, now follow the directions below

0 km (0 mi)
Starting west on Pike Mtn. FS road, departing Hwy 5A near a small lake.

1 km (0.6 mi)
Stay straight, passing A&P Guest Ranch on the right.

1.9 km (1.2 mi)
Reach a triangular junction and go right. Follow the sign for W H Ranch. Pass Robertson Lake Road on the left.

3.9 km (2.4 mi)
Reach another triangular junction and go left. See more signs for W H Ranch.

4.3 km (2.7 mi)
Fork right.

7.6 km (4.7 mi)
Pass an overnight pullout next to a meadowy hill.

9.2 km (5.7 mi)
Reach another triangular junction. Straight continues across the plateau. Turn sharply left to quickly reach Lodwick Lake North campground. If you're lucky, you might hear the loons in a yodeling frenzy.

LODWICK LAKE NORTH RECREATION SITE #56
Weekend / Moderate
3 tables
Inaccessible by motorhomes and trailers

Continuing generally west on the main road, passing the turnoff to Lodwick Lake North campground.

11.8 km (7.3 mi)
Reach a fork. Left continues across the plateau. Turn right to enter Thalia Lake campground. It's set in aspen and pines. Nearby glades are bright with wildflowers in early summer.

THALIA LAKE SOUTH RECREATION SITE #54
Weekend / Moderate
Elev: 1052 m (3450 ft) / Lake: 19 ha
8 tables
Inaccessible by motorhomes and trailers

Continuing generally south on the main road, passing the turnoff to Thalia Lake South campground.

12.4 km (7.7 mi)
Straight continues across the plateau. Turn left to reach Goose Lake campground in just over 1 km (0.6 mi).

GOOSE LAKE SOUTH RECREATION SITE #55
Weekend / Moderate
Elev: 1036 m (3400 ft) / Lake: 13.5 ha
8 tables
Inaccessible by motorhomes and trailers

Continuing generally west on the main road, passing the turnoff to Goose Lake South campground.

12.6 km (7.8 mi)
Reach Rickey Lake campground on the right, beside the main road. There are two grassy areas near the shore. The lake is cluttered with cattails and deadfall.

RICKEY LAKE RECREATION SITE #51
Weekend / Moderate
3 tables
Inaccessible by motorhomes and trailers

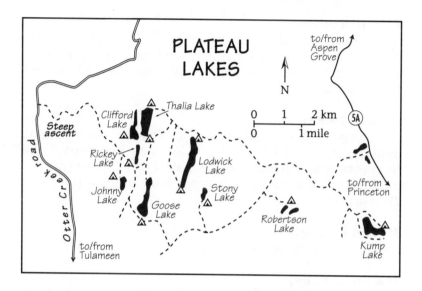

Continuing generally northwest on the main road, passing Rickey Lake campground, then descending the rough road on the plateau's west side.

22.4 km (13.9 mi)
Reach a T-junction in Otter Creek valley. Turn left (south) to reach Tulameen in another 29.6 km (18.4 mi), Coalmont in 38.6 km (23.9 mi), and Princeton in 58.6 km (36.3 mi).

PRINCETON TO MERRITT

Hwy 5A links Princeton and Merritt. At about the midpoint, west of the highway, are the Plateau Lakes campgrounds, described on page 164. East of the highway is Missezula Lake campground, described here. Other campgrounds between Princeton and Merritt are farther from the highway, have rough access, or both, but the turnoffs to several are also listed here.

If you're heading north on Hwy 5A from Princeton

0 km (0 mi)
Starting northwest on Bridge Street in Princeton, departing Hwy 3 at the Petro Canada station by the blue bridge over the Similkameen River. Set your tripometer to 0 and follow the sign for Hwy 5A. Turn right onto Tapton Ave., signed for Merritt.

1 km (0.6 mi)
After crossing a bridge over the Tulameen River, reach a junction. Right is the Old Hedley Road and the Princeton-Summerland Road. Bear left (north) onto Hwy 5A, toward Merritt (90 km).

9.3 km (5.8 mi)
Pass Summers Creek Road on the right. Follow it north (bearing right at about 8.5 km / 5.3 mi) to reach **Rampart Lake Recreation Site #68** at about 14.7 km (9.1 mi). There are two small camping areas on this minor lake; the first should be 2WD accessible.

31.7 km (19.7 mi)
Pass the north end of Allison Lake.

35.6 km (22.1 mi)
Pass Hornet Lake FS road on the right. This is the rough access to three small campgrounds on dinky lakes. The first, **Loosemore Lake Recreation Site #62**, is about 3.2 km (2 mi) off pavement, has four campsites, and should be 2WD accessible. Just beyond, requiring 4WD, are **Deadman Lake South Recreation Site #63** (5 campsites) and **Prosser Lake Recreation Site #61** (2 campsites).

37.8 km (23.5 mi)
Pass Gulliford Lake Rest Area.

39 km (24.2 mi)
Turn left (west) onto Pike Mtn. FS road for the **Plateau Lakes campgrounds**; directions continue on page 165.

48.8 km (30.3 mi)
Pass a yellow sign warning of trucks entering the highway.

49.1 km (30.5 mi)
Turn right (southeast) onto Dillard Creek FS road for **Missezula Lake campground**; directions continue on page 170.

60.1 km (37.3 mi)
Reach Aspen Grove and pass Connector Hwy 97C, which leads east to the Okanagan.

83.1 km (51.5 mi)
Intersect Hwy 5 at the Merritt Interchange.

If you're heading south on Hwy 5A from Merritt

0 km (0 mi)
Starting south on Hwy 5A, from the junction with Hwy 5 at the Merritt Interchange. Set your tripometer to 0.

23 km (14.3 mi)
Reach Aspen Grove and pass Connector Hwy 97C, which leads east to the Okanagan.

34 km (21.1 mi)
Turn left (southeast) onto Dillard Creek FS road for **Missezula Lake campground**; directions continue on page 170.

44.1 km (27.3 mi)
Turn right (west) onto Pike Mtn. FS road for the **Plateau Lakes campgrounds**; directions continue on page 165.

45.3 km (28.1 mi)
Pass Gulliford Lake Rest Area.

47.5 km (29.5 mi)
Pass Hornet Lake FS road on the left. This is the rough access to three small campgrounds on dinky lakes. The first, **Loosemore Lake Recreation Site #62**, is about 3.2 km (2 mi) off pavement, has four campsites, and should be 2WD accessible. Just beyond, requiring 4WD, are **Deadman Lake South Recreation Site #63** (5 campsites) and **Prosser Lake Recreation Site #61** (2 campsites).

51.4 km (31.9 mi)
Pass the north end of Allison Lake.

73.8 km (45.8 mi)
Pass Summers Creek Road on the left. Follow it north (bearing right at about 8.5 km / 5.3 mi) to reach **Rampart Lake Recreation Site #68** at about 14.7 km (9.1 mi). There are two small camping areas on this minor lake; the first should be 2WD accessible.

Missezula Lake

82.1 km (50.9 mi)
Reach a junction in Princeton. Left is the Old Hedley Road and the Princeton-Summerland Road. Turn right, cross a bridge over the Tulameen River, and continue through town.

83.1 km (51.5 mi)
Intersect Hwy 3. Turn left for Hedley and Keremeos. Turn right for Manning Provincial Park.

For MISSEZULA LAKE, now follow the directions below.

0 km (0 mi)
Starting southeast on Dillard Creek FS road, departing Hwy 5A.

1.6 km (1 mi)
Stay straight at the fork. The wide road passes through unimpressive forest.

4.2 km (2.6 mi)
Reach a fork. Stay left on Dillard Creek FS road.

6.7 km (4.2 mi)
Reach a fork. Go right for Missezula Lake. Left (north) is a 4WD road to **Bluey Lake Recreation Site #40**.

7.6 km (4.7 mi)
Reach a fork. Go right for Missezula Lake. Left (north) is a rough road to Loon Lake and eventually Connector Hwy 97C.

9.7 km (6 mi)
Turn right and descend to reach Missezula Lake campground, at the lake's north end.

MISSEZULA LAKE RECREATION SITE #48
Weekend / Moderate
Elev: 1052 m (3450 ft) / Lake: 6.2 km (3.8 mi) long, 241 ha
8 tables, boat launch
Accessible by small motorhomes and trailers

Continue to Loon Lake Exit on Connector Hwy 97C by turning right when leaving Missezula campground. In about 2.4 km (1.5 mi), turn left (northeast) onto Dillard-Galena Creek FS road. En route to the highway, pass **Buck Lake Recreation Site #46.**

PRINCETON TO SUMMERLAND

Don't come here in search of a quiet, lonely campsite. Much of the land is settled. Private cabins crowd the lakes. The biggest campground, on Chain Lake, is often a hive of activity. Yet the terrain through this corridor is scenically substandard for beautiful British Columbia. Driving Princeton - Summerland Road, however, is an enjoyable alternative to the major highways. The generally smooth gravel surface allows comfortable cruising. And, unlike the highways, this backroad has several very convenient FS campgrounds along the way.

If you're heading east, from Princeton to Summerland

In Princeton, drive northwest on Bridge Street. It departs Hwy 3 at the Petro Canada station by the blue bridge over the Similkameen River. Follow the sign for Hwy 5A. Turn right onto Tapton Avenue, signed for Merritt. Cross a bridge over the Tulameen River and reach a junction. Left (north) is Hwy 5A. Turn right onto Old Hedley Road and set your tripometer to 0.

0 km (0 mi)
Starting on Old Hedley Road in Princeton.

0.3 km (0.2 mi)
Turn left (north) onto Princeton - Summerland Road, signed for Osprey Lake.

3.2 km (2 mi)
Stay straight (north) on the main road for Summerland. Turn left (west), then fork right to quickly reach Martin's Lake campground.

Intended primarily for day use, this small campground is very close to the road. Other drawbacks: the lake is just a pond, the forest is sparse, and homes are nearby. But it's a handy place for a brief overnight stay near Princeton.

MARTIN'S LAKE RECREATION SITE #77
Overnight / Easy
3 tables
Accessible by small motorhomes and trailers

Continuing north on the main road, passing the turnoff to Martin's Lake campground.

36.6 km (22.6 mi)
Reach Chain Lake West campground, beside the road, on the right.

CHAIN LAKE WEST RECREATION SITE #69
Weekend / Difficult (due only to distance)
Elev: 1036 m (3400 ft) / Lake: 42 ha
20 tables, boat launch
Accessible by motorhomes and 5th-wheels

Continuing northeast on the main road, passing Chain Lake West campground.

41.6 km (25.7 mi)
Stay straight (east) on the main road for Summerland. Turn right (south) onto Agur Road to reach Link Lake campground in 0.8 km (0.5 mi).

This small lake and campground have little appeal. Private cabins are nearby. The access road loops around the lake, back to the main road.

LINK LAKE RECREATION SITE #70
Overnight / Difficult (due only to distance)
Elev: 1100 m (3608 ft) / Lake: 15 ha
5 tables, more campsites, boat launch
Accessible by small motorhomes and trailers

Continuing east on the main road, passing the turnoff to Link Lake campground.

42.4 km (26.3 mi)
Pass Link Lake Road, on the right. To access Link Lake campground this way, immediately go left, then right at the junction. At the fork with Osprey Lake on the left, go right on the main road. Pass the boat launch. Go right at the T-junction. After reaching the campground, you can rejoin the main road just beyond.

43.8 km (27.2 mi)
Stay straight (east) on the main road for Summerland. Turn right to enter Osprey Lake campground.

The densely forested hillside here is prettier than the scenery at Link Lake. The campground is far enough below the main road that noise is minimal.

OSPREY LAKE RECREATION SITE #71
Overnight / Difficult (due only to distance)
Elev: 1082 m (3550 ft) / Lake: 39 ha
6 tables, rough boat launch
Accessible by small motorhomes and trailers

Continuing east on the main road, passing the turnoff to Osprey Lake campground.

46.6 km (28.8 mi)
Reach a junction. Stay straight (east) on the main road for Summerland. Trout Creek FS road forks left (northeast) eventually accessing Okanagan Connector Hwy 97C and several campgrounds en route.

52 km (32.3 mi)
Reach a junction. Bear right (east) on the main road for Summerland.

52.8 km (32.8 mi)
Reach Thirsk Lake campground, beside the road, on the right. Irrigation drops the water level significantly in summer.

THIRSK LAKE RECREATION SITE #18
Overnight / Difficult (due only to distance)
Elev: 1020 m (3346 ft) / Lake: 59 ha
5 tables, beach
Accessible by small motorhomes and trailers

Continuing east on the main road, passing Thirsk Lake campground.

53.1 km (33 mi)
Pass more Thirsk Lake campsites.

54.1 km (33.6 mi)
Watch for possible **overnight pullouts** beside Trout Creek.

70.5 km (43.8 mi)
Stay straight (southeast) on the main road for Summerland. Turn left for Trout Creek Crossing campground, just before a bridge and switchback.

Set in pines and cottonwoods, beside the rushing creek, this small, intimate campground is delightful. But it's often ignored, because most campers prefer lakes.

TROUT CREEK CROSSING RECREATION SITE #17
Weekend / Difficult (due only to distance)
4 tables, 3 campsites
Too small for motorhomes and trailers

*Continuing southeast on the main road, passing the turnoff to Trout
Creek Crossing campground.*

82 km (50.8 mi)
Pass a viewpoint overlooking Okanagan Valley to the east.

82.8 km (51.3 mi)
Pavement resumes.

84.3 km (52.3 mi)
Stay straight (southeast) for Summerland. Fish Lake Road forks
left (north) to Darke Lake Provincial Park.

90.3 km (56 mi)
Reach a junction. Go left and curve downhill.

94 km (58.3 mi)
Arrive at the junction of Prairie Valley and Victoria Roads, at
Giant's Head in Summerland. Continue east on Prairie Valley
Road, toward Okanagan Lake.

94.4 km (58.5 mi)
Proceed through the 4-way intersection, on Prairie Valley Road.

95.3 km (59.2 mi)
Intersect Hwy 97, by the IGA shopping centre. Turn left for
Peachland and Kelowna. Turn right for Penticton.

If you're heading west, from Summerland to Princeton

Driving the first 11 km (6.8 mi) west from Summerland is
worthwhile just for the scenery. The road ascends a lovely, cul-
tivated valley above Okanagan Lake. The rest of the way to
Princeton isn't special, but it's an enjoyable alternative to the
major highways. And you can camp free en route. Read page
171 for details. The following route description is general.

Summerland is beside Hwy 97, south of Peachland, north of Penticton, near the southwest shore of Okanagan Lake. Begin this backroad drive to Princeton by heading west on Prairie Valley Road. It departs Hwy 97 at the IGA shopping centre, 5.4 km (3.3 mi) south of Sun Oka Beach Provincial Park.

0 km (0 mi)
Starting west on Prairie Valley Road in Summerland, departing Hwy 97 at the IGA shopping centre.

0.9 km (0.5 mi)
Reach a 4-way intersection. Proceed left on Prairie Valley Road.

1.3 km (0.8 mi)
Reach a junction with Victoria Road. Stay straight on Prairie Valley Road, toward Rutherford Farms.

2.4 km (1.5 mi)
Begin ascending.

4.6 km (2.9 mi)
Curve right.

5 km (3 mi)
Go left on Bathfield Road. Follow the yellow line on the pavement. At the white signs outlined in red, curve right.

10.9 km and 11 km (6.8 mi)
Stay straight on the main road, signed for Osprey Lake and Princeton.

12.5 km (7.8 mi)
Pavement ends.

17.6 km (10.9 mi)
Stay straight.

24.7 km (15.3 mi)
Turn right for **Trout Creek Crossing campground**, just after a bridge and switchback. Read page 175 for details.

Old Hedley Road campsite above Similkameen River

42.5 km (26.4 mi)
Reach **Thirsk Lake campground**, beside the road, on the left. Read page 174 for details.

51.5 km (32 mi)
Turn left for **Osprey Lake campground**. Read page 173 for details.

53.7 km (33.3 mi)
Turn left for **Link Lake Campground**. Read page 173 for details.

58.7 km (36.4 mi)
Reach **Chain Lake West campground**, beside the road, on the left. Read page 172 for details.

92.1 km (57.1 mi)
Turn right for **Martin's Lake campground**. Read page 172 for details.

95.3 km (59.2 mi)
Intersect Old Hedley Road, in Princeton. Go right 300 meters, then turn left to proceed through town and reach Hwy 3.

PRINCETON TO HEDLEY

Travelling between Princeton and Hedley, you can take your pick: water, pavement, or dirt. The Similkameen River is a boating playground, a delicious sight in such dry, hot country. Hwy 3 follows the river's south bank for most of this short stretch. Along the river's north bank is Old Hedley Road. Initially paved, it soon lapses into a dusty track. But it offers you three FS campgrounds on the sparkling river. See photo on page 177.

The Old Hedley Road campgrounds are unremarkable. They afford no privacy from fellow campers or passing vehicles. Highway traffic is audible despite the river's throaty attempts to muffle it. Still, rafters, canoeists and fisherfolk who want to launch their boats or wet their lines will find these campgrounds convenient and useful.

If you're heading southeast, from Princeton to Hedley

In Princeton, drive northwest on Bridge Street. It departs Hwy 3 at the Petro Canada station by the blue bridge over the Similkameen River. Follow the sign for Hwy 5A. Turn right onto Tapton Avenue, signed for Merritt. Cross a bridge over the Tulameen River and reach a junction. Left (north) is Hwy 5A. Turn right onto Old Hedley Road. It follows the Similkameen River's north bank, rejoining Hwy 3 in about 35 km (21.7 mi). Reach **Dewdney Recreation Site #78** in about 7 km (4.3 mi). Reach **Old Hedley Road West Recreation Site #79** and **Old Hedley Road East Recreation Site #80** just before rejoining Hwy 3. All are on the right, above the riverbank. All have tables. Dewdney is small. Old Hedley West is big, with room for motorhomes and trailers. Old Hedley East is medium size.

If you're heading northwest, from Hedley to Princeton

From Hedley, drive Hwy 3 northwest 6.5 km (4 mi). Just before a bridge over the Similkameen River, turn right onto Old Hedley Road. It follows the river's north bank, reaching Princeton in about 35 km (21.7 mi). Reach **Old Hedley Road East Recreation Site #80** and **Old Hedley Road West Recreation Site #79** shortly after departing the highway. Reach **Dewdney Recreation Site #78** in about 28 km (17.4 mi). All are on the left, above the riverbank. All have tables. Old Hedley East is medium size. Old Hedley West is big, with room for motorhomes and trailers. Dewdney is small.

NEAR KEREMEOS

With Hwy 3 in pursuit, the Similkameen River rushes southeast from Princeton, past Hedley and Keremeos. A tributary, the Ashnola River, races down from mountainous Cathedral Provincial Park, flowing north into the Similkameen just west of Keremeos. A backroad departs Hwy 3 and follows the Ashnola

Ashnola River campsite

upstream, where you'll find two FS campgrounds, plus a BC Parks trailhead campground (walk in, tenters only) for backpackers heading to or from the Cathedral lakes. The campgrounds are within sight and sound of the lusty Ashnola, making them very conducive to a couple days of R&R.

Keremeos is dry, sunny, orchard country, so the Ashnola River's lower canyon has a comfortable camping climate from April until November. The Cathedral lakes, however, are high above at 2100 m (6888 ft), where it can snow even in summer. Hiking to the lakes is a steep grunt. The trail gains 1200 m (3936 ft) in 14 km (8.7 mi). And the ascent is worse than the numbers indicate, because there's no scenery en route to fuel motivation. But the heavenly alpine country in the Park's core area is a generous reward. Allow at least three days. For details, read *Don't Waste Your Time in the North Cascades*, described on page 395. If your preferred method of payment is a credit card, instead of sweat, you can ride a jeep up to the lakes. For prices, departure times, and reservations, phone Cathedral Lakes Resort: 1-888-255-4453. Visit their website at www.cathedral-lakes-lodge.com. Directions to the parking lot for the resort's private jeep road are included here.

If you're heading east or west on Hwy 3, near Keremeos

The Ashnola River road departs Hwy 3 at the west edge of Keremeos, or 66 km (40.5 mi) southeast of Princeton. Turn south at the sign for Cathedral Lakes Provincial Park. Immediately cross the Similkameen River. Set your tripometer to 0 on the bridge.

For ASHNOLA RIVER, now follow the directions below

0 km (0 mi)
Starting west on the red bridge over the Similkameen River, heading for Ashnola River and Cathedral Park.

10 km (6.2 mi)
Pavement ends. From here on, watch for **unofficial campsites** along the river. Camp at one only if the FS or BC Parks campgrounds are full, and only if you'll leave no trace of your stay.

Goat Lake and Denture Ridge, Cathedral Provincial Park

12.2 km (7.6 mi)
Turn left to enter Red Bridge campground on Ashnola River.

> The campsites are treed, beside the river. A beautiful pool invites swimming but requires caution. The riversong is just loud enough to mask other campers' noise.

RED BRIDGE RECREATION SITE #12
Weekend / Easy
8 tables
Accessible by motorhomes and 5th-wheels

Continuing south on the main road, passing the turnoff to Red Bridge campground.

15.9 km (9.9 mi)
Reach a junction at the Ewart Creek / Ashnola River confluence. Bear right (west). You're now in Cathedral Park.

18.8 km (11.7 mi)
Pass the Cathedral Park kiosk.

22.2 km (13.8 mi)
Pass Cathedral Lakes Resort Base parking lot, on the left. The resort is high in the mountains, at Quiniscoe Lake. Their private jeep road begins here.

23.8 km (14.8 mi)
Reach **Lakeview trailhead** on Ashnola River, at 900 m (2952 ft) elevation. The **tenters-only, walk-in campground** here is administered by BC Parks but was fee-free in 1999. It's primarily for backpackers entering or exiting Cathedral Park.

Continuing west on the main road, passing the turnoff to Lakeview trailhead and campground.

37.8 km (23.4 mi)
Turn left to enter Ashnola River campground, in a grassy clearing.

ASHNOLA RIVER RECREATION SITE #34
Weekend / Easy
6 tables
Accessible by motorhomes and 5th-wheels

Continuing west on the main road, passing the turnoff to Ashnola River campground.

49.5 km (30.7 mi)
Reach Cathedral Park's Wall Creek trailhead, on the left.

61.5 km (38.1 mi)
Reach Easygoing Creek trailhead, on the right. The trail climbs the west side of Ashnola River canyon, to Trapper and Border lakes.

KEREMEOS TO OLIVER

Dependably clear skies make Kobau Observatory, southeast of Keremeos, one of Canada's prime stargazing sites. A decent gravel road (with sections of severe washboard) climbs to the 1874-m (6147-ft) summit of Mt. Kobau, where you'll find a tiny but remarkable FS campground and a 5-km (3-mi) hiking trail network. Earthgazing is enjoyable here too. The view encompasses Similkameen River valley (west and northwest), Okanagan Falls (north), and Washington's Okanagan country (south). Motorhomes or trucks pulling trailers can handle the ascent if they have brawny engines.

About a 15-minute drive northwest of Oliver is small Burnell Lake. Locals call it Sawmill Lake. The campground here is convenient for a brief overnight stay, accessible by motorhomes and trailers, and attractive for fly fishing. The lake has a reputation for lunker rainbow trout. Catch-and-release rules apply.

For MT. KOBAU, now follow the directions below

Drive Hwy 3 northwest 11.2 km (6.9 mi) from the junction of Hwys 3 and 97 in Osoyoos. Or drive Hwy 3 south then north-east 23 km (14.3 mi) from the junction of Hwy 3 and the road south out of Cawston. From either approach, turn northwest onto Mt. Kobau Road. It departs Hwy 3 near the pass. Follow the serpentine, gravel road 19.8 km (12.3 mi) to the observatory and campground on the summit.

MT. KOBAU RECREATION SITE #10
Weekend / Easy
2 tables, hiking trails, extensive views
Accessible by motorhomes and trailers

For BURNELL LAKE, now follow the directions below

0 km (0 mi)
Starting west on paved Seacrest Road, departing Hwy 97 in downtown Oliver

3.9 km (2.4 mi)
Turn right (north) on Fairview - White Lake Road.

7.5 km (4.7 mi)
Turn left (west) onto Burnell Lake Road. It's rough, but passable in a 2WD car.

11.3 km (7 mi)
Arrive at Burnell Lake campground.

BURNELL LAKE RECREATION SITE #13
Weekend / Easy
6 tables, rough boat launch
Elev: 762 m (2500 ft)
Accessible by motorhomes and trailers

HOPE TO MERRITT

Coquihalla Hwy 5 is B.C.'s only toll highway. It's the newer, straighter, smoother, faster alternative to a circuitous stretch of Trans-Canada Hwy 1. Driving the Coquihalla will cost you $10 (1999), whether you're behind the wheel of a Winnebago or a Miata. The southern segment, between Hope and Merritt, climbs through the husky Cascade Mountains. Farther inland the topography goes slack and the forests wither, but the scenery is impressively vast the entire way. Equally awesome is the highway itself. Observant travellers marvel at snow sheds, diversion trenches, avalanche dams, and dozens of bridges and overpasses crossing roads, rivers and railways. The Coquihalla is a monument to engineering prowess. It also defines the west side of the South Thompson Plateau, where all the campgrounds described here are reached by turning off the highway at well signed, easy-to-see exits.

Murray Lake is a narrow, unremarkable, water-filled gap in the woods. Yet opulent cabins belly-up to the east shore. The access road is rough—passable in a 2WD car but problematic for big RVs. Approaching the lake, beware of potholes the size of kiddy pools. Avoid Murray Lake after heavy rain, when the road can be a muddy morass. Of the two campgrounds here, the one on the north shore is bigger and better.

Gillis Lake is in a tight bowl. Forest rises abruptly from the shore. The campground is on a treed bench well below the main road. Some campers will enjoy hunkering down in this tiny pocket, others will feel squeezed. The approach road poses no difficulties. Small RVs can access Gillis Lake campground, but motorhomes and trailers will find Boss and Davis lakes much bigger and more accommodating.

Shea, Tahla, Boss and Davis lakes are small and close together. Their attendant campgrounds range in size from pee-wee to jumbo. It's easy to check them all out, then settle in at your favourite. Variety of choice and relatively easy access make this the most attractive camping area near Hwy 5 between Hope and Merritt. Shea and Tahla are fine for small motorhomes and trailers. Boss and Davis accommodate land yachts. But beware of mud in early season.

If you're heading northeast on Hwy 5 from Hope

0 km (0 mi)
Starting northeast on Hwy 5 from the junction of Hwys 3 and 5, just east of Hope. Set your tripometer to 0.

50 km (31 mi)
Proceed through the toll plaza near 1240-m (4067-ft) Coquihalla Pass. The toll for cars and RVs is $10 (1999).

63 km (39 mi)
Reach the Juliet Exit. Proceed northeast for more campgrounds en route to Merritt. Turn off the highway here for **Murray Lake campgrounds;** directions continue on page 187.

80 km (50 mi)
Reach the Coldwater Exit (Kingsvale Interchange). Proceed northeast for Merritt. Turn off the highway here for **Gillis Lake campground** (directions continue on page 187), and for **campgrounds at Shea, Tahla, Boss and Davis lakes** (directions continue on page 188).

110 km (68 mi)
Reach the junction of Hwys 5 and 5A, at the Merritt Interchange.

If you're heading southwest on Hwy 5 from Merritt

0 km (0 mi)
Starting southwest from the junction of Hwys 5 and 5A, at the Merritt Interchange. Set your tripometer to 0.

30 km (19 mi)
Reach the Coldwater Exit (Kingsvale Interchange). Proceed southwest for Murray Lake campgrounds and for Hope. Turn

Campers cheer on their straggling buddy near Gillis Lake.

off the highway here for **Gillis Lake campground** (directions continue on page 187), and for campgrounds at **Shea, Tahla, Boss and Davis lakes** (directions continue on page 188).

47 km (29 mi)
Reach the Juliet Exit. Proceed southwest for Hope. Turn off the highway here for **Murray Lake campgrounds**; directions continue on page 187.

60 km (37 mi)
Proceed through the toll plaza near 1240-m (4067-ft) Coquihalla Pass. The toll for cars and RVs is $10 (1999).

110 km (68 mi)
Reach the junction of Hwys 5 and 3, just east of Hope.

For MURRAY LAKE, now follow the directions below

0 km (0 mi)
After departing Hwy 5 at the Juliet Exit, go straight toward the
hill. Set your tripometer to 0 and turn right after the big cattle
guard. Head north on Maka-Murray FS road. Stay left, above
the canyon on your right.

0.9 km (0.5 mi)
Proceed through a hairpin turn and climb steeply.

5 km (3 mi)
Turn left to enter Murray Lake South campground. Or continue
to the larger, more attractive campground on the north shore.

MURRAY LAKE SOUTH RECREATION SITE #65
Weekend / Difficult
Elev: 1143 m (3750 ft) / Lake: 2 km (1.2 mi) long, 25 ha
3 tables
Inaccessible by motorhomes and trailers

~∙∕

6.9 km (4.3 mi)
Turn left to enter Murray Lake North campground. It has a
small, mucky beach and a view down the forest-enclosed lake.

MURRAY LAKE NORTH RECREATION SITE #64
Weekend / Difficult
10 tables, level grassy area for tents, boat launch
Inaccessible by motorhomes and trailers

~∙∕

For GILLIS LAKE, now follow the directions below

0 km (0 mi)
After departing Hwy 5 at the Coldwater Exit (Kingsvale
Interchange), set your tripometer to 0 and head north on the
paved road paralleling the highway's west side.

2.6 km (1.6 mi)
In Kingsvale, turn left before the railway overpass. Cross the bridge then go left on Maka - Murray FS road.

6.5 km (4 mi)
Begin ascending.

7.1 km (4.4 mi)
Bear left at the fork.

7.9 km (4.9 mi)
Gillis Lake is visible below. Left is the first and longer of the campground's two entrances. It descends steeply then skirts the shore to reach the campground in 1 km (0.6 mi). Proceed straight on the main road for the second, shorter entrance.

8.9 km (5.6 mi)
Turn left for the second, shorter entrance to Gillis Lake campground.

GILLIS LAKE RECREATION SITE #35
Weekend / Moderate
Elev: 1143 m (3750 ft) / Lake: 19 ha
6 tables, rough boat launch, crude dock, level ground for tents
Too small for motorhomes and trailers

~

For SHEA, TAHLA, BOSS and DAVIS LAKES, now follow the directions below

After departing Hwy 5 at the Coldwater Exit (Kingsvale Interchange), head north on the paved road paralleling the highway's west side. At 2.6 km (1.6 mi), in Kingsvale, proceed straight beneath the railway overpass. Shortly beyond, turn right (east) onto unpaved Kane Valley Road. Follow it about 10 km (6.2 mi), then turn right (southeast) onto Voght Valley Road and set your tripometer to 0. Kane Valley Road continues northeast, passing campgrounds at Harmon and Kane lakes (page 200) en route to Hwy 5A.

0 km (0 mi)
Starting southeast on Voght Valley Road.

5.3 km (3.3 mi)
Proceed south on Voght Valley Road for campgrounds at Tahla,
Boss and Davis lakes. Turn left (northeast) onto Shea Lake FS
road to reach Shea Lake campground in 2 km (1.2 mi).

SHEA LAKE RECREATION SITE #36
Weekend / Moderate
5 tables, boat launch
Accessible by small motorhomes and trailers

~

6.5 km (4 mi)
Proceed south on Voght Valley Road for Boss and Davis lakes.
Turn right to enter Tahla Lake campground. It's not on the shore.

TAHLA LAKE RECREATION SITE #37
Weekend / Moderate
3 tables
Accessible by small motorhomes and trailers

~

7.1 km (4.4 mi)
Proceed south on Voght Valley Road for Davis Lake. Turn right
to enter Boss Lake campground.

BOSS LAKE RECREATION SITE #38
Weekend / Moderate
15 tables, boat launch
Accessible by motorhomes and 5th-wheels

~

9.5 km (5.9 mi)
Turn right to enter Davis Lake campground.

DAVIS LAKE RECREATION SITE #39
Weekend / Moderate
55 tables, boat launch
Accessible by motorhomes and 5th-wheels

~

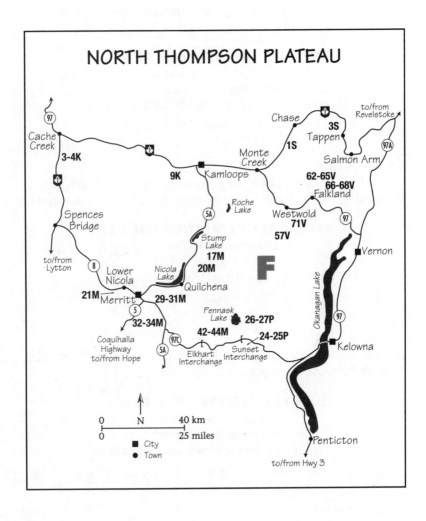

NORTH THOMPSON PLATEAU

to/from Revelstoke

Chase

3S
Tappen

1S

Salmon Arm

97A

97

Cache Creek

3-4K

9K

Monte Creek

Kamloops

62-65V

66-68V

Falkland

Spences Bridge

5A

Roche Lake

Westwold

71V

57V

97

to/from Lytton

8

Lower Nicola

Stump Lake

17M

20M

Nicola Lake

F

Vernon

21M

Merritt

29-31M

Quilchena

Pennask Lake

26-27P

97

5

42-44M

24-25P

32-34M

97C

5A

Elkhart Interchange

Sunset Interchange

Kelowna

Coquihalla Highway to/from Hope

Okanagan Lake

0   N   40 km

0   25 miles

■ City

● Town

Penticton

to/from Hwy 3

F: North Thompson Plateau

The letter indicates which FS district the campground is in. **K** stands for Kamloops FS District. **M** stands for Merritt FS District. **P** stands for Penticton FS District. **S** stands for Salmon Arm FS District. **V** stands for Vernon FS District.

1S	Harper Lake	32M	Kane Lake
3K	Willard Lake	33M	Harmon Lake West
3S	Skimikin Lakes	34M	Harmon Lake East
4K	Barnes Lake	42M	Bob's Lake
9K	Duffy Lake	43M	Island Lake
17M	Peter Hope Lake	44M	Elkhart Lake
20M	Glimpse Lake	62V	Charcoal Creek
21M	N'Kwala	63V	Chase Creek
24P	MacDonald Lake	64V	Pillar Lake
25P	Brenda Lake	65V	Joyce Lake
26P	Pinnacle Lake	66V	Spa Lake
27P	Hatheume Lake	67V	Arthur Lake
29M	Marquart Lake	68V	Bolean Lake
30M	Lundbom Lake West	57V	Woods Lake
31M	Lundbom Lake East	71V	Pinaus Lake

North Thompson Plateau

Harmon Lake, in Kane Valley, south of Merritt

Aspen, ponderosa pines and other conifers cloak much of this region. The rest is grassland. An all-you-can-eat smorgasbord for cows. Some of the nation's largest cattle ranches sprawl across the rolling hills and gentle valleys near Nicola, Quilchena, and Douglas Lake. A gaggle of this industry's hapless victims, loitering on a backroad, will occasionally slow your progress to a crawl. They'll stare at you for minutes with uncomprehending eyes, then suddenly bolt—stiff-legged and scared. You'll be aware of their presence even when they're not in sight: cattle mementos collage many campgrounds.

The lakes, marshes and springs of the plateau, especially along Hwy 5A between Merritt and Kamloops, are optimal nesting grounds for thousands of waterfowl. In addition to the ducks that delight kids playing on shorelines, look for larger, more elegant species: trumpeter swans, Canada geese, snow geese, and great blue herons. The habitat that attracts birds also nurtures moose. Though huge, these homely creatures are shy. You'll be lucky to see one.

At many plateau lakes, the horizon is not serrated. It's a level line of trees. This gives the land a pre-Columbus appearance, a flatness that some people find dull compared to the magnanimous mountains of B.C.'s Coast Range, Kootenays, or Rockies. But camped beside a plateau lake, you'll have a unique perspective. The sky is a blue dome, filling your field of vision. The earth is just a sliver. It seems you're on top of the world. Or on the edge of the universe.

FS campgrounds are strewn throughout the region. You'll find as much variety in campground size, quality and accessibility here as elsewhere in the province. A choice of easy-to-reach campgrounds along Hwys 5A and 97 invites you to venture off the major thoroughfares, slow down, and explore.

NEAR CACHE CREEK

Trans-Canada Hwy 1 turns abruptly at Cache Creek, creating a right angle. From an abstract perspective, it resembles an open nut cracker. The nut is the town of Ashcroft. Nearby are FS campgrounds at Willard and Barnes lakes. Both are convenient to Hwy 1, accessed via paved road, and easily reached by any vehicle, so they're heavily used. But late some night while driving across the province, you too might appreciate how handy they are. You can be there in 15 minutes from Ashcroft. The surrounding grassland is scattered with pines. Think of it as a vast openness, rather than emptiness.

If you're heading south on Hwy 1 from Cache Creek

From the junction of Hwys 1 and 97 at Cache Creek, drive Hwy 1 south 4.2 km (2.6 mi). Turn left (southeast) at the north access to Ashcroft. Proceed 6.2 km (3.8 mi) into town. Set your tripometer to 0 on the northwest side of the Thompson River bridge.

If you're heading north on Hwy 1 from Spences Bridge

From Spences Bridge, drive Hwy 1 north about 39 km (24 mi). Turn right (east) at the south access to Ashcroft. Proceed 5 km (3.1 mi) into town. Set your tripometer to 0 on the northwest side of the Thompson River bridge.

For either approach above, now follow the directions below

0 km (0 mi)
Starting southwest on Hwy 97C, leaving Ashcroft and crossing the Thompson River bridge.

7.8 km (4.8 mi)
After heading generally south, the highway jogs north.

9.2 km (5.7 mi)
Where the highway veers south again, turn left (north) onto paved Barnes Lake Road.

10 km (6.2 mi)
Reach Willard Lake campground on the south shore. Proceed north for Barnes Lake.

WILLARD LAKE RECREATION SITES #3
Weekend / Easy
Elev: 700 m (2296 ft)
2 campsites without tables, cartop boat launch
Accessible by small motorhomes and trailers

~

11.1 km (6.9 mi)
Reach the sound end of Barnes Lake.

12.8 km (7.9 mi)
Arrive at Barnes Lake campground on the northwest shore.

BARNES LAKE RECREATION SITES #4
Weekend / Easy
Elev: 687 m (2253 ft)
8 tables, boat launch
Accessible by motorhomes and 5-wheels

NORTHWEST OF MERRITT

N'Kwala. Nicola. The latter is obviously an English speaker's version of the Native place name. The only easy-to-reach campground northwest of Merritt still bears the original name: N'Kwala. It's on the Nicola River, just off paved Hwy 8, which links Trans-Canada Hwy 1 at Spences Bridge with Hwys 97C, 5 and 5A at Merritt.

The other FS campgrounds in this general area are much harder to reach—way north of Hwy 8. It's a tediously long backroad journey made confusing by extensive recent logging. Those who persist can choose from nearly a dozen tiny campgrounds on small lakes reputed to offer good fishing. The final access to most is rough. A few require 4WD. Only the initial directions are included in the route description below. If you're going, take a Merritt FS District recreation map. Their office is listed in the back of this book. Call to ask if and where maps are available.

If you're heading northwest on Hwy 97C from Merritt

0 km (0 mi)
Starting northwest on Hwy 97C, from the junction of Hwys 5 and 97C at the Merritt Interchange near the Tourist Info Centre.

4 km (2.5 mi)
Follow signs for Spences Bridge, Logan Lake and Cache Creek.

9 km (5.6 mi)
Proceed west on Hwy 8 for N'Kwala campground and Spences Bridge. Hwy 97C forks right (north) to Logan Lake, Ashcroft, and Cache Creek on Trans-Canada Hwy 1.

12.6 km (7.8 mi)
Proceed west on Hwy 8 through Lower Nicola to reach N'Kwala campground and Spences Bridge. Turn right (north) onto initially-paved Aberdeen Road for **Roscoe Lake Recreation Site #3, Billy Lake Recreation Site #4, Leroy Lakes Recreation Site #5, Tupper Lake Recreation Site #6, Gump Lake Recreation Site #7, Antler Lake Recreation Site #8, Dot Lake Recreation Site #9, Gypsum Lake Recreation Site #10, Tyner Lake Recreation Site #11, Abbott Lake Recreation Site #12, and Gordon Lake Recreation Site #13.** At the 14-km (8.7-mi) junction, turn left (northwest) to reach Tyner Lake at about 20 km (12.4 mi). Most of the others are more than 10 km (6.2 mi) farther north. Access is rough. Abbott and Gordon lakes (4WD only) are southwest of Tyner.

26.2 km (16.2 mi)
Proceed northwest on Hwy 8 for Spences Bridge. Turn left (south) to enter N'Kwala campground on the Nicola River. It's before a cement barrier and an abrupt curve north. Two big, dark boulders mark the entry road.

N'KWALA RECREATION SITE #21
Weekend / Easy
9 tables
Accessible by small motorhomes and trailers

Nicola River, from N'Kwala campground

Continuing northwest on Hwy 8, passing the turnoff to N'Kwala campground.

69 km (42.8)
Reach Spences Bridge and Trans-Canada Hwy 1.

If you're heading southeast on Hwy 8 from Spences Bridge

0 km (0 mi)
Starting southeast on Hwy 8, from Spences Bridge and Trans-Canada Hwy 1.

42.8 km (26.5 mi)
Proceed southeast on Hwy 8 for Merritt. Turn right (south) to enter **N'Kwala campground** on the Nicola River, described on page 196. It's by a cement barrier, immediately after an abrupt curve east. Two big, dark boulders mark the entry road.

56.3 km (34.9)
Proceed southeast on Hwy 8 through Lower Nicola to reach Merritt. Turn left (north) onto Aberdeen Road for rough access to nearly a dozen campgrounds at small, distant lakes. Initial directions continue on page 196.

60 km (37.2 mi)
Proceed southeast for Merritt. Hwy 97C forks left (north) to Logan Lake, Ashcroft, and Cache Creek on Trans-Canada Hwy 1.

65 km (40.3 mi)
Arrive in Merritt.

69 km (42.8 mi)
Reach the junction of Hwys 97C and 5 at the Merritt Interchange near the Tourist Info Centre.

EAST AND SOUTH OF MERRITT

The campgrounds at Marquart and Lundbom lakes are a short drive east of Merritt and only a few kilometers off pavement. They're very convenient for a brief overnight stay. Though both lakes are small, Lundbom is bigger, has two spacious campgrounds, and offers a choice of treed or open campsites. The Marquart setting is barren.

If you want to settle in for a couple days near Merritt, look south of town, where campgrounds at Kane and Harmon lakes offer a prettier mixture of grassland, aspen, and ponderosa pines; a more intimate camping atmosphere; a short interpretive trail; and the Kane Valley cross-country ski trails—a 37-km (23-mi) network available to equestrians and mountain bikers in summer. Check out the photo on page 192. These campgrounds are slightly farther off pavement than Marquart and Lundbom, but the Kane Valley Road is smoother. Cows can be a nuisance here— a reminder that this isn't wilderness. At least they're wandering, instead of imprisoned in factory farms.

If you're heading east on Hwy 5A from Merritt

0 km (0 mi)
Starting east on Hwy 5A, from the junction with Hwy 5 at the Merritt Interchange. The highway soon bends southeast.

9.4 km (5.8 mi)
Proceed south on Hwy 5A for Kane and Harmon lakes. Turn left (east) near a cattleguard, reset your tripometer to 0, and follow the directions on page 199 for **Marquart and Lundbom lakes**.

14.3 km (8.9 mi)
Pass a sign announcing the turn for Kane Valley.

14.5 km (9 mi)
Proceed south on Hwy 5A to reach Hwy 97C or Princeton. Turn right (west) at the top of the rise, reset your tripometer to 0, and follow the directions on page 200 for **Kane and Harmon lakes**.

23 km (14.3 mi)
Reach the junction with Hwy 97C, which leads east to the Okanagan. Hwy 5A continues south to Princeton and Hwy 3.

If you're heading north on Hwy 5A from Hwy 97C

0 km (0 mi)
Starting north on Hwy 5A, from the junction with Hwy 97C near Aspen Grove.

8.5 km (5.3 mi)
Proceed north on Hwy 5A for Marquart and Lundbom Lakes.

Turn left (west), reset your tripometer to 0, and follow the directions on page 200 for **Kane and Harmon lakes**.

13.6 km (8.4 mi)
Proceed north on Hwy 5A for Merritt. Turn right (east) near a cattleguard, reset your tripometer to 0, and follow the directions below for **Marquart and Lundbom lakes**.

23 km (14.3 mi)
Reach the junction with Hwy 5 at the Merritt Interchange.

For MARQUART and LUNDBOM LAKES, now follow the directions below

0 km (0 mi)
Starting east, departing Hwy 5A. Quickly reach a junction and go left on the rough road through rolling grassland. Pass the day-use area on Marquart Lake's southwest shore.

2.7 km (1.7 mi)
Reach Marquart Lake campground, on the northeast shore. The lake is shallow; the campground shadeless.

MARQUART LAKE EAST RECREATION SITE #29
Overnight / Easy
Elev: 1123 m (3683 ft) / Lake: 22 ha
6 tables, boat launch
Accessible by small motorhomes and trailers

~

4.7 km (2.9 mi)
Reach Lundbom Lake West campground, spread around the southwest shore.

LUNDBOM LAKE WEST RECREATION SITE #30
Weekend / Easy
Elev: 1128 m (3700 ft) / Lake: 49 ha
35 tables, boat launch, horse corral
Accessible by motorhomes and 5th-wheels

~

5.7 km (3.5 mi)
Reach Lundbom Lake East campground, spread around the northeast shore.

LUNDBOM LAKE EAST RECREATION SITE #31
Weekend / Easy
Elev: 1128 m (3700 ft) / Lake: 49 ha
14 tables, boat launch
Accessible by motorhomes and 5th-wheels

~

For KANE and HARMON LAKES, now follow the directions below

0 km (0 mi)
Starting west, departing Hwy 5A. The road soon bends southwest and continues in that general direction until past the campgrounds.

3.7 km (2.3 mi)
Bear right on the main road. Pass several tiny lakes.

9 km (5.6 mi)
Reach Kane Lake campground on the left.

KANE LAKE RECREATION SITE #32
Weekend / Easy
Elev: 1100 m (3608 ft) / Lake: 8 ha
5 tables, open grassy area
Accessible by motorhomes and trailers

~

9.2 km (5.7 mi)
Reach Harmon Lake West campground on the left.

HARMON LAKE WEST RECREATION SITE #33
Weekend / Easy
Elev: 1120 m (3675 ft) / Lake: 27 ha
6 tables
Accessible by motorhomes and trailers

~

Campfire Questions

Add spark to your evening powwow by asking your campfire mates unusual questions. Go around in a circle. Limit answers to a few minutes, to keep everyone involved. No judging allowed. The person who asks is the last person to answer. Here are suggestions. If you had time to learn and money to hire the best instructors, what would you like to master? What character in what movie would you most like to be? What was your most embarrassing moment? If you could experience the outcome of a path you didn't take, what juncture in life would you return to? Of anyone in the world, past or present, who would you most like to be friends with? What personal trait would you like to improve? When did you feel most proud of yourself?

9.8 km (6.1 mi)
Turn left just before the cattleguard to reach Harmon Lake East campground in about 200 meters.

HARMON LAKE EAST RECREATION SITE #34
Weekend / Easy
Elev: 1120 m (3675 ft) / Lake: 27 ha
18 tables
Accessible by motorhomes and 5th-wheels

11.9 km (7.4 mi)
Pass Englishmen Lake. Proceed southwest on Kane Valley Road to reach Coquihalla Hwy 5 at the Coldwater Exit (Kingsvale Interchange). En route, Voght Valley Road forks left (southeast) to campgrounds at Shea, Tahla, Boss and Davis lakes, described on page 188.

WEST OF KAMLOOPS

Duffy Lake campground is no place for family frolic. It's just a clearing plastered with cow pies. But it's close enough to Kamloops that it's worth knowing about in case you need a place to sleep. A 10-minute drive on Hwy 1, then 15 minutes off pavement will get you there. Convenience is Duffy's only asset. Though big RVs will find adequate room, the backroad is bumpy enough to loosen a few screws. It gets muddy too, so avoid it after heavy rain.

If you're heading west on Hwy 1 from Kamloops

0 km (0 mi)
Starting west on Trans-Canada Hwy 1, from the junction with Hwy 5A at Kamloops.

6.5 km (4 mi)
Stay in the far right lane on Hwys 1/97 where Hwy 5 bears left.

14.5 km (9 mi)
Pass the gas station at Cherry Creek.

23.5 km (14.6 mi)
Turn left onto Greenstone Mtn. Road (signed for Dominic Lake Resort) and reset your tripometer to 0.

If you're heading east on Hwy 1 from Savona

0 km (0 mi)
Starting east on Trans-Canada Hwy 1, from Savona.

24 km (14.9 mi)
Pass Rodeo Drive and the green highway sign stating the distance to Kamloops (22 km).

27.5 km (17.1 mi)
Turn right onto Greenstone Mtn. Road (signed for Dominic Lake Resort) and reset your tripometer to 0.

For either approach above, now follow the directions below

0 km (0 mi)
Starting on Greenstone Mtn. Road.

2.4 km (1.5 mi)
Go right. Proceed through a burned area.

9.7 km (6 mi)
Turn left and ascend steeply.

12.3 km (7.6 mi)
Turn right.

13.5 km (8.4 mi)
Arrive at Duffy Lake campground. The best campsite is 300 meters farther, on a grassy knoll overlooking the lake.

DUFFY LAKE RECREATION SITE #9
Weekend / Moderate
Elev: 1158 m (3800 ft) / Lake: 24 ha
4 tables, more campsites
Accessible by motorhomes and 5th-wheels

MERRITT TO KAMLOOPS

Lakes, like a string of sausages, line the bottom of a sweeping valley between Merritt and Kamloops. The land is vast and open, as if the earth is baring itself to the sky. It feels lonely. Looks like cowboys should be riding the range. And they do. This is cattle country. Huge ranches lay claim to the grassland. Driving here on Hwy 5A is a peaceful alternative to the more hectic Trans-Canada Hwy 1 or Coquihalla Hwy 5. You can't cruise quite as fast, but the blacktop is straight enough to let you make good time—unless you exit eastward to visit the area's large, lakeside campgrounds. They're not far from pavement, close enough for a brief overnight stay, via access roads that even big RVs can handle.

Glimpse Lake has a cabin community, and campgrounds on its south and north shores. It's a pretty lake. A few stately Douglas firs add elegance to the surrounding forest. But enough people

B.C. stands for Boating Country.

come here to get away from it all that it often feels they've brought it all with them.

Peter Hope Lake is attractive though unremarkable. The campground is pleasant. Bring your own shade in summer; the setting is only lightly treed. Kids can play in the lumpy grass, and a meadowy forest across the road. As at many lakes throughout the province, there's a fishing lodge here. It might give you a smug chuckle to think that most of what the lodge guests are paying for, you're enjoying free at the FS campground.

If you're heading northeast on Hwy 5A from Merritt

0 km (0 mi)
Starting northeast on Hwy 5A, from the junction with Hwy 5, just north of Merritt.

8.4 km (5.2 mi)
Proceed through Nicola.

20.5 km (12.7 mi)
Proceed through Quilchena.

25.5 km (15.8 mi)
Proceed north on Hwy 5A for Peter Hope Lake campground and Kamloops. Turn right (east) onto Douglas Lake Road and reset your tripometer to 0 for the **Glimpse Lake campgrounds**; directions continue on page 206. Beyond Douglas Lake, the road heads northeast, eventually intersecting Hwy 97 at Westwold.

31.4 km (19.5 mi)
Pass Nicola Lake rest area.

42.2 km (26.2 mi)
Proceed north on Hwy 5A for Kamloops. Turn right (east) onto Peter Hope Road and reset your tripometer to 0 for **Peter Hope Lake campground**; directions continue on page 208.

49.8 km (30.9 mi)
Pass Stump Lake rest area.

68.1 km (42.2 mi)
Proceed north on Hwy 5A for Kamloops. Just past Trapp Lake, turn right (east) for Roche Lake Provincial Park.

74.1 km (45.9 mi)
Pass Shumway Lake on the right.

91.8 km (56.9 mi)
Intersect Trans-Canada Hwy 1 at Kamloops.

If you're heading south on Hwy 5A from Kamloops

0 km (0 mi)
Starting south on Hwy 5A, from Trans-Canada Hwy 1 at Kamloops.

17.7 km (11 mi)
Pass Shumway Lake on the left.

23.7 km (14.7 mi)
Proceed south on Hwy 5A for campgrounds at Peter Hope and Glimpse lakes, and for Merritt. Turn left (east) for Roche Lake Provincial Park.

37.4 km (23.2 mi)
Stump Lake is visible.

42 km (26 mi)
Pass Stump Lake rest area.

49.6 km (30.8 mi)
Proceed south on Hwy 5A for the Glimpse Lake campgrounds and for Merritt. Turn left (east) onto Peter Hope Road and reset your tripometer to 0 for Peter Hope Lake campground; directions continue on page 208.

60.4 km (37.4 mi)
Pass Nicola Lake rest area.

66.3 km (41.1 mi)
Proceed south on Hwy 5A for Merritt. Turn left (east) onto Douglas Lake Road and reset your tripometer to 0 for the Glimpse Lake campgrounds; directions continue below. Beyond Douglas Lake, the road heads northeast, eventually intersecting Hwy 97 at Westwold.

71.3 km (44.2 mi)
Proceed through Quilchena.

83.4 km (51.7 mi)
Proceed through Nicola.

91.8 km (56.9 mi)
Intersect Hwy 5 just north of Merritt.

For GLIMPSE LAKE, now follow the directions below

0 km (0 mi)
Starting east on Douglas Lake Road, departing Hwy 5A.

8 km (5 mi)
Proceed straight (southeast) for Douglas Lake. Just beyond the power station, turn left (east) onto Lauder Creek FS road. It soon bends northeast and continues in that general direction all the way to Glimpse Lake.

Watch for moose along Hwy 5A.

23 km (14.3 mi)
Reach the west end of 93.5-hectare Glimpse Lake. The camp-grounds are on the south and north shores, at 950 m (3116 ft) elevation.

GLIMPSE LAKE SOUTH RECREATION SITE #20
Weekend / Moderate
7 tables
Inaccessible by motorhomes and trailers

~

GLIMPSE LAKE NORTH RECREATION SITE #19
Weekend / Moderate
11 tables
Accessible by small motorhomes and trailers

~

For PETER HOPE LAKE, now follow the directions below

0 km (0 mi)
Starting east on Peter Hope Road, departing Hwy 5A.

6.5 km (4 mi)
Bear left on the main road.

7.6 km (4.7 mi)
Arrive at Peter Hope Lake campground. The first camping area has a few tables in an open, grassy clearing on the shore. The main campground is 200 meters farther, on the reedy side of the lake.

PETER HOPE LAKE RECREATION SITE #17
Weekend / Easy
1082 m (3550 ft) / Lake: 116 ha
16 tables, boat launch
Accessible by motorhomes and 5th-wheels

The road continuing along Peter Hope Lake's east shore soon forks. Left (northeast) is 4WD access to **Plateau Lake Recreation Site #18**. Right (south) is 4WD access to the **Glimpse Lake campgrounds** (described on pages 204 and 206).

OKANAGAN CONNECTOR HWY 97C

Hwy 97C, between Merritt and Okanagan Lake, is an efficient but despotic structure, rigidly commanding motorists to travel nonstop. But there are a few exits. Use them to escape. They quickly access several campgrounds at higher elevations (about 1525 m / 5000 ft) where even the hottest summer day is comfortably cool.

The Elkhart Interchange accesses campgrounds at Bob's and Island lakes. The Sunset Interchange accesses campgrounds at Pinnacle, Hatheume, Brenda and MacDonald lakes.

Consider the tiny campground at puny Bob's Lake for only a brief overnight stay. The others are small or medium-size campgrounds on pretty, forested lakes, where a couple days of relaxation might be enjoyable. All are quickly reached via good backroads that won't alarm RV pilots.

If you're heading east on Hwy 97C from Hwy 5A

0 km (0 mi)
Starting east on Hwy 97C, departing Hwy 5A near Aspen Grove, southeast of Merritt.

27.7 km (17.2 mi)
Reach the Elkhart Interchange. Proceed east on Hwy 97C for campgrounds at Pinnacle, Hatheume, Brenda or MacDonald lakes, or for the Okanagan. Exit the highway here for **campgrounds at Bob's and Island lakes**; directions continue on page 210.

39.5 km (24.5 mi)
Reach the Sunset Interchange. Proceed east on Hwy 97C for the Okanagan. Exit the highway here for **campgrounds at Pinnacle and Hatheume lakes** (directions continue on page 211), or **Brenda and MacDonald lakes** (directions continue on page 213).

48.7 km (30.2 mi)
Proceed east over 1728-m (5668-ft) Pennask Summit.

82 km (50.8 mi)
Intersect Hwy 97 on the west side of Okanagan Lake. Turn left (north) for Kelowna. Turn right (south) for Peachland, Summerland or Penticton

If you're heading west on Hwy 97C from the Okanagan

0 km (0 mi)
Starting west on Hwy 97C from the west side of Okanagan Lake, departing Hwy 97 between Peachland and Westbank.

33.3 km (20.7 mi)
Proceed west over 1728-m (5668-ft) Pennask Summit. Pennask Lake is visible north.

42.5 km (26.4 mi)
Reach the Sunset Interchange. Proceed west on Hwy 97C for campgrounds at Bob's and Island lakes, or for Hwy 5A. Exit the

Typical backroad junction, near Bob's Lake

highway here for **campgrounds at Pinnacle and Hatheume lakes** (directions continue on page 211), or **Brenda and MacDonald lakes** (directions continue on page 213).

54.3 km (33.7 mi)
Reach the Elkhart Interchange. Proceed west on Hwy 97C to reach Hwy 5A. Exit the highway here for **campgrounds at Bob's and Island lakes;** directions continue below.

82 km (50.8 mi)
Intersect Hwy 5A near Aspen Grove. Turn right (north) for Merritt. Turn left (south) for Princeton.

For BOB'S and ISLAND LAKES, now follow the directions below

From the eastbound exit, turn left (north) and go under the highway, then reset your tripometer to 0. From the westbound exit, ignore the first right fork, descend toward the tunnel, then turn right (north) and reset your tripometer to 0.

0 km (0 mi)
Starting north on Bob's Lake Pit Road.

5 km (3.3 mi)
Pass an unnamed lake on the right.

5.7 km (3.5 mi)
Proceed straight for Island Lake. Turn right to enter Bob's Lake campground. It's convenient for a brief overnight stay, but the lake is just a pond in the woods.

BOB'S LAKE RECREATION SITE #42
Overnight / Easy
Elev: 1524 m (5000 ft) / Lake: 5 ha
2 tables
Accessible by small motorhomes and trailers

Continuing on the main road, passing the turnoff to Bob's Lake campground.

7.2 km (4.5 mi)
Pass the turnoff to Paradise Lake.

7.5 km (4.7 mi)
Go left at the four-way junction.

7.7 km (4.8 mi)
Turn left to enter Island Lake campground. This is a larger, prettier lake than Bob's. The campsites here are much more appealing.

ISLAND LAKE RECREATION SITE #43
Weekend / Easy
Elev: 1524 m (5000 ft)
5 tables, boat launch
Accessible by small motorhomes and trailers

For PINNACLE and HATHEUME LAKES,
now follow the directions below

From the eastbound exit, proceed straight (east) and reset your tripometer to 0 where left (north) goes under the highway. From the westbound exit, turn left (south), go under the highway, then turn left (east) at the T-junction and reset your tripometer to 0.

0 km (0 mi)
Starting east on the frontage road paralleling the south side of the highway.

5 km (3.1 mi)
Go left at the junction.

6.1 km (3.8 mi)
Curve left.

6.4 km (4 mi)
Bear right.

6.8 km (4.2 mi)
Reach a T-junction. Right (south) on Sunset FS road leads to Brenda and MacDonald lakes (page 213). Turn left (northeast) on Bear FS road and go under the highway for Pinnacle and Hatheume lakes.

9.3 km (5.8 mi)
Go right.

13.7 km (8.5 mi)
Proceed straight where Pennask FS road forks left.

14.2 km (8.8 mi)
Proceed straight where a rough road forks left to reach Pennask Lake Recreation Area in 6 km (3.7 mi).

19 km (11.8 mi)
Turn left at the junction.

21.3 km (13.2 mi)
Proceed right for Hatheume Lake. Turn left to quickly reach Pinnacle Lake campground.

PINNACLE LAKE RECREATION SITE #26
Weekend / Moderate
Elev: 1433 m (4700 ft) / Lake: 10.5 ha
5 tables, boat launch
Accessible by small motorhomes and trailers

~

The Successful Camping Trip

You didn't starve. Or freeze. Or get washed away in a deluge. Or eaten by wild animals. You still have all your fingers and toes. You can still see out of both eyes. You're still on speaking terms with your campmates. You didn't end up throwing rocks at the campers in the next site. You didn't fall into the outhouse, or the campfire, or the creek. You didn't run out of gas, or have a flat tire, or get stuck in the mud. You didn't lose the dog, the kids, the car keys, your wallet, your lunch, your spouse, or your mind. And despite everything else that did happen, or maybe because of it, you arrived safely at home feeling better about life than you did before you left.

Continuing on the main road, passing the turnoff to Pinnacle Lake campground.

22.2 km (13.8 mi)
Fork right.

22.9 km (14.2 mi)
Arrive at Hatheume Lake campground.

HATHEUME LAKE RECREATION SITE #27
Weekend / Moderate
Elev: 1402 m (4600 ft) / Lake: 106 ha
14 tables, 1 walk-in tent site, boat launch
Accessible by motorhomes and 5th-wheels

For BRENDA and MACDONALD LAKES,
now follow the directions below

Follow the directions for Pinnacle and Hatheume lakes (page 211) as far as the T-junction at 6.8 km (4.2 mi), then turn right (south) on Sunset FS road and continue following the directions on page 214.

11.8 km (7.3 mi)
Reach a junction. Turn left (northeast) onto Brenda FS road. Right (southeast) leads to **Headwater Lakes Recreation Site #21** and **Peachland Lake Recreation Site #22**. Both are inferior to other campgrounds nearby, and are in settings ravaged by mining and logging.

13.5 km (8.4 mi)
Reach a junction. Stay straight on the main road.

14 km (8.7 mi)
Proceed straight for MacDonald Lake. Turn left to reach Brenda Lake campground.

BRENDA LAKE RECREATION SITE #25
Weekend / Easy
Elev: 1707 m (5600 ft) / Lake: 20 ha
5 tables, cartop boat launch
Accessible by small motorhomes and trailers

Continuing on the main road, passing the turnoff to Brenda Lake campground.

14.8 km (9.2 mi)
Reach a junction and turn left. Soon bear right at the fork to reach MacDonald Lake campground.

MACDONALD LAKE RECREATION SITE #24
Weekend / Easy
Elev: 1707 m (5600 ft) / Lake: 11 ha
5 tables, cartop boat launch
Accessible by small motorhomes and trailers

SOUTHWEST OF SALMON ARM

Between Kamloops and Salmon Arm, Trans-Canada Hwy 1 drunkenly wanders north and bumps into Shuswap Lake. At Monte Creek, just east of Kamloops, Hwy 1 loses touch with its equally inebriated little buddy, Hwy 97, which veers southeast, waking up the towns of Monte Lake, Westwold and Falkland

Funky RV at Pinaus Lake

before smacking into the Okanagan just north of Vernon. The campgrounds described here are south and north of Hwy 97. You can pinpoint the area on maps by looking southwest of Salmon Arm. It's picturesque ranching country. A good place for a leisurely, exploratory drive.

(1) **Woods Lake** is south of Westwold. **Pinaus Lake** is southeast. (Ah, go ahead. Enjoy the bawdy pronunciation.) Both lakes are handsome, bearded with forest. Pinaus is larger. A rocky escarpment high on the treed slope opposite the campground adds interest to the view. The Woods campsites are more comfortably spaced, however, and the access road is better. The final few kilometers to Pinaus are narrow, rough, and can be dangerously muddy. A high-clearance vehicle is preferable. After heavy rain, 4WD might be necessary. Big RVs (motorhomes, trucks pulling trailers) should opt for Woods.

(2) **Bolean, Arthur and Spa lakes** (page 218) are on a 1525-m (5000-ft) plateau northeast of Falkland. All are small (about 1.6 km / 1 mi long), peaceful, and laced with forest. Bring a fishing rod, a good book, or your meditation cushion. These campgrounds are fine for an overnight stop and a peaceful morning, but none has a setting likely to keep you entertained. Bolean is

a steep, 30-minute drive from Hwy 97. The narrow, bumpy road has sections of washboard. Your 2WD car will make it—in first gear much of the way. Big RVs (motorhomes, trucks pulling trailers) need after burners to surmount the ascent. There are pullouts for passing, and viewpoints overlooking the Salmon River valley.

(3) **Joyce and Pillar lakes** (page 220) are on the good gravel road linking Falkland (Hwy 97) with Chase (Hwy 1). Pillar is a small lake. Joyce is extra small. Both have recreation sites that are little more than day-use pullouts. They'll suffice for an overnight stop only if you arrive late and leave early. The same is true of the recreation site at **Chase Creek**. The only inviting campground along here is at **Charcoal Creek**, where you can get well off the road, into a creekside clearing, but it's too small for motorhomes and trailers.

(1) WOODS AND PINAUS LAKES

If you're heading southeast on Hwy 97 from Monte Creek

From Trans-Canada Hwy 1 at Monte Creek, drive Hwy 97 south-east. At 30.2 km (18.7 mi) pass Westwold School on the right. At 32.2 km (20 mi) turn right (south) onto Ingram Creek FS road and reset your tripometer to 0.

If you're heading west on Hwy 97 from Falkland

From the junction with Falkland-Chase Road (near the Falkland store and pub) drive Hwy 97 west 13.4 km (8.3 mi), then turn left (south) onto Ingram Creek FS road and reset your tripometer to 0.

For either approach above, now follow the directions below

0 km (0 mi)
Starting south on Ingram Creek FS road, departing Hwy 97.

6.4 km (4 mi)
Reach a junction. Proceed right (southwest) for Woods Lake; directions continue at the bottom of page 217. For Pinaus Lake, turn left (northeast) and reset your tripometer to 0.

0 km (0 mi)
Starting left (northeast) for Pinaus Lake.

2.4 km (1.5 mi) and **2.7 km (1.7 mi)**
Bear left.

3.9 km (2.4 mi)
Fork left.

6.7 km (4.2 mi)
Go right at the T-junction. The road deteriorates.

7.2 km (4.5 mi)
Stay straight and begin descending.

9.3 km (5.8 mi)
Bear left where right descends to a resort. Beware of mud. The road narrows on a high slope.

9.9 km (6.1 mi)
Pinaus Lake is visible.

12.1 km (7.5 mi)
Turn right and descend to reach Pinaus Lake campground in 200 meters. Pass a couple individual campsites. Bear left to reach the main campground in another 200 meters. Beware of further mud.

PINAUS LAKE RECREATION SITE #71
Weekend / Difficult
Elev: 1006 m (3300 ft) / Lake: 3.3 km (2 mi) long, 162 ha
5 tables, 7 campsites, gravel boat launch
Inaccessible by motorhomes and trailers

Continuing southwest at the 6.4-km (4-mi) junction, passing the turnoff to Pinaus Lake campground.

10.2 km (6.3 mi), **11.3 km (7 mi)**, and **11.4 km (7.1 mi)**
Fork right.

15.3 km (9.5 mi)
Stay straight on the main road. Ignore a minor right fork.

15.6 km (9.7 mi)
Proceed under the powerline.

15.8 km (9.8 mi)
Bear right and ascend north, beneath the powerline.

16.5 km (10.2 mi)
Re-enter forest.

18.2 km (11.3 mi)
Reach Woods Lake. The first campsite is on the right.

18.7 km (11.6 mi)
Pass more campsites.

19.5 km (12.1 mi)
Arrive at the main Woods Lake campground.

WOODS LAKE RECREATION SITE #57
Weekend / Moderate
Elev: 1151 m (3775 ft) / Lake: 27 ha
6 tables, boat launch
Accessible by small motorhomes and trailers

(2) BOLEAN, ARTHUR & SPA LAKES

If you find a vacant campsite at Bolean Lake, stay there. Arthur Lake is pretty, but the campsites are at the weedy end and have a limited view. Endure the rough road to Spa Lake only in search of solitude.

If you're heading southeast on Hwy 97 from Monte Creek

From Trans-Canada Hwy 1 at Monte Creek, drive Hwy 97 southeast about 47 km (29 mi). Just east of Falkland, turn left (north) onto Silvernails Road and reset your tripometer to 0.

If you're heading northwest on Hwy 97 from near Vernon

From the junction of Hwys 97 and 97A (about 9 km north of Vernon) drive Hwy 97 northwest about 29 km (18 mi). Just before Falkland, turn right (north) onto Silvernails Road and reset your tripometer to 0.

For either approach above, now follow the directions below

0 km (0 mi)
Starting north on Silvernails Road, departing Hwy 97.

0.3 km (0.2 mi)
Turn left onto Ord Road. The lakes are above the hill visible ahead. The gravel road switchbacks steeply.

8.9 km (5.5 mi)
Reach a junction and proceed on the main road. Shortly after, fork left for Bolean Lake campground; directions continue on page 220. Stay straight and reset your tripometer to 0 for campgrounds at Arthur and Spa lakes.

0 km (0 mi)
Proceeding straight on the main road, heading for Arthur and Spa lakes.

2.9 km (1.8 mi)
Reach a junction. Go right, on the higher road, for Arthur Lake. Left is the rough road (4WD recommended) to **Spa Lake Recreation Site #66**.

4.2 km (2.6 mi)
Turn right

4.9 km (3 mi)
Arrive at Arthur Lake campground.

ARTHUR LAKE RECREATION SITE #67
Weekend / Difficult
Elev: 1563 m (5127 ft) / Lake: 76 ha
1 table, many campsites, rough boat launch
Inaccessible by motorhomes and trailers

Bolean Lake

Continuing left, shortly after the 8.9-km (5.5-mi) junction, where straight leads to Arthur and Spa lakes.

9.2 km (5.7 mi)
Reach Bolean Lake Lodge. Go left.

9.7 km (6 mi)
Arrive at Bolean Lake campground.

BOLEAN LAKE RECREATION SITE #68
Weekend / Moderate
Elev: 1437 m (4713 ft) / Lake: 71 ha
4 tables, 5 campsites, rough boat launch
Accessible by small motorhomes and trailers

(3) FALKLAND-CHASE ROAD

If you're heading southeast on Hwy 97 from Monte Creek

From Trans-Canada Hwy 1 at Monte Creek, drive Hwy 97 southeast about 45.6 km (28.3 mi) to Falkland. Turn left (north) onto Falkland-Chase Road and reset your tripometer to 0.

If you're heading northwest on Hwy 97 from near Vernon

From the junction of Hwys 97 and 97A (about 9 km north of Vernon) drive Hwy 97 northwest about 30.4 km (18.8 mi) to Falkland. Turn right (north) onto Falkland-Chase Road and reset your tripometer to 0.

For either approach above, now follow the directions below

0 km (0 mi)
Starting north on Falkland-Chase Road. It's paved to Pillar Lake.

7.2 km (4.5 mi)
Stay straight. Pass a sign stating the distance to Chase: 43 km.

10.1 km (6.3 mi)
Reach Joyce Lake day-use area / overnight pullout, on the left, just after crossing the small bridge over Bolean Creek.

> The first site has room for a tent, in trees, away from the road. The second site is 100 meters farther, at a large pull-out near the lake.

JOYCE LAKE RECREATION SITE #65
Overnight / Easy
Elev: 853 m (2800 ft) / Lake: 6.5 ha
2 tables, boat launch
Accessible by motorhomes and 5th-wheels

Continuing north on Falkland-Chase Road, passing Joyce Lake.

13 km (8 mi)
Pillar Lake is visible on the left.

13.4 km (8.3 mi)
Reach Pillar Lake day-use area / overnight pullout, on the left, below the road. Across the road, a short trail leads to the pillar —a geologic curiosity.

PILLAR LAKE RECREATION SITE #64
Overnight / Easy
Elev: 853 m (2800 ft) / Lake: 38 ha
No tables, boat launch
Accessible by motorhomes and 5th-wheels

Continuing north on Falkland-Chase Road, passing Pillar Lake.

15.8 km (9.8 mi)
Reach Chase Creek campground, on the right, just before a small bridge.

CHASE CREEK RECREATION SITE #63
Overnight / Easy
3 roadside campsites
Too small for motorhomes and trailers

Continuing north on Falkland-Chase Road, passing Chase Creek campground.

19.8 km (12.3 mi)
Reach Charcoal Creek campground, on the right. About 50 meters behind the roadside campsite are several more sites in a creekside meadow wedged between low hills.

CHARCOAL CREEK RECREATION SITE #62
Weekend / Moderate
3 tables, level tent sites
Too small for motorhomes and trailers

Continuing north on Falkland-Chase Road, passing Charcoal Creek campground.

39.5 km (24.5 mi)
Reach a junction. Left intersects Hwy 1 at Chase in 10 km (6.2 mi). Right, then right at the next junction, leads generally east 19 km (11.8 mi) to Skimikin Lakes campground (described on page 224) before intersecting Hwy 1 at Tappen.

NEAR CHASE

Harper Lake is just off Trans-Canada Hwy 1, near Chase. But it's not convenient, because the access road is rough and steep, quickly gaining 495 m (1625 ft). It's narrow too, with a sheer drop-off. Motorhome pilots and trailer tuggers should opt for Skimikin Lakes (page 224). With patience and persistence, however, you can reach Harper in a 2WD car. Only if it's muddy might you need 4WD. Your reward is a small, attractive, forested lake with cattails along the north shore. It's a peaceful haven from the combat atmosphere on the highway. Come up for a swim on a hot afternoon. Or a pleasant overnight stay.

If you're heading northeast on Hwy 1 from Monte Creek

From the junction with Hwy 97 at Monte Creek, drive Trans-Canada Hwy 1 northeast 25.2 km (15.6 mi). Turn right (south) onto Harper Lake Road and reset your tripometer to 0. If you reach Shuswap-Chase Creek Road, you're 300 meters too far.

If you're heading southwest on Hwy 1 from Chase

From Chase, drive Trans-Canada Hwy 1 southwest. Just out of town, set your tripometer to 0 at the green highway sign: KAMLOOPS 55 KM. At 1.4 km (0.9 mi) pass Shuswap-Chase Creek Road on the left. At 1.7 km (1.1 mi) turn left (south) onto Harper Lake Road and reset your tripometer to 0.

For either approach above, now follow the directions below

0 km (0 mi)
Starting south on Harper Lake Road.

3.4 km (2.1 mi)
Go right at the junction.

5.8 km (3.6 mi)
Arrive at Harper Lake. Fork left to enter the campground.

HARPER LAKE RECREATION SITE #1
Overnight / Difficult
Elev: 840 m (2755 ft) / Lake: 27 ha
5 tables
Inaccessible by motorhomes and trailers

NEAR SALMON ARM

Skimikin Lakes campground, just northwest of Salmon Arm, is a rarity: reached via paved road, a short distance from the Trans-Canada. You can also get there on a well-maintained backroad via bucolic Turtle Valley. Each of the two small lakes has a camping area. The scenery isn't beautiful, but the atmosphere can be soothing. Choose from campsites in grassy clearings, or among pines, alders and aspen. The area is open enough to accommodate land yachts.

The paved access to Skimikin Lakes, if you're heading east on Hwy 1

From Chase, drive Trans-Canada Hwy 1 (northeast along Shuswap Lake, then south) 35 km (21.7 mi). Turn right (northwest) onto Tappen Valley Road, signed for Turtle Valley. It's across from the lumber mill at Tappen Bay. Reset your tripometer to 0.

The paved access to Skimikin Lakes, if you're heading west on Hwy 1

From the Salmon River bridge, on the west edge of Salmon Arm, drive Trans-Canada Hwy 1 north 10.8 km (6.7 mi). Turn left (northwest) onto Tappen Valley Road, signed for Turtle Valley. It's across from the lumber mill at Tappen Bay. Reset your tripometer to 0.

For either approach above, now follow the directions below

0 km (0 mi)
Starting northwest on Tappen Valley Road, departing Hwy 1.

4 km (2.5 mi)
Turn left (west) at the junction.

10.1 km (6.3 mi)
Turn left (south) to enter the first Skimikin Lakes campground, on the south lake. Big RVs will find room here in a large clearing.

10.8 km (6.7 mi)
Turn left (south) to enter the second Skimikin Lakes campground, on the north lake. Choose from campsites up to the right in trees, or ahead on an open point.

SKIMIKIN LAKES RECREATION SITE #3
Weekend / Easy
Elev: 525 m (1722 ft) / Lake: 11 ha
6 tables
Accessible by motorhomes and 5th-wheels

The backroad access to Skimikin Lakes, if you're heading east on Hwy 1

From the rest area beside Chase Creek, near the north entrance to Chase, drive Trans-Canada Hwy 1 northeast. At 9.1 km (5.6 mi) pass a BC Parks sign for Roderick Haig-Brown. Get in the right turn lane. At 9.4 km (5.8 mi) turn right (south) following the sign for North Shuswap Resort Area, Adams Lake, and Squilax-Anglemont Rd. Reset your tripometer to 0.

For many excellent campgrounds north of Hwy 1, on nearby Adams Lake, read Camp Free in B.C. Volume Two, *described on page 394.*

0 km (0 mi)
Starting south, departing Hwy 1.

0.3 km (0.2 mi)
Fork left onto Turtle Valley Road for Skimikin Lakes campground.
Right crosses Hwy 1 on an overpass and leads to excellent FS
campgrounds on Adams Lake. For details, read *Camp Free in
B.C. Volume Two.* It's described on page 394.

1.3 km (0.8 mi)
Pavement ends.

3.7 km (2.3 mi)
Pass a sign: WELCOME TO TURTLE VALLEY.

6 km (3.7 mi)
Fork left. Chum Lake is right.

7.3 km (4.5 mi) and **9.3 km (5.8 mi)**
Stay straight, following signs for Tappen.

10 km (6.2 mi)
Bear left on the main road. In the next 8.2 km (5.1 mi) stay
straight, ignoring right forks.

18.3 km (11.3 mi)
Turn right (south) to enter the first Skimikin Lakes campground.
Read page 225 for details.

19 km (11.7 mi)
Turn right (south) to enter the second Skimikin Lakes campground. Read page 225 for details.

25.1 km (15.6 mi)
Turn right (east) at the junction.

29.1 km (18 mi)
Intersect Hwy 1, across from the lumber mill at Tappen Bay.
Turn right (south) for Salmon Arm. Turn left (north) for
Kamloops.

~

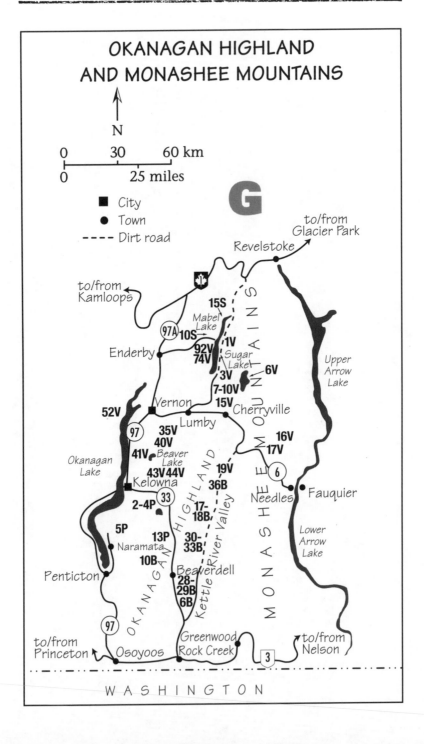

OKANAGAN HIGHLAND
AND MONASHEE MOUNTAINS

N

| 0 | 30 | 60 km |

0   25 miles

■ City
● Town
- - - - Dirt road

G

to/from
Glacier Park

Revelstoke

to/from
Kamloops

15S

Mabel
Lake

97A 10S

92V
74V

Enderby

Sugar
Lake

1V

6V

3V

7-10V

15V

Upper
Arrow
Lake

Vernon   Lumby   Cherryville

52V

97

35V
40V

41V Beaver
Lake

16V

17V

43V 44V

Okanagan
Lake

Kelowna

19V

36B

6

Needles   Fauquier

2-4P   33

17-
18B

Lower
Arrow
Lake

5P

13P

30-
33B

Naramata

10B

28-
29B
6B

Beaverdell

Penticton

97

to/from
Princeton

Osoyoos

Greenwood
Rock Creek

3

to/from
Nelson

MONASHEE MOUNTAINS

OKANAGAN HIGHLAND

Kettle River Valley

WASHINGTON

G: Okanagan Highland and Monashee Mountains

The letter indicates which FS district the campground is in. **B** stands for Boundary FS District. **P** stands for Penticton FS District. **V** stands for Vernon FS District.

1V	Cottonwood Bay	19V-a	Bruer Creek
2P	Browne Lake	19V-b	Kettle River
3V	Cascade South	28B	Canyon Flats
3P	Hydraulic Lake	29B	Canyon Creek
4P	Minnow Lake	30B	Thone Lake
5P	Chute Lake	31B	Kettle Bench
6B	Taurus Lake	32B	Kettle Canyon
6V	Sugar Creek	33B	State Creek
7-10V	Sugar Lake	35V	Doreen Lake
10B	Saunier Lake	36B	Nevertouch Lake
10S	Dale Lake	40V	Island Lake
13P	Arlington Lakes	41V	Beaver Lake
15S	Noisy Creek	43V	Postill Lake
15V	Cherryville	44V	Ideal Lake
16V	Holmes Lake	52V	Okanagan Lake
17B	Lassie Lake	74V	Hidden Lake
17V	Monashee Kettle River	92V	Cooke Creek
18B	Cup Lake		

Okanagan Highland and Monashee Mountains

Kettle Valley Railway trestle spans Myra Canyon, near Chute Lake

Every summer, after enduring perpetual cold and damp elsewhere in the province, wave upon wave of British Columbians rolls into the sunny Okanagan Valley seeking resuscitation of the senses. Like hypothermic shipwreck survivors, they wash onto the beaches of **Okanagan Lake**. It's an inland sea measuring 125 km (78 mi) long, 2 to 5 km (1.2 to 3.1 mi) wide, up to 550 m (1805 ft) deep, and covering 35,008 hectares. That much water is difficult to cool, which contributes to a dreamy climate, which supports thriving orchards and vineyards. Among people who shovel snow all winter, the Okanagan Valley's mythic Mediterranean image is understandable.

As a result of its popularity and subsequent development, the Okanagan Valley has undergone a rapid character shift—from rural to urban. Finding an unofficial free campsite here used to be easy. Now you have to be a crafty stealth-camper to pull it off. That's no fun. And the FS maintains just one campground on Okanagan Lake. But many more are nearby, above and east of the valley, in the **Okanagan Highland**.

If you're unfamiliar with the region, *highland* might suggest Scottish moors carpeted with blazing-green grass. Give your head a shake. Most of the Okanagan Highland is dry forest. Unsightly clearcuts are prevalent. The remaining trees look emaciated. They're nothing like the proud Ponderosa pines and stately Doug firs closer to Okanagan Lake. And here, *high* simply refers to relative elevation. The highland is really just a 1310-m (4300-ft) plateau. It's way above the Okanagan Valley, but it's not impressively mountainous. To complete this accurate but dull picture, the highland lakes are small, mere birdbaths compared to Okanagan Lake. Yet the highland offers campers a cool refuge from the valley heat. Driving to some, you'll gain a panoramic perspective on the celebrated lake and valley below. Several campgrounds are near Hwy 33, which traverses the highland. And a few highland campgrounds accommodate behemoth RVs.

East of the Okanagan Highland is **Kettle River Valley**, at about 720 m (2360 ft) elevation. You'll find eleven FS campgrounds here, several on a healthy river with glorious swimming holes. The south end of the valley is actually Boundary Country. It's described in this Okanagan chapter because of the RV-passable backroad access departing Hwy 33 at Beaverdell, reaching more highland lakes campgrounds along the way.

East of **Enderby**, the topography is more rambunctious, the climate wetter, the vegetation lusher. Cedars and hemlocks rise among the deciduous trees. An irresistible camping destination here is 35-km (21.7-mi) long **Mabel Lake**, in a trough scooped by an ice-age glacier. Noisy Creek campground, on the lake's northwest shore, is provincial-park quality. It has plenty of room for big RVs but the final approach is a steep descent. On the southeast shore is Cascade South campground, where you can walk in and pitch your tent on a sandy beach. Another RV-accessible campground is farther up the east shore, at Cottonwood Bay.

Hwy 6 links **Vernon** with **Lower Arrow Lake**. En route it swoops through the **Monashee Mountains**. Turn north at Cherryville to reach lovely **Sugar Lake**, in a verdant bowl at the foot of the Monashees. The lake is ringed by several FS campgrounds ranging in size from dwarf to giant. One is provincial-park quality and easily absorbs big RVs. Hwy 6 also obliges travellers in need of a quick, easy overnight stop, offering convenient camprounds on the Shuswap River near Cherryville, and the Kettle River farther southeast.

OKANAGAN LAKE

Don't count on finding a vacant site at Okanagan Lake's lone FS campground. Do be prepared for an overnight fee to help pay for increased maintenance. Your annual BC Camping Pass will grant you a 50% discount, so this is still your cheapest option on the lake. And this is a great place to camp: shady pines, pocket beaches scattered along the shore, water lapping at your feet, and the ever-enticing possibility of a refreshing plunge. The campground is on the lake's quiet northwest shore, with a more comfortable buffer from pavement than you'll find at the pricier provincial parks. Access is via the paved Westside Road.

If you're heading north on Hwy 97 from Vernon

From Vernon, drive Hwy 97 north about 9 km (5.6 mi) to the junction with Hwy 97A near the north end of Swan Lake. Proceed east on Hwy 97 another 5.7 km (3.5 mi), then turn left (southwest) onto Westside Road and reset your tripometer to 0. It's 1 km (0.6 mi) past O'Keefe Ranch. It's signed for Westshore, Killiney and Fintry.

If you're heading south on Hwy 97A from Enderby

From Enderby, drive Hwy 97A south to the junction with Hwy 97 near the north end of Swan Lake. Turn right (east) onto Hwy 97, proceed 5.7 km (3.5 mi), then turn left (southwest) onto Westside Road and reset your tripometer to 0. It's 1 km (0.6 mi) past O'Keefe Ranch. It's signed for Westshore, Killiney and Fintry.

If you're heading southeast on Hwy 97 from Hwy 1

From Trans-Canada Hwy 1 at Monte Creek, drive Hwy 97 generally southeast about 70 km (43 mi), then turn right (southwest) onto Westside Road and reset your tripometer to 0. It's signed for Westshore, Killiney and Fintry. It's just before O'Keefe Ranch and well before the junction with Hwy 97A.

For any approach above now follow the directions below

0 km (0 mi)
Starting southwest on Westside Road.

18.3 km (11.3 mi)
After cresting a rise and attaining a viewpoint, turn left (across from Sugarloaf Mtn. Road) and descend to reach Okanagan Lake campground in 1 km (0.6 mi).

OKANAGAN LAKE RECREATION SITE #52
Destination / Easy / Overnight Fee
Elev: 342 m (1122 ft)
30 campsites, 17 tables, boat launch
Accessible by small motorhomes and trailers

ABOVE OKANAGAN VALLEY

Pastel palaces crawling up every hillside. Visually dominant highways. Traffic. The Okanagan Valley resembles Southern California. But the B.C. bush is not far away. Head for the hills east of the valley. Aim for one of these campgrounds.

Chute Lake is an underwhelming sight. It's small (1 km / 0.6 mi long), edged by scrawny lodgepole-pine forest. A nearby resort prevents any sense of seclusion. But the access from Penticton, through Naramata, is a tour of picture-perfect orchard and vineyard country overlooking Okanagan Lake. And Chute Lake campground, accessible by small motorhomes and trailers, is an ideal base for exploring the historic Kettle Valley Railway (KVR). The towering trestle bridges spanning sheer-sided chasms are a fantastic sight. Drive the abandoned railbed from Chute Lake to Myra Canyon, then hike or cycle beyond.

In terms of size and scenery, **Postill Lake** (page 236) is typical of others in the Okanagan Highland. But the campground is tiny, cramped, unlevel, without tables. Just maneuvering a truck is difficult here, so don't bring your motorhome or trailer. Until the FS upgrades this campground, think of it as merely a parking area with a cartop boat launch. Be aware that the lake level fluctuates; this is a domestic water supply.

East of Hwy 97, about halfway between Vernon and Kelowna, is a cluster of highland lakes. You'll find more than 20 campgrounds here—the heaviest concentration in Vernon FS District. The three easiest to reach are **Beaver (Swalwell) Lake**, **Island Lake**, and **Doreen Lake** (page 237). They have room for big RVs. Rough access, possibly requiring 4WD, precludes most of the other nearby campgrounds from this book. Be aware that the Beaver and Island lake levels fluctuate; they supply domestic water. Returning to Winfield from Beaver Lake, cyclists can enjoy a wicked downhill ride with aerial views of the Okanagan Valley. All you need is an agreeable companion to drive your vehicle while you ride your bike.

CHUTE LAKE

If you're heading north or south on Hwy 97 to Penticton

Exit Hwy 97 at the north end of Penticton, following the CITY CENTRE sign onto Westminster Avenue. It leads northeast toward Okanagan Lake's south shore. Follow signs for Naramata. Angle left onto Front Street. It soon intersects Lakeshore Drive (west) and Vancouver Avenue (east) at the waterfront. Turn right onto Vancouver Avenue. Where it becomes Lower Bench Road, set your tripometer to 0 and continue following signs for Naramata.

0 km (0 mi)
Starting on Lower Bench Road in Penticton.

1.7 km (1.1 mi), 2.8 km (1.7 mi), and **3.1 km (1.9 mi)**
Curve left.

4 km (2.5 mi)
Proceed on Naramata Road.

13 km (8.1 mi)
Bear right and ascend. Robinson Road descends left.

13.5 km (8.4 mi)
Proceed straight on the main road, leaving the vineyards, entering
ponderosa-pine and sage country overlooking Okanagan Lake.
Smethurst Road, ascending right, leads to a KVR trailhead.
From there, the abandoned railbed climbs 915 m (3000 ft) and
passes through two tunnels.

20 km (12.4 mi)
Fork right onto Chute Lake Road. Pavement ends.

23 km (14.3 mi)
Go right. The road narrows.

25 km (15.5 mi)
Go right. Left leads to Okanagan Mountain Park in 1.6 km (1 mi).

27.3 km (16.9 mi)
Stay straight.

28.2 km (17.5 mi)
Stay straight. The road levels.

30 km (18.6 mi)
Bear left.

30.7 km (19 mi)
Go right to reach Chute Lake campground, on the south shore.
Chute Lake Resort is straight ahead, on the west shore. The
road north along the west shore, is the KVR railbed leading to
Myra Canyon.

30.9 km (19.2 mi)
Reach a 4-way intersection. Proceed straight onto Elinor Lake FS
road, then immediately bear right.

31.1 km (19.3 mi)
Turn sharply left to arrive at Chute Lake campground in 100
meters.

CHUTE LAKE RECREATION SITE #5
Weekend / Moderate
Elev: 1180 m (3870 ft) / Lake: 3 ha
4 well-spaced tables, boat launch
Accessible by small motorhomes and trailers

POSTILL LAKE

If you're heading north on Hwy 97 from Kelowna

From Hwy 33 in Kelowna, drive Hwy 97 north 4.1 km (2.5 mi). Where Sexsmith goes left (west), turn right (east) onto Old Vernon Road. Continue 7.4 km (4.6 mi), curving north, then turn right (northeast) onto Postill Drive and set your tripometer to 0.

If you're heading south on Hwy 97 from Winfield

Drive Hwy 97 south to the community of Postill, just past Ellison Lake. Turn left (east) onto Old Vernon Road and set your tripometer to 0. It's signed for Postill Lake Lodge (19 km). Soon enter the community of Ellison. At 1.1 km (0.7 mi) turn right at Ellison Market. At 1.3 km (0.8 mi) turn left (northeast) onto Postill Drive and reset your tripometer to 0.

For either approach above, now follow the directions below

0 km (0 mi)
Starting northeast on Postill Drive.

1.2 km (0.7 mi)
Turn left onto Post Lake Road

2.5 km (1.6 mi)
Go left onto gravel.

3.3 km (2 mi)
Cross a bridge

6.1 km (3.8 mi)
Proceed straight.

7.9 km (4.9 mi) and **8.4 km (5.2 mi)**
Pass **overnight pullouts**.

10.8 km (6.7 mi)
Bear right. The road levels.

12.2 km (7.6 mi) and **13.2 km (8.2 mi)**
Bear right.

16 km (10 mi)
Proceed straight.

17.3 km (10.7 mi)
Go right. The road deteriorates.

17.5 km (10.8 mi)
Arrive at Postill Lake campground.

POSTILL LAKE RECREATION SITE #43
Overnight / Moderate
Elev: 1326 m (4350 ft) / Lake: 2 km (1.2 mi) long, 70 ha
2 campsites, no tables, cartop boat launch
Inaccessible by motorhomes and trailers

BEAVER, ISLAND and DOREEN LAKES

If you're driving Hwy 97 south from Vernon
or north from Kelowna

Drive Hwy 97 to the town of Winfield. Turn east onto Beaver Lake Road, signed for Beaver Lake (17 km) and Dee Lake (26 km). There's a Turbo gas station here. It's just north of Voyageur RV Center, just south of Winfield Industrial Park. Set your tripometer to 0.

0 km (0 mi)
Starting east on Beaver Lake Road. Cross railroad tracks and proceed straight.

8.5 km (5.3 mi)
Pavement ends. The road is wide and well-graded.

15.6 km (9.7 mi)
Go left at the junction. Follow the sign for Dee Lake. Ignore the right fork to Beaver Lake Resort.

18.4 km (11.4 mi)
Proceed straight (northeast) for campgrounds at Island and Doreen lakes. Turn right (south) to quickly reach Beaver Lake campground.

BEAVER LAKE RECREATION SITE #41
Weekend / Moderate
Elev: 1348 m (4420 ft) / Lake: 4 km (2.5 mi) long, 305 ha
11 tables, 2 laveview campsites, boat launch
Accessible by motorhomes and 5th-wheels

~

Continuing northeast on the main road, passing the turnoff to Beaver Lake campground.

24.3 km (15.1 mi)
Proceed straight (northeast) for Doreen Lake campground. Turn right to enter Island Lake campground.

ISLAND LAKE RECREATION SITE #40
Weekend / Moderate
Elev: 1524 m (5000 ft) / Lake: 1.5 km (0.9 mi) long, 45 ha
7 tables, boat launch
Accessible by motorhomes and 5th-wheels

~

Continuing northeast on the main road, passing the turnoff to Island Lake campground. Proceed on the main road as it veers southeast.

28.5 km (17.7 mi)
Reach Doreen Lake campground, on the south shore.

DOREEN LAKE RECREATION SITE #35
Weekend / Moderate
Lake: 1.8 km (1.1 mi) long, 60 ha
20 campsites, 10 tables, boat launch
Accessible by motorhomes and 5th-wheels

~

South and east of Doreen Lake are 10 campgrounds, most of which are accessed via rough roads: **Aberdeen Lake Recreation Site # 29, Haddo Lake North Recreation Site #30, Specs Lakes Recreation Site #31, Haddo Lake West Recreation Site #32, Aileen Lake Recreation Site #33, Loon Lake Recreation Site #34, Flyfish Lakes Recreation Site #36, Ruth Lake Recreation Site #37, Brunette Lake Recreation Site #38, and Flyfish Lakes Recreation Site #39.** To reach them, you need a 4WD vehicle and a Vernon FS District recreation map. Call to ask if and where maps are available. The office is listed in the back of this book.

KELOWNA TO ROCK CREEK

Access these campgrounds from Hwy 33. Most are not far from pavement. After reading the brief descriptions below and choosing your destination, check where to turn off the highway. Then turn to the page indicated for route details. Read page 242 for directions heading north on Hwy 33, from Hwy 3 at Rock Creek.

Ideal Lake is about 23 km (14.3 mi) off Hwy 33. Ideal it definitely is not. The access is extremely rocky much of the way and has severe sections of washboard. The area's vicious clearcuts are a disturbing sight. The campground and setting are unappealing. Many of the campsites do not have lakeviews. Space is sufficient for big RVs, but the rough road will deter all but the smallest.

Hydraulic Lake is 5 km (3 mi) off Hwy 33. **Minnow Lake** is just beyond. Both campgrounds are handy for a brief overnight stop, but a longer stay can be enjoyable if you don't mind paying the per-night fee. Small RVs will find sufficient room. Locals refer to the entire reservoir system as McCulloch Lake—the name of a Kettle Valley Railway engineer. The KVR grazes Hydraulic Lake, so this is a good base for exploring (on foot or mountainbike) the abandoned railbed and marvelous trestle bridges. The campground at small **Browne Lake** is north of Hydraulic, on a rough access road unsuitable for big RVs.

Arlington Lakes are 3.4 km (2.1 mi) off Hwy 33. Campsites on both sides of the south lake are accessible by small motorhomes and trailers. The lake and setting are unremarkable. Other than convenience, the attraction here is the nearby KVR.

Beaverdell Creek FS road departs Hwy 33 at Beaverdell, about 81 km (50 mi) southeast of Kelowna. Follow it northeast to access FS campgrounds at several **more highland lakes**. Some will accommodate RVs. From there, you can descend into **Kettle River Valley**, passing excellent riverside campgrounds south on Kettle River Road. Rejoin Hwy 33 at Westbridge. The other Kettle River Valley access is from Hwy 3 at Rock Creek, between Osoyoos and Greenwood. Starting at Rock Creek, more than 30 km (18.6 mi) of Kettle River Road is paved. It's virtually level, has a wide shoulder, and traffic is minimal, making it ideal for road cycling.

Saunier Lake is 6 km (3.7 mi) from Hwy 33. The lake is small (just 3 hectares) and marshy, but it's pretty. The lonely atmosphere is soothing. With luck, you'll have the tiny campground all to yourself. It's not big enough for motorhomes or trailers.

If you're heading southeast on Hwy 33 from Kelowna

0 km (0 mi)
Starting east on Hwy 33, departing Hwy 97 in Kelowna.

21 km (13 mi)
Proceed east on Hwy 33 for more campgrounds. Turn left (northeast) onto paved Philpot Road and reset your tripometer to 0 for **Ideal Lake campground**; directions continue on page 244.

23.3 km (14.4 mi)
Cross a bridged creek at the community of Three Forks.

33.5 km (20.8 mi)
Pass the road to Big White ski area, on the left.

35.3 km (22 mi)
Reach the highway's 1265-m (4150-ft) summit.

40 km (24.8 mi)
Proceed south on Hwy 33 for more campgrounds. Turn right (west) near a large pullout and reset your tripometer to 0 for campgrounds at **Hydraulic, Minnow and Browne lakes**; directions continue on page 245.

56 km (34.7 mi)
Pass through a shallow canyon.

Saunier Lake

58 km (36 mi)
Proceed south on Hwy 33 for more campgrounds. Turn right (west) and reset your tripometer to 0 for **Arlington Lakes campground**; directions continue on page 246.

73.7 km (46 mi)
Proceed south through the community of Carmi.

80.6 km (50 mi)
Proceed south on Hwy 33 for more campgrounds. Turn left (northeast) onto Beaverdell Creek Road and reset your tripometer to 0 for **highland lakes campgrounds** on the backroad to Kettle River Valley; directions continue on page 247.

82 km (50.8 mi)
Pass the Beaverdell Hotel.

89 km (55.2 mi)
Proceed south on Hwy 33 for more campgrounds. Turn right (west) onto Tuzo Creek FS road and reset your tripometer to 0 for **Saunier Lake campground**; directions continue on page 250.

98.6 km (61.1 mi)
Proceed south on Hwy 33 for more campgrounds. Turn left (northeast) onto Taurus Lake FS road to reach **Taurus Lake campground** in 8.3 km (5.1 mi). This is the shortest access, but it's unsuitable for big rigs. The campground, and the RV-passable access from Kettle River Road, are described on page 251.

115.3 km (71.5 mi)
Reach the community of Westbridge. Proceed south on Hwy 33 to intersect Hwy 3. Turn sharply left (northeast) onto paved Kettle Valley Road and reset your tripometer to 0 for the **Kettle River campgrounds**; directions continue on page 251.

129 km (80 mi)
Intersect Hwy 3 at Rock Creek. Turn left (east) for Greenwood. Turn right (west) for Osoyoos.

If you're heading north on Hwy 33
from Hwy 3 at Rock Creek

0 km (0 mi)
Starting north on Hwy 33, departing Hwy 3 at Rock Creek.

13.7 km (8.5 mi)
Reach the community of Westbridge. Proceed north on Hwy 33 for numerous campgrounds. Turn right (northeast) onto paved Kettle Valley Road and reset your tripometer to 0 for the **Kettle River campgrounds**; directions continue on page 251.

30.4 km (18.8 mi)
Proceed north on Hwy 33 for more campgrounds. Turn right (northeast) onto Taurus Lake FS road to reach **Taurus Lake campground** in 8.3 km (5.1 mi). This is the shortest access, but it's unsuitable for big rigs. The campground, and the RV-passable access from Kettle River Road, are described on page 251.

40 km (24.8 mi)
Proceed north on Hwy 33 for more campgrounds. Turn left (west) onto Tuzo Creek FS road and reset your tripometer to 0 for **Saunier Lake campground**; directions continue on page 250.

47 km (29.1 mi)
Pass the Beaverdell Hotel.

48.4 km (30 mi)
Proceed north on Hwy 33 for more campgrounds. Turn right (northeast) onto Beaverdell Creek Road and reset your tripometer to 0 for **highland lakes campgrounds** on the backroad to Kettle River Valley; directions continue on page 247.

55.3 km (34.3 mi)
Proceed north through the community of Carmi.

71 km (44 mi)
Proceed north on Hwy 33 for more campgrounds. Turn left (west) and reset your tripometer to 0 for **Arlington Lakes campground**; directions continue on page 246.

89 km (55.2 mi)
Proceed north on Hwy 33 for Kelowna. Turn left (west) near a large pullout and reset your tripometer to 0 for **campgrounds at Hydraulic, Minnow and Browne lakes**; directions continue on page 245.

Free the Caveperson within You

Technology has not delivered on its promise to reduce toil. Everywhere, people are working harder than ever. In a recent poll, 88% of workers said their jobs require them to work longer. 68% said they have to work faster. And 80% said their lives are more stressful now than five years ago, largely due to pressure at work. The result is a society of stressed-out wage slaves failing to keep pace in a techno-world where efficiency is everything. The solution to this crisis is complex. But the major symptom—stress—is easy to understand. According to brain research, humans have a Stone Age psychology that's struggling to adapt to modern life. So, whenever possible, turn your back on modern life. Go wild. Go camping. Embrace the simple life of your aboriginal ancestors. Become a hunter-gatherer. Gather a few essentials, then go hunt for a comfortable campsite. Cull your concerns down to food, water, warmth and shelter. You'll find the simple, outdoor life can relieve stress better than anything on pharmacy or video-store shelves.

93.7 km (58.1 mi)
Reach the highway's 1265-m (4150-ft) summit.

95.5 km (59.2 mi)
Pass the road to Big White ski area, on the right.

105.7 km (65.5 mi)
Cross a bridged creek at the community of Three Forks.

108 km (67 mi)
Proceed west on Hwy 33 for Kelowna. Turn right (northeast) onto paved Philpot Road and reset your tripometer to 0 for **Ideal Lake campground**; directions continue below.

129 km (80 mi)
Intersect Hwy 97 in Kelowna.

For IDEAL LAKE, now follow the directions below

0 km (0 mi)
Starting northeast on initially paved Philpot Road, departing Hwy 33. Pass several country homes.

2.4 km (1.5 mi)
Pass Cardine Creek FS road on the left.

6.6 km (4.1 mi)
Proceed generally north on rough, rocky Philpot Main FS road.

7.7 km (4.8 mi)
Pass Darley Creek FS Road on the left.

16 km (10 mi)
Proceed north on Philpot Main FS road. Soon Pass Mugford FS road on the left.

19.6 km (12.2 mi)
Turn left to reach Ideal Lake in about 3.6 km (2.2 mi). The campground is beneath Belgo Dam.

IDEAL LAKE RECREATION SITE #44
Weekend / Difficult
Elev: 1300 m (4265 ft) / Lake: 1.8 km (1.1 mi) long, 132 ha
30 campsites, a few tables, boat launch
Accessible by small motorhomes and trailers

~

For HYDRAULIC, MINNOW and BROWNE LAKES, now follow the directions below

0 km (0 mi)
Starting west on McCulloch Road, departing Hwy 33.

0.8 km (0.5 mi)
Proceed straight at the junction. Follow the sign for McCulloch Lake Resort.

4.5 km (2.7 mi)
Turn left (south) and cross the KVR railbed for Hydraulic and Minnow lakes. Proceed straight (northwest) and reset your tripometer to 0 for Browne Lake.

0 km (0 mi)
Continuing northwest on McCulloch Road, passing the turnoff to Hydraulic and Minnow lakes.

3 km (1.9 mi)
Turn right (east) onto rough Browne Lake FS road. It heads northeast, then veers north along the west shore of Long Meadow Lake.

6.6 km (4.1 mi)
Reach Browne Lake campground.

BROWNE LAKE RECREATION SITE #2
Weekend / Moderate
5 tables, cartop boat launch
Inaccessible by motorhomes and trailers

~

Turning left (south) at the 4.5-km (2.7-mi) junction, heading for Hydraulic and Minnow lakes.

5 km (3 mi)
Reach Hydraulic Lake campground.

HYDRAULIC LAKE RECREATION SITE #3
Weekend / Easy / Overnight Fee
Elev: 1257 m (4123 ft) / Lake: 2.5 km (1.6 mi) long, 286 ha
14 campsites, many with tables, cartop boat launch
Accessible by small motorhomes and trailers

Continuing south through Hydraulic Lake campground. Slow down. The road deteriorates.

6 km (3.7 mi)
Reach Minnow Lake campground. It's on the channel between Minnow and Hydraulic lakes.

MINNOW LAKE RECREATION SITE #4
Weekend / Easy / Overnight Fee
12 campsites, many with tables
Accessible by small motorhomes and trailers

For ARLINGTON LAKES, now follow the directions below

0 km (0 mi)
Starting west, departing Hwy 33.

2.9 km (1.8 mi)
Fork right or left to quickly reach Arlington Lakes campground. Campsites are on both sides of the south lake.

ARLINGTON LAKES RECREATION SITE #13
Weekend / Easy
Elev: 1052 m (3450 ft) / South lake: 7 ha
12 tables, cartop boat launch
Accessible by small motorhomes and trailers

Kettle River Valley

For MORE HIGHLAND LAKES,
now follow the directions below

0 km (0 mi)
Starting northeast on Beaverdell Creek Road, departing Hwy 33 just north of the Beaverdell Hotel.

5.6 km (3.5 mi)
Bear right where Wallace Lake FS road forks left. Proceed generally east on the main Beaverdell-State FS road. Ignore Sago Creek FS road on the left.

10.6 km (6.6 mi)
Stay right on the main road.

11.2 km (6.9 mi)
Stay left on the main road where Crouse FS road forks right.

13.8 km (8.6 mi), 14.5 km (9 mi), and **17.7 km (11 mi)**
Proceed straight (north-northeast) on the main road.

18 km (11.2 mi)
Reach Sago Creek campground.

This is a handy place for a brief overnight stay, but it's beside the road, with no buffer from passing vehicles. A trail leads east 1 km to a walk-in campsite at Lower Collier Lake, then continues 500 meters southeast to another walk-in campsite at Upper Collier Lake.

SAGO CREEK RECREATION SITE #12
Overnight / Moderate
3 tables
Accessible by motorhomes and 5th-wheels

Continuing north-northeast on the main road, passing Sago Creek campground.

20.2 km (12.5 mi)
Bear right on the main road. Proceed through clearcuts.

23.8 km (14.8 mi)
Proceed straight, ignoring a right fork.

24.4 km (15.1 mi)
Reach a stop sign at a 3-way junction. Proceed straight (east) on State Creek FS road to descend into Kettle River Valley; directions continue on page 249. Turn left (north) onto Lassie Lake FS road and reset your tripometer to 0 for campgrounds at Cup and Lassie lakes.

0 km (0 mi)
Starting north and ascending on Lassie Lake FS road.

3.4 km (2.1 mi)
Proceed north on Lassie Lake FS road, passing a right fork signed for State Creek.

5.1 km (3.2 mi)
Pass a long pullout on the right, beside Cup Lake.

5.3 km (3.3 mi)
Bear right to quickly reach tiny Cup Lake campground on the right. The entry road rejoins the main road in 100 meters. This is a pretty lake, with an island.

CUP LAKE RECREATION SITE #18
Weekend / Difficult (due only to distance)
Elev: 1295 m (4248 ft) / Lake: 9 ha
2 well-spaced tables, rough boat launch, small dock
Accessible by small motorhomes and trailers

Continuing north on Lassie Lake FS road, passing Cup Lake campground.

8.4 km (5.2 mi)
Reach a junction and a map-sign indicating campsites and trails in the area. Turn right and descend to reach Lassie Lake campground in 100 meters. The entry road gets very muddy when wet. Pass a lone table, then proceed left for more campsites on the west shore.

LASSIE LAKE RECREATION SITE #17
Weekend / Difficult (due only to distance)
Elev: 1295 m (4248 ft) / Lake: 36 ha
7 tables, rough boat launch, 2 docks
Accessible by small motorhomes and trailers

Continuing east on State Creek FS road, from the 24.4-km (15.1-mi) junction, passing Lassie Lake FS road on the left.

25.6 km (15.9 mi)
Proceed straight at the triangular junction. Pass Lower State FS road on the left.

31 km (19.2 mi)
Curve left.

31.5 km (19.5 mi)
Intersect Kettle River Road, across from a barn in Kettle River Valley. Reset your tripometer to 0. Turn left (north), following directions on page 254 from the 44.6-km (27.7-mi) point, for campgrounds in the upper Kettle River Valley. Turn right (south), following directions on page 250, to reach campgrounds in the lower Kettle River Valley before intersecting Hwy 33 at Westbridge in 44.6 km (27.7 mi).

For SAUNIER LAKE, now follow the directions below

0 km (0 mi)
Starting west on Tuzo Creek FS road. Proceed northwest through a narrow valley. The forest is a pleasing mix of cottonwoods, aspen and larch. Beware of rocks on the road that fall from the steep hillside on the right.

6.1 km (3.8 mi)
Reach Saunier Lake campground on the left, just before the bridged outlet stream. A short trail leads south to a tiny, potable spring.

SAUNIER LAKE RECREATION SITE #10
Weekend / Easy
2 tables
Too small for motorhomes and trailers

For KETTLE RIVER VALLEY, now follow the directions below

If you're heading south on Kettle River Road from State Creek

0 km (0 mi)
Starting south on Kettle River Road, from the junction with State Creek FS road on page 249.

3.7 km (2.3 mi)
Proceed south on Kettle River Road for more campgrounds and to reach Hwy 33. Turn left for **Kettle Canyon campground**, described on page 254.

5.2 km (3.2 mi)
Proceed south on Kettle River Road for more campgrounds and to reach Hwy 33. Turn left for **Kettle Bench campground**, described on page 254.

6.5 km (4 mi)
Proceed south on Kettle River Road.

12.8 km (7.9 mi)
Pavement begins. Proceed south on Kettle River Road, passing Fourth of July Creek FS road on the right.

13 km (8.1 mi)
Proceed south on Kettle River Road for more campgrounds and to reach Hwy 33. Turn left for **Canyon Creek campground**, described on page 253.

14 km (8.7 mi)
Proceed south on Kettle River Road for more campgrounds and to reach Hwy 33. Turn left for **Canyon Flats campground**, described on page 252.

17.4 km (10.8 mi)
Proceed south on Kettle River Road for one more campground and to reach Hwy 33. Turn left for **Thone Lake campground**, described on page 252.

30.6 km (19 mi)
Proceed south on Kettle River Road to reach Hwy 33. Turn right for **Taurus Lake campground**, described on page 252.

44.6 km (27.7 mi)
Intersect Hwy 33 and reach the community of Westbridge, at the bridge over West Kettle River. Right (northwest) leads to Kelowna. Proceed south for Hwy 3.

51.7 km (32.1 mi)
Pass Kettle River Provincial Park on the left.

58.2 km (36.1 mi)
Intersect Hwy 3. Turn right (west) for Osoyoos. Turn left (east) for Greenwood.

~

If you're heading north on Kettle River Road from Westbridge

0 km (0 mi)
Starting north on Kettle River Road, departing Hwy 33 at the community of Westbridge.

14 km (8.7 mi)
Proceed north on Kettle River Road for more campgrounds. Turn left onto Ouellette Creek FS road and follow it generally

northwest to reach Taurus Lake campground in about 10 km (6.2 mi). Campsites are on the east and west shores of the tiny lake.

TAURUS LAKE RECREATION SITE #6
Weekend / Moderate
9 tables, cartop boat launch
Accessible by small motorhomes and trailers

~

Continuing north on Kettle River Road, passing the turnoff to Taurus Lake.

27.2 km (16.9 mi)
Proceed north on Kettle River Road for more campgrounds. Turn right onto Thone Lake - Lost Horse Creek FS road, cross a bridge over the Kettle River, and immediately turn left (northeast) to reach Thone Lake campground in about 14 km (8.7 mi). Campsites are on the south and northwest shores of the tiny lake.

THONE LAKE RECREATION SITE #30
Weekend / Moderate
7 tables, cartop boat launch
Accessible by motorhomes and 5th-wheels

~

Continuing north on Kettle River Road, passing the turnoff to Thone Lake.

30.6 km (19 mi)
Proceed north on Kettle River Road for more campgrounds. Turn right to reach Canyon Flats campground in 200 meters.

Two campsites are on the riverbank. Others are wide, flat, grassy, surrounded by forest. There's a swimming hole here, and a sandy beach just downstream.

CANYON FLATS RECREATION SITE #28
Weekend / Easy
7 campsites, 2 tables
Accessible by motorhomes and 5th-wheels

~

Continuing north on Kettle River Road, passing the turnoff to Canyon Flats campground.

31.6 km (19.6 mi)
Proceed north on Kettle River Road for more campgrounds. Turn right (just before Fourth of July Creek FS road forks left) to quickly reach Canyon Creek campground.

> This stretch of river is slow and quiet, so you won't be lulled to sleep by water music. But there's a big swimming hole here and a sandy beach.

CANYON CREEK RECREATION SITE #29
Weekend / Easy
2 tables
Accessible by small motorhomes and trailers

Continuing north on Kettle River Road, passing the turnoff to Canyon Creek campground.

31.8 km (19.7 mi)
Pavement ends.

Swimming hole at Kettle Canyon campground

38.1 km (23.6 mi)
Proceed north on Kettle River Road.

39.4 km (24.4 mi)
Proceed north on Kettle River Road for more campgrounds. Turn right to quickly reach Kettle Bench campground.

> This is a spacious, grassy, riverside clearing. There's a swimming hole here, and a sandy beach just downstream.

KETTLE BENCH RECREATION SITE #31
Weekend / Easy
2 tables
Accessible by small motorhomes and trailers

Continuing north on Kettle River Road, passing the turnoff to Kettle Bench.

41 km (25.4 mi)
Proceed north on Kettle River Road for more campgrounds. Turn right to quickly reach Kettle Canyon campground.

> This steep-sided canyon harbours huge swimming holes, a small waterfall, and large, flat rocks for lounging. The riverside campsites are treed.

KETTLE CANYON RECREATION SITE #32
Weekend / Easy
3 tables
Accessible by small motorhomes and trailers

Continuing north on Kettle River Road, passing the turnoff to Kettle Canyon campground.

44.6 km (27.7 mi)
Reach a junction across from a barn. Proceed north on Kettle River Road for campgrounds in the upper Kettle River Valley. Turn left (west) onto State Creek FS road and reset your tripometer to 0 for highland lakes campgrounds on the backroad access to Hwy 33 at Beaverdell; directions continue on page 256.

46.8 km (29 mi)
Proceed north on Kettle River Road for more campgrounds. Reach State Creek campground on the right.

STATE CREEK RECREATION SITE #33
Overnight / Easy
4 campsites, 2 tables
Accessible by motorhomes and 5th-wheels

~

Continuing north on Kettle River Road, passing State Creek campground. Proceed through Christian Valley. Pass FS roads forking right and left.

66 km (41 mi)
Pass Copperkettle Lake trailhead on the left. The 3-km (1.9-mi) trail ascends to a campsite on the tiny lake.

68 km (42.2 mi)
Proceed north on Kettle River Road for more campgrounds. Reach Damfino Creek campground on the right. One campsite is on each side of the creek, near its confluence with Kettle River.

DAMFINO CREEK RECREATION SITE #35
Weekend / Moderate
3 tables
Accessible by motorhomes and 5th-wheels

~

Continuing north on Kettle River Road, passing Damfino Creek campground.

68.2 km (42.3 mi)
Proceed north on Kettle River Road for more campgrounds. Turn left onto Nevertouch FS road and follow it generally northwest then northeast to reach Nevertouch Lake campground in about 14 km (8.7 mi). Campsites are on the north shore.

NEVERTOUCH LAKE RECREATION SITE #36
Weekend / Difficult (due only to distance)
10 tables, cartop boat launch
Accessible by motorhomes and 5th-wheels

~

Continuing north on Kettle River Road, passing the turnoff to Nevertouch Lake campground.

79.5 km (49.3 mi)
Proceed north on Kettle River Road for one more campground. Reach Sandy Bend campground on the right.

SANDY BEND RECREATION SITE #37
Weekend / Difficult (due only to distance)
2 tables, swimming hole, sandy beach
Accessible by small motorhomes and trailers

~

Continuing northeast on Kettle River Road, passing Sandy Bend campground.

80 km (49.6 mi)
Reach Kettle River crossing campground on the right. Campsites are on both sides of the bridge.

KETTLE RIVER CROSSING RECREATION SITE #38
Weekend / Difficult (due only to distance)
1 table, grassy area
Accessible by small motorhomes and trailers

~

If you're heading west on the backroad to Hwy 33 from Kettle River Valley

0 km (0 mi)
Starting west on State Creek FS road, departing Kettle River Road at 44.6 km (27.7 mi), across from a barn. Begin ascending.

0.5 km (0.3 mi)
Curve right.

5.9 km (3.7 mi)
Stay left.

7.1 km (4.4 mi)
Reach a 3-way junction. Proceed straight (west) on the main Beaverdell-State FS road for Hwy 33 at Beaverdell. Turn right

(north) onto Lassie Lake FS road and reset your tripometer to 0 for **campgrounds at Cup and Lassie lakes**; directions continue on page 248.

7.7 km (4.8 mi)
Proceed west on the main road.

11.3 km (7 mi)
Bear left (south) on the main road.

13.5 km (8.4 mi)
Reach **Sago Creek campground**, beside the road. Read page 248 for details.

13.8 km (8.6 mi), 17 km (10.5 mi), and **17.7 km (11 mi)**
Proceed straight (south-southwest) on the main road.

20.3 km (12.6 mi)
Stay right on the main road.

20.9 km (13 mi)
Stay left on the main road.

26 km (16.1 mi)
Curve left (south) on the main road where Wallace Lake FS road forks right.

31.5 km (19.6 mi)
Intersect Hwy 33, just north of the Beaverdell Hotel. Turn right (north) for Kelowna. Turn left (south) for Kettle Valley Road at Westbridge, or Hwy 3 at Rock Creek.

ENDERBY TO MABEL LAKE

Enderby is on Hwy 97A, about midway between Okanagan Lake and Shuswap Lake. Travelling east to Mabel Lake, your choice of FS campgrounds ranges from puny to colossal. You can take your pick of settings, too: pond, river or lake. The area even offers you a selection of lake sizes: medium or XXL.

Hidden Lake is about a 20-minute drive from Enderby. It's surrounded by low hills and a forest peppered with cedars. Though not memorably scenic, it's very accommodating, with about 40 campsites in three separate camping areas, good boat launches, and room for big rigs. A few minutes east of Hidden Lake is much smaller **Baird Lake**. It has two, tiny, separate camping areas. Check it out if you can't find peace at Hidden Lake.

Cooke Creek is about a 15-minute drive from Enderby, on pavement the whole way. The campground is a lovely, tranquil, shady haven where the creek flows into Shuswap River. Big rigs will find adequate space. The slow-moving river allows easy canoeing. Come here in fall to watch surging salmon.

Dale Lake is about a 20-minute drive from Enderby. It's north of Cooke Creek campground, in a group of dinky, shallow, marshy lakes. Ponds, really. The others are Elbow, Grassy and Spruce lakes. All have small campgrounds with insufficient room for motorhomes or trailers. Dale has the best access and is the one you'll reach first. The road deteriorates beyond.

Noisy Creek helps keep massive Mabel Lake's fluid level topped up. It gurgles into the lake at the far northwest shore. The sprawling campground here is provincial-park quality. The view is world class. And in mid-summer, it seems the whole world has heard about this place. Expect a crowd. Also be prepared for a per-night camping fee to help defray the cost of increased maintenance. But it's worth it—if you have an annual Camping Pass, which entitles you to a 50% discount. A short loop trail, the creek, broad beaches and pretty forest give you more to appreciate than at most FS campgrounds. The water's warm enough for a plunge in summer. The peninsula between the two camping areas offers a grand perspective on the lake. A minor drawback: beachcombing bovines; better keep your sandals on. The major drawback: overpopularity; try to come before the long May weekend, or after mid-September. Noisy is about an hour's drive from Enderby. The final approach is a steep descent. Exiting, the stiff ascent could bully a weakling motorhome or trailer-tugger into backing down.

0 km (0 mi)
Starting east on Cliff Avenue, departing Hwy 97 in Enderby. Follow the sign for North Mabel Lake (37 km).

Shuswap River, from Cooke Creek campground

0.3 km (0.2 mi)
Cross a bridge over Shuswap River.

0.6 km (0.4 mi)
Proceed straight.

8.1 km (5.1 mi)
Cross a bridge over Brash Creek.

9.4 km (5.8 mi)
Pass Ashton General Store and curve right.

9.6 km (5.9 mi)
Reach a junction. Bear left (east) for Cooke Creek, Dale Lake, and Noisy Creek (Mabel Lake); directions continue on page 261. Turn right (south) and reset your tripometer to 0 for Hidden Lake.

> **0 km (0 mi)**
> Starting south, heading for Hidden Lake.

> **1.2 km (0.7 mi)**
> Cross a bridge over Shuswap River and bear left.

5.8 km (3.6 mi)
Reach a junction. Turn left. Pavement ends. Proceed east.

13.4 km (8.3 mi), 15 km (9.3 mi), and **15.9 km (9.9 mi)**
Stay straight.

16.7 km (10.4 mi)
Bear right. Pass a KM 11 sign.

17.6 km (10.9 mi)
Bear left.

18.4 km (11.4 mi)
Hidden Lake is visible.

18.8 km (11.7 mi)
Arrive at Hidden Lake. Camping areas are on the south-west, southeast, and north shores.

HIDDEN LAKE RECREATION SITE #74
Weekend / Moderate
Elev: 655 m (2150 ft) / Lake: 2.2 km (1.4 mi) long, 131 ha
40 campsites, many with tables, boat launch
Accessible by motorhomes and 5th-wheels

Fork right (east), departing Hidden Lake's east shore road, to quickly reach tiny Baird Lake. The north and south shores each have one campsite.

BAIRD LAKE RECREATION SITE #75
Weekend / Moderate
Lake: 9 ha
2 tables, cartop boat launch
Inaccessible by motorhomes and trailers

Continuing east at the 9.6-km (5.9-mi) junction, heading for Cooke Creek, Dale Lake, and Noisy Creek (Mabel Lake).

23 km (14.3 mi)
Cross a bridge over Fall Creek.

26.1 km (16.2 mi)
Proceed east on pavement for Noisy Creek (Mabel Lake). Turn left (north) onto Cooke Creek FS road to reach small **Dale Lake Recreation Site #95** in 4 km (2.5 mi)—it's just beyond the creek crossing, on the right fork. Turn right (south) to reach Cooke Creek campground on Shuswap River, 200 meters off pavement.

COOKE CREEK RECREATION SITE #92
Weekend / Easy
11 tables, boat launch
Accessible by motorhomes and 5th-wheels

Continuing east on pavement, passing the turnoffs to Dale Lake and Cooke Creek campgrounds.

30.6 km (19 mi)
Turn left onto Three Valley - Mabel FS road and reset your tripometer to 0 for Noisy Creek campground on Mabel Lake's northwest shore. East on pavement is the short, direct route to Mabel Lake's west shore.

0 km (0 mi)
Turning left onto Three Valley - Mabel FS road.

11.9 km (7.4 mi)
Proceed straight and cross a small bridge.

13.7 km (8.5 mi)
Fork right. Beware of cattle.

20 km (12.4 mi)
Cross another small bridge.

21 km (13 mi)
Fork right. Begin the long, steep, final descent.

Noisy Creek campground on Mabel Lake

26.1 km (16.2 mi)
Arrive at Noisy Creek campground on Mabel Lake. Fork right or left for campsites.

NOISY CREEK RECREATION SITE #15
Destination / Difficult (due only to distance)
Elev: 393 m (1290 ft)
Lake: 35 km (21.7 mi) long, 2.2 km (1.4 mi) wide, 5942 ha
55 tables, 5 tent sites, cement boat launch
sandy beach, hiking trail
Accessible by motorhomes and 5th-wheels

VERNON TO LOWER ARROW LAKE

From Vernon, Hwy 6 plies pastoral valleys cradled by forested slopes, then gradually climbs through the Monashee Mountains before plummeting to Lower Arrow Lake. Standing between the Okanagan and Kootenay regions, the rounded Monashee peaks are indistinct. But the range is so lonesome, it feels wilder than some that are more photogenic. On a sunny, summer day, driving the highway as it spasms through the mountains southeast of Cherryville can be exhilarating.

If your direction of travel is flexible, drive Hwy 6 east. The scenery builds in that direction, climaxing with a view of Lower Arrow Lake—762 m (2500 ft) below. The Selkirk Mountains leap from the far shore and swagger off to the eastern horizon.

Two FS campgrounds on the east shore of **Mabel Lake** are your invitation to turn north off Hwy 6 at Lumby. Much of the way is paved. The lake is a whopper: 34.5 km (21.4 mi) long, 2.2 km (1.4 mi) wide, covering 5942 hectares. The elevation is 393 m (1290 ft). The setting is dramatic. Several walk-in campsites on the southeast shore allow you to pitch your tent in relative seclusion, and perhaps be monarch of your own beach for a day. Much farther north is Cottonwood Bay campground, accessible by big rigs if you can endure the paint-shaker effect for that distance.

Sugar Lake—12 km (7.5 mi) long, 4 km (2.5 mi) wide, covering 2130 hectares—is smaller than Mabel. But it's still big, and comparably beautiful. The elevation is slightly higher: 595 m

(1952 ft). On the west shore are three tiny FS campgrounds, plus a huge one where even a converted school-bus can lumber in and out. On the east shore is a medium-size campground suitable for small motorhomes and trailers. Some campsites are treed, others are in the open. A few choice parcels of real estate have lake and mountain views. The pebble beaches allow your body to comfortably absorb all the harmful rays your brain will permit. When you're toasted on both sides, chill down in the lake.

Several campgrounds are located along the Kettle River, southwest of where Hwy 6 crosses Monashee Summit. The first two—**Bruer Creek and Kettle River**—are close together, about a 15-minute drive off pavement. Bruer Creek has a swimming hole. Kettle has a large grassy area. The well-maintained backroad continues south into Kettle River Valley, described on page 265.

If Hwy 6 is simply part of your route between A and B, and a night's sleep is all you ask, a detour isn't necessary. Try Cherryville campground on Shuswap River, the spacious overnight pullout near Monashee Summit, or Monashee Kettle River campground. Considering how convenient they are, all three are surprisingly agreeable.

Remember that camping in the vicinity of Hwy 6, especially farther east toward Lower Arrow Lake, you'll be sharing the forest with bears. Black bears are prevalent. And the Monashee Mountains are grizzly bear habitat. Read *B.C. Stands for Bear Country* on page 27.

If you're heading southeast on Hwy 6 from Vernon

0 km (0 mi)
Starting east on Hwy 6, departing Hwy 97 at the east edge of Vernon, just before Polson Place Mall.

24.5 km (15.2 mi)
Reach Lumby. Proceed east on Hwy 6 for Sugar Lake and Lower Arrow Lake. Turn left (north) for **Mabel Lake's east shore campgrounds**; directions continue on page 267.

49 km (30.4 mi)
Pass a sign stating the Monashee turnoff is 2 km ahead.

51 km (31.6 mi)

Reach Cherryville. Proceed southeast on Hwy 6 for Lower Arrow Lake. Turn left (northeast) onto Sugar Lake Road for **campgrounds on Shuswap River and Sugar Lake**; directions continue on page 269.

83 km (51 mi)

Proceed southeast on Hwy 6 for Lower Arrow Lake. Turn right (south) onto Kettle River FS road and follow it southwest to reach **Bruer Creek Recreation Site #19a** (just before a bridge) in about 13 km (8.1 mi). Just beyond (across the bridge, then left) is **Kettle River Recreation Site #19b**. Together they have about 6 campsites. The main road continues south 98 km (60 mi) through Kettle River Valley (page 250) to Hwy 33, passing more campgrounds en route.

87 km (54 mi)

Proceed southeast on Hwy 6 for Lower Arrow Lake. Pass an **overnight pullout** on the right, just before the Kettle River bridge.

> You can drive well off pavement here. There's room for big RVs, and for others to spread out. It's quiet at night because traffic is minimal. The Kettle River (just a stream here in its upper reaches) and the open forest make this a pleasant area even during the day. There are no trash cans or toilets here. Please leave no trace of your stay, or access will be blocked. Use the toilets at nearby Lost Lake Rest Area.

89 km (55.2 mi)

Cross 1241-m (4070-ft) Monashee Summit. Lost Lake Rest Area is on the right. Proceed southeast on Hwy 6 for Lower Arrow Lake. Turn left (north) onto Keefer Lake Road for **campgrounds on Kettle River and Holmes Lake**; directions continue on page 272.

130.1 km (80.7 mi)

Proceed southeast on Hwy 6 to quickly reach Lower Arrow Lake. Turn left (north) onto Whatshan Lake FS road (following directions on page 302 in the Arrow and Kootenay Lakes chapter) to reach **Whatshan Lake campgrounds** on the north end in about 26 km (16 mi).

Lower Arrow Lake ferry links Needles and Fauquier.

134.5 km (83.4 mi)
Reach Needles, on the west shore of Lower Arrow Lake. A free ferry crosses the lake to Fauquier, where Hwy 6 continues north along the east shore to Nakusp.

If you're heading northwest on Hwy 6 from Arrow Lake

0 km (0 mi)
Resuming on Hwy 6 from Needles, after disembarking the Lower Arrow Lake ferry on the west shore.

4.4 km (2.7 mi)
Proceed west on Hwy 6 for Sugar Lake, Mabel Lake, and Vernon. Turn right (north) onto Whatshan Lake FS road (following directions on page 302 in the Arrow and Kootenay Lakes chapter) to reach **Whatshan Lake campgrounds** on the north end in about 26 km (16 mi).

45.5 km (28.2 mi)
Cross 1241-m (4070-ft) Monashee Summit. Lost Lake Rest Area is on the left. Proceed west on Hwy 6 for Sugar Lake, Mabel Lake, and Vernon. Turn right (north) onto Keefer Lake Road for **campgrounds on Kettle River and Holmes Lake**; directions continue on page 272.

47.5 km (29.5 mi)
Proceed west on Hwy 6 for Sugar Lake, Mabel Lake, and Vernon. Pass an **overnight pullout** on the left, just after the Kettle River bridge; read page 265 for details.

51.5 km (31.9 mi)
Proceed northwest on Hwy 6 for Sugar Lake, Mabel Lake, and Vernon. Turn left (south) onto Kettle River FS road for **Bruer Creek and Kettle River campgrounds**; directions continue on page 265

83.5 km (51.8 mi)
Reach Cherryville. Proceed west on Hwy 6 for Mabel Lake and Vernon. Turn right (northeast) onto Sugar Lake Road for **campgrounds on Shuswap River and Sugar Lake**; directions continue on page 269.

110 km (68.2 mi)
Reach Lumby. Proceed west on Hwy 6 for Vernon. Turn right (north) for **Mabel Lake's east shore campgrounds**; directions continue below.

134.5 km (83.4 mi)
Intersect Hwy 97 at the east edge of Vernon, just after Polson Place Mall.

For MABEL LAKE'S EAST SHORE, now follow the directions below

0 km (0 mi)
Starting north, departing Hwy 6 in Lumby. Follow signs for Mabel Lake.

17 km (10.5 mi)
Proceed on the main road past Shuswap Falls.

28 km (17.4 mi)
Pavement ends. Proceed north on Mabel Lake FS road.

35 km (21.7 mi)
Mabel Lake is visible.

38 km (23.6 mi)
Pass Mabel Lake Provincial Park.

42.5 km (26.4 mi)
Reach trails on the left leading to Cascade South walk-in tent sites on Mabel Lake. They start near a sharp bend in the road. The first (south) site is a couple minutes from the road; others are a bit farther.

CASCADE SOUTH RECREATION SITE #3
Weekend / Moderate
3 walk-in tent sites, good beaches
Parking accessible by all vehicles

Continuing north on Mabel Lake FS road, passing Cascade South walk-in tent sites.

43.2 km (26.8 mi)
Reach a trail on the right leading to Cascade Falls. It's about a 10-minute ascent to the picnic table at the falls.

43.5 km (27 mi)
Reach a trail on the left leading to another Mabel Lake **walk-in tent site**.

55.3 km (34.3 mi)
Turn left and descend to quickly reach Cottonwood Bay campground on Mabel Lake. Mabel Lake FS road continues generally north, passing campgrounds at Wap Lake and Frog Falls (described on page 295) shortly before intersecting Trans-Canada Hwy 1 at Three Valley Gap in about 55 km (34 mi).

COTTONWOOD BAY RECREATION SITE #1
Destination / Difficult (due only to distance)
10 tables, many more campsites, sandy beach
cartop boat launch
Accessible by motorhomes and 5th-wheels

Sugar Lake

For SHUSWAP RIVER and SUGAR LAKE, now follow the directions below

0 km (0 mi)
Starting (northeast) on Sugar Lake Road, departing Hwy 6 at Cherryville.

2.6 km (1.6 mi)
Cross a bridge over Cherry Creek.

5.5 km (3.4 mi)
Proceed northeast for Sugar Lake. Turn left to reach Cherryville campground in 0.5 km (0.3 mi). It's a pretty, quiet, grassy clearing beside Shuswap River.

CHERRYVILLE RECREATION SITE #15
Overnight / Easy
2 tables, many more campsites
Accessible by small motorhomes and trailers

Continuing northeast on Sugar Lake Road, passing the turnoff to Cherryville campground.

13.2 km (8.2 mi)
Pavement ends.

16.3 km (10.1 mi)
Reach a junction near the south end of Sugar Lake. Proceed left for several campgrounds on the west shore. Turn right onto Kate Creek FS road and reset your tripometer to 0 for Sugar Creek campground on the lake's east shore.

0 km (0 mi)
Starting east on Kate Creek FS road. Soon cross the bridge over Outlet Creek, then bear left and head north. After paralleling Sugar Lake's southeast shore, the road veers east again.

12 km (7.4 mi)
Cross the bridge over Sitkum Creek, then bear left (west).

14 km (8.7 mi)
Fork left to quickly reach Sugar Creek campground. Fork right and ascend about 3 km (1.7 mi) to a trailhead just past Sugar Creek. From there you can hike about 7 km to either the summit of Sugar Mountain or a campsite at Kate Lake.

SUGAR CREEK RECREATION SITE #6
Destination / Moderate
10 campsites, a few tables, cartop boat launch, good beach
Accessible by small motorhomes and trailers

Continuing left at the 16.3-km (10.1-mi) junction, passing the turnoff to Sugar Creek campground.

16.8 km (10.4 mi)
Go left, following the sign for Monashee Provincial Park. Pass a commercial fishing camp on the right.

17.4 km (10.8 mi)
Go right at the junction.

18.2 km (11.3 mi)
Proceed north along the west shore for more campgrounds. Turn right to enter Sugar 1-Mile campground.

SUGAR 1-MILE RECREATION SITE #10
Weekend / Easy
1 table, cartop boat launch
Accessible by small motorhomes and trailers

~

20.1 km (12.5 mi)
Proceed north along the west shore for two small campgrounds.
Turn right to enter Sugar 2-Mile campground.

SUGAR 2-MILE RECREATION SITE #9
Destination / Easy
20 tables, many more campsites, tent sites, boat launch
Accessible by motorhomes and 5th-wheels

~

21.7 km (13.5 mi)
Proceed north along the west shore for another small campground. Turn right to enter Sugar 3-Mile campground.

SUGAR 3-MILE RECREATION SITE #8
Weekend / Easy
1 table, creeklet, cartop boat launch
Accessible by small motorhomes and trailers

~

22.5 km (14 mi)
Proceed north for Monashee Provincial Park trailhead. Turn
right to enter Sugar $3\frac{1}{2}$-Mile campground.

SUGAR $3\frac{1}{2}$-MILE RECREATION SITE #7
Weekend / Easy
1 table, creeklet, cartop boat launch
Accessible by small motorhomes and trailers

~

For KETTLE RIVER and HOLMES LAKE, now follow the directions below

0 km (0 mi)
Starting north on Keefer Lake Road, departing Hwy 6.

1 km (0.6 mi)
Reach Monashee Kettle River campground on the left, just after crossing a bridge to the river's northwest bank.

MONASHEE KETTLE RIVER RECREATION SITE #17
Overnight / Easy
1 table, 2 campsites, grassy area for tents
Accessible by motorhomes and 5th-wheels

Keefer Lake Road continues generally northeast, following the river about another 15 km (9.3 mi) to its source at Keefer Lake. Fork left at the lake's west end, then proceed east along the north shore. A few minutes beyond Keefer Lake is an FS campground on smaller Holmes Lake.

HOLMES LAKE RECREATION SITE #16
Weekend / Moderate
Lake: 34 ha
4 campsites, a couple tables
Inaccessible by motorhomes and trailers

Watch for swimming holes along backroads throughout B.C.

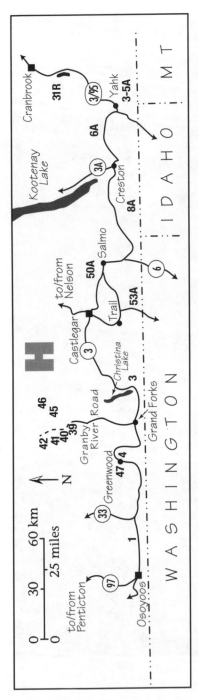

H: Boundary Country

Most of these campgrounds are in the Boundary FS District. **A** stands for Arrow and Kootenay Lake FS Districts. **R** stands for Cranbrook FS District.

1	Jolly Creek
3	Trout Creek
3 A	America Creek
4 A	Canuck Creek
4	Providence Lake
5 A	Hawkins Creek
6 A	Goat River Canyon
8 A	Boundary Lake
31 R	Monroe Lake
39	Granby-Burrell
40	Gable Creek
41	Eight-Mile Flats
42	Howe Creek
45	Bluejoint Creek
46	St. Annes Meadow
47	Greenwood
50 A	Erie Creek
53 A	Seven Mile Reservoir

Boundary Country

Boundary Lake

In its east-west journey along the Canada-U.S. boundary, Hwy 3 ricochets north and south like a cartoon bullet. Between Cranbrook in the east, Osoyoos in the west, it travels up and down passes, in and out of valleys, offering numerous access points for FS campgrounds.

Read the brief campground descriptions below. After choosing your destination, check where to turn off the highway. Then turn to the page indicated for route details.

Near Bridesville is a small, little-used campground on **Jolly Creek**. It's in a lush, lumpy meadow, wedged in a ravine, beneath rolling mountains. Trees are few. There's sufficient space for small motorhomes and trailers. Tenters will appreciate all the grass if they can find a level patch. You'll see wild rose here in spring; golden larches in fall.

Departing Hwy 3 at Rock Creek, Hwy 33 heads north, accessing **Kettle River Valley** at Westbridge. The Kettle River has excellent riverside campgrounds and enticing swimming holes.

Though the Kettle is in Boundary Country, we describe it with the rest of Hwy 33, in the Okanagan Highland and Monashee Mountains chapter (page 242).

The community of **Greenwood** generously offers free overnight camping to visitors. The campground has a cooking shelter, tables, and plenty of room for gargantuan RVs. It's in a creekside clearing near the north end of the business district. Please act respectfully. Say thanks to any locals you meet, so they know you appreciate this rare privilege. Greenwood is charming, well worth a stop even if you don't camp. It flourished during an 1890's mining boom. Many historic buildings have been restored. If you prefer lonelier camping, but want to stay near Greenwood, a ten-minute drive east into the hills will bring you to a mediocre FS campground at **Providence (Marshall) Lake**. The road is paved much of the way, but motorhomes and trailers will struggle on the steep ascent, only to be thwarted by the final, rough approach.

North of Grand Forks is the beautiful **Granby River valley**. The hilly terrain is a crazy quilt of meadows, forest, and rock outcroppings. Road cyclists should take advantage of the paved road probing the valley for more than 40 km (25 mi). Granby-Burrell and Bluejoint Creek campgrounds have enough space for small motorhomes and trailers. Up valley are more FS campgrounds. At road's end, hikers can venture north into Granby Provincial Park. A 4.5-km (2.8-mi) riverside trail through hemlock-and-cedar forest pierces the park boundary then forges 8 km (5 mi) deeper. Call BC Parks for details.

The **Christina Lake** area is highly developed, so free-camping options are severely limited. The only nearby FS campground is a small, grim one at **Trout Creek**. It's high above the lake. Though passable in a 2WD car, the long, steep access road is demanding. Don't coax your motorhome or tug your trailer up here; there's insufficient room. But if you prefer the company of pines to people, Trout Creek is tolerable for a night. It's huddled beside the creek, in a dark forest, at a hairpin turn.

Southeast of Trail, the Pend-d'Oreille River loops into B.C. for just 24 km (15 mi). Canadians seized the opportunity, damming the river before it joins the Columbia and escapes back into the U.S. The result is called **Seven Mile Reservoir**. In a meadow beside the dam is Buckley campground, managed by BC Hydro. Like all their campgrounds, this one is smartly organized, well maintained, roomy enough for big RVs, and free to the public.

The campground on sparkling clear **Erie Creek** is about a ten-minute drive west of Salmo. Though its in mixed forest, a clearcut hillside is visible. Two individual, treed campsites offer privacy from the main camping area. Space is inadequate for motorhomes and trailers. The creek bank has sandy beaches. The area's roadside berry bushes offer fruitful picking in season.

Boundary Lake is in a narrow mountain basin just inside Canada, southeast of Stagleap Park. The campground has several sites on the lakeshore and accommodates motorhomes and 5th-wheels. The forest has enough big trees to be admirable. Come here to fish, canoe or swim. It gets buggy, so bring your anti-insect arsenal.

Between Creston and Yahk is a campground in **Goat River Canyon**. It's spacious enough to lay out the welcome mat for your small motorhome or trailer. The forest is open, but there's little to look at. From the campsites, you can't even see the river, though it's audible. The deep pool by the bridge is a swimmer's delight. There's also a short trail along the riverbank.

The campgrounds along gentle **Hawkins Creek**, just outside Yahk, are handy for cross-province travellers. Access is quick and easy. Stop here overnight, or just to rest your road-weary brain. The campsites are suitable for only the smallest motorhomes and trailers.

Monroe Lake is a very convenient campground: south of Cranbrook, just off the highway, near the provincial park at the north end of Moyie Lake. Space is adequate for small motorhomes and trailers. The access road is even paved. But the lake is small, private cabins are nearby, and the area is busy, so don't expect a wilderness experience.

If you're heading east on Hwy 3, between Osoyoos and Cranbrook

For **Jolly Creek**, drive Hwy 3 east 2.7 km (1.7 mi) from the hamlet of Bridesville. Turn left (north) just before Rock Creek Canyon bridge and reset your tripometer to 0. Directions continue on page 280.

For **Greenwood,** drive Hwy 3 east 22 km (13.6 mi) from the village of Rock Creek at the junction of Hwys 3 and 33. For **Providence Lake**, turn right (east) onto Greenwood Road (in the business district) and reset your tripometer to 0. Directions continue on page 281.

For **Granby River valley**, drive Hwy 3 east of Greenwood to Grand Forks. Just after crossing the Granby River bridge, turn left (north) onto Granby Road and reset your tripometer to 0. Directions continue on page 281.

For **Trout Creek**, drive Hwy 3 east of Grand Forks to the town of Christina Lake, at the lake's south end. Turn right (southeast) onto Santa Rosa Road and reset your tripometer to 0. Directions continue on page 284.

For **Seven Mile Reservoir**, drive Hwy 3 northeast of Christina Lake to Castlegar, then Hwy 22 south to Trail, then Hwy 3B southeast to Waneta Junction, and finally Hwy 22A south. Just north of Waneta, turn left (southeast) onto Seven Mile Dam road. Directions continue on page 285.

For **Erie Creek**, drive Hwy 3 east of Castlegar. Proceed 7 km (4.3 mi) past the Hwy 3B junction. Just after crossing the small bridge over Erie Creek, turn left (north) onto Second Relief Road and reset your tripometer to 0. Directions continue on page 285.

For **Boundary Lake**, drive Hwy 3 east of Salmo. Proceed 16.2 km (10 mi) beyond Kootenay Pass summit in Stagleap Provincial Park. Turn sharp right (southwest) onto Maryland Creek FS road and reset your tripometer to 0. Directions continue on page 286.

For **Goat River Canyon**, drive Hwy 3 east 21 km (13 mi) from Hwy 3A at the north end of Creston. Turn left (north) onto Leadville Road at the Kitchener store and restaurant. Reset your tripometer to 0. Directions continue on page 287.

For **Hawkins Creek**, drive Hwy 3 northeast 1 km (0.6 mi) from Yahk Provincial Park. Immediately after crossing the bridge over Moyie River, turn right (southeast) onto Yahk Meadow Creek Road and reset your tripometer to 0. Directions continue on page 288.

For **Monroe Lake** drive Hwy 3 north 12.5 km (7.8 mi) from the community of Moyie. Turn left (southwest) onto Monroe Lake Road (signed for Moyie Lake Provincial Park) and reset your tripometer to 0. Directions continue on page 289.

If you're heading west on Hwy 3, between Cranbrook and Osoyoos

For **Monroe Lake** drive Hwy 3 southwest 17 km (10.5 mi) from the Travel Info Centre on the southwest edge of Cranbrook. Turn right (southwest) onto Monroe Lake Road (signed for Moyie Lake Provincial Park) and reset your tripometer to 0. Directions continue on page 289.

For **Hawkins Creek**, drive Hwy 3 southwest 32.5 km (20 mi) from the community of Moyie. Just before the bridge over Moyie River, turn left (southeast) onto Yahk Meadow Creek Road and reset your tripometer to 0. Directions continue on page 288.

For **Goat River Canyon**, drive Hwy 3 west 19.5 km (12.1 mi) from Hwy 95 just southwest of Yahk. Turn right (north) onto Leadville Road at the Kitchener store and restaurant. Reset your tripometer to 0. Directions continue on page 287.

For **Boundary Lake**, drive Hwy 3 west from Hwy 3A at the north end of Creston. At 4.2 km (2.6 mi) cross the Kootenay River bridge. At 22 km (13.6 mi) pass a rest area on the left. At 28.7 km (17.8 mi) turn left (southwest) onto Maryland Creek FS road and reset your tripometer to 0. Directions continue on page 286.

For **Erie Creek**, drive Hwy 3 west 3.6 km (2.2 mi) from Salmo. Just before the small bridge over Erie Creek, turn right (north) onto Second Relief Road and reset your tripometer to 0. Directions continue on page 285.

For **Seven Mile Reservoir**, drive Hwy 3 west of Salmo, then Hwy 3B southwest to Waneta Junction, and finally Hwy 22A

south. Just north of Waneta, turn left (southeast) onto Seven
Mile Dam road. Directions continue on page 285.

For **Trout Creek,** drive Hwy 3 west of Castlegar to the town of
Christina Lake, at the lake's south end. Turn left (southeast)
onto Santa Rosa Road and reset your tripometer to 0. Directions
continue on page 284.

For **Granby River valley,** drive Hwy 3 west of Christina Lake
to Grand Forks. Just before crossing the Granby River bridge,.
turn right (north) onto Granby Road and reset your tripometer
to 0. Directions continue on page 281.

For **Greenwood,** drive Hwy 3 west of Grand Forks. For Providence
Lake, turn left (east) onto Greenwood Road (in the business district)
and reset your tripometer to 0. Directions continue on page 281.

For **Jolly Creek,** drive Hwy 3 west 12.7 km (7.9 mi) from the
village of Rock Creek at the junction of Hwys 3 and 33. Turn
right (north) just after Rock Creek Canyon bridge and reset your
tripometer to 0. Directions continue on page 280.

For JOLLY CREEK, now follow the directions below

0 km (0 mi)
Starting north on the road signed for Mt. Baldy Ski Area, departing
Hwy 3 just west of Rock Creek Canyon bridge.

2.9 km (1.8 mi)
Turn right onto Canyon Road and descend to the canyon floor.

4 km (2.4 mi)
Turn right to enter Jolly Creek campground, across from an
historic cabin.

JOLLY CREEK RECREATION SITE #1
Weekend / Easy
3 tables
Accessible by small motorhomes and trailers

~

For PROVIDENCE LAKE, now follow the directions below

0 km (0 mi)
Starting east on Greenwood Street, departing Hwy 3 in Greenwood. Pass the historic post office and ascend.

6.8 km (4.2 mi)
Pavement ends.

7.7 km (4.8 mi) and **8.2 km (5.1 mi)**
Turn left.

8.4 km (5.2 mi)
Reach a clearing beside Providence Lake. Skirt the west shore on a rough, potentially very muddy road to reach the small campground across the lake.

8.6 km (5.3 mi)
Arrive at Providence Lake campground.

PROVIDENCE LAKE RECREATION SITE #4
Overnight / Easy
Elev: 1386 m (4546 ft) / Lake: 5.5 ha
2 tables, cooking shelter
Inaccessible by motorhomes and trailers

For GRANBY RIVER VALLEY, now follow the directions below

0 km (0 mi)
Starting north on Granby Road, departing Hwy 3 in Grand Forks, just east of the Granby River bridge.

16.2 km (10 mi)
Reach a junction. Turn right and proceed north, up valley, along Granby River's east bank.

44.3 km (27.5 mi)
Pavement ends. Turn left onto Granby River FS road and cross Burrell Creek bridge. Granby-Burrell campground is immediately on the left, at the river/creek confluence. Proceed northwest, along the river's east bank, to reach four more campgrounds en route to Granby Provincial Park. Just beyond Burrell

Confluence of Granby River and Burrell Creek

Creek bridge, turn right (north) onto Burrell Creek FS road and reset your tripometer to 0 for two more campgrounds.

A rocky bluff called Bunch Grass Hill is visible from the campground. There's a deep swimming hole beneath the bridge.

GRANBY - BURRELL RECREATION SITE #39
Weekend / Easy
2 tables, grassy tent sites
Accessible by small motorhomes and trailers

Turning right (north) onto Burrell Creek FS road, just beyond Granby-Burrell campground.

0 km (0 mi)
Starting north on Burrell Creek FS road, soon following the west bank of Burrell Creek.

7 km (4.3 mi)
Bear left onto Franklin Mine road, staying on the creek's west bank. Burrell Creek FS road goes right, crossing a bridge to the

east bank. It continues northeast, eventually reaching Edgewood, on Lower Arrow Lake. From there, a paved road leads north to Hwy 6 and the Needles - Fauquier ferry.

11 km (6.8 mi)
Reach Bluejoint Creek campground on the right.

BLUEJOINT CREEK RECREATION SITE #45
Overnight / Moderate
1 table, grassy area
Accessible by small motorhomes and trailers

14.5 km (9 mi)
Reach St. Annes Meadow campground on the right.

ST. ANNES MEADOW RECREATION SITE #46
Overnight / Moderate
2 tables
Inaccessible by motorhomes and trailers

Continuing northwest on Granby River FS road, passing Granby-Burrell campground and Burrell Creek FS road.

49.4 km (30.6 mi)
Proceed north on Granby River FS road for three more campgrounds and the provincial park. Fork left and descend to reach tiny Gable Creek campground in 1.5 km (0.9 mi). It's on the Granby River, near the confluence with Gable Creek. Even in summer, it's shaded here by mid afternoon.

GABLE CREEK RECREATION SITE #40
Weekend / Easy
1 table
Accessible by small motorhomes and trailers

Continuing north on Granby River FS road, passing the turnoff to Gable Creek campground.

59.3 km (36.8 mi)
Proceed north on Granby River FS road for one more camp-ground (4WD access only) and the provincial park. Fork left to reach two campgrounds on Granby River's west bank.

> Descend, cross a bridge over Granby River, and reach a T-junction. Turn left (south) to reach small **Eight Mile Flats Recreation Site #41** in about 3 km (1.9 mi). Turn right (north), then right at the next junction, to reach large **Howe Creek Recreation Site #42** in about 3 km (1.9 mi).

Continuing north on Granby River FS road, passing the turnoff to Eight Mile Flats and Howe Creek campgrounds.

61 km (37.8 mi)
Reach a junction. Bear right for the 2WD-accessible provincial park trailhead. Left is a rough 4WD road fording Howe Creek— only possible in summer, when the water's low. Beyond the ford, bear left and proceed north to reach small **Traverse Creek Recreation Site #44**, at the actual provincial-park trailhead, in about 4 km (2.5 mi).

61.5 km (38.1 mi)
Turn left, cross the Howe Creek bridge, and look for a signed trail on the left. Park here to begin hiking to the provincial park. In about 1 km (0.6 mi) the trail intersects a small road. Follow it left. Soon join the road that fords Howe Creek. Bear right and pro-ceed north to reach small **Traverse Creek Recreation Site #44**, at the actual provincial-park trailhead, in about 4 km (2.5 mi).

~

For TROUT CREEK, now follow the directions below

0 km (0 mi)
Starting southeast on Santa Rosa Road, departing Hwy 3 across from the Travel Info Centre in the town of Christina Lake.

1.5 km (0.9 mi)
Pavement ends. Begin ascending. Pass a viewpoint overlooking Christina Lake. Stay on the old Cascade Highway all the way to the campground.

10 km (6 mi)
Fork right.

14 km (8.7 mi)
Arrive at Trout Creek campground. The Dewdney hiking trail crosses the road here. This section links Christina Lake with Rossland.

TROUT CREEK RECREATION SITE #3
Overnight / Moderate
1 table, hiking trail
Inaccessible by motorhomes and trailers

~

For SEVEN MILE RESERVOIR,
now follow the directions below

0 km (0 mi)
Starting south on Hwy 22A, departing Hwy 3B at Waneta Junction.

6.3 km (3.9 mi)
Turn left (southeast) onto Seven Mile Dam Road.

19.3 km (12 mi)
Pass Seven Mile Dam.

20.8 km (12.9 mi)
Reach Buckley campground, on the right.

BUCKLEY CAMPGROUND #53
Weekend / Easy
8 campsites, 12 tables, beach, grassy area
rough boat launch, garbage cans
Accessible by motorhomes and 5th-wheels

~

For ERIE CREEK, now follow the directions below

0 km (0 mi)
Starting north on Second Relief Road, departing Hwy 3. Pavement ends in 200 meters.

0.8 km (0.5 mi)
Go left onto Erie Creek FS road.

7 km (4.3 mi)
Fork left.

8.5 km (5.3 mi)
Bear left and descend into the valley.

10 km (6.2 mi)
Turn left and cross Erie Creek. The campground is on the right, just after the bridge.

ERIE CREEK RECREATION SITE #50
Weekend / Easy
5 tables
Too small for motorhomes and trailers

For BOUNDARY LAKE, now follow the directions below

0 km (0 mi)
Starting southwest on Maryland Creek FS road, departing Hwy 3. It drops below the highway, across from Jordan's historic log cabin.

1.1 km (0.7 mi)
Cross a bridge over Summer Creek.

2.7 km (1.7 mi)
Go right at the junction and ascend steeply.

6.9 km (4.3 mi)
Go right at the junction.

9.1 km (5.6 mi)
Stay right on the main road. It levels out in a meadow. Proceed through an upper valley and descend gradually.

13.7 km (8.5 mi)
Fork left.

13.9 km (8.6 mi)
Stay straight on the main road.

16.7 km (10.4 mi)
Bear left on the main road.

17.7 km (11 mi)
Boundary Lake is visible below to the right.

18 km (11.2 mi)
Turn sharply right and descend.

18.2 km (11.3 mi)
Arrive at Boundary Lake campground. Go either way to reach campsites.

BOUNDARY LAKE RECREATION SITE #8
Weekend / Moderate
Elev: 1220 m (4000 ft) / Lake: 25 ha
11 tables, 3 wharves, small beach
Accessible by motorhomes and 5th-wheels

For GOAT RIVER CANYON, now follow the directions below

0 km (0 mi)
Starting north on Leadville Road, departing Hwy 3 at Kitchener.

0.5 km (0.3 mi)
Cross a bridge over Meadow Creek. Immediately after, stay straight on the main road.

3.9 km (2.4 mi)
Pass an **overnight pullout** on the riverbank.

7.4 km (4.6 mi)
Proceed straight on the main road. Anchor Creek FS road forks right.

8.1 km (5 mi)
Stay left. Leadville Creek FS road forks right.

Goat River

10.9 km (6.8 mi)
Cross a wooden bridge over a deep swimming hole on Goat River.

11 km (6.8 mi)
Turn left (south) just before another bridge. This final approach is narrow, but the road is good.

11.7 km (7.3 mi)
Arrive at Goat River Canyon campground.

GOAT RIVER CANYON RECREATION SITE #6
Weekend / Easy
7 tables
Accessible by small motorhomes and trailers

For HAWKINS CREEK, now follow the directions below

0 km (0 mi)
Starting southeast on Yahk Meadow Creek Road, departing Hwy 3 at Yahk. In 100 meters proceed straight where River Avenue forks right. Pavement ends 700 meters beyond.

3.8 km (2.4 mi)
Reach **Hawkins Creek Recreation Site #5**, on the right. It has 4 tables. For more campgrounds, proceed southeast on the main road, staying on the northeast side of Hawkins Creek.

7.2 km (4.5 mi)
Turn right through a clearing to reach **Canuck Creek Recreation Site #4** in 200 meters. It has 4 tables at well-spaced campsites beside the creek. A scenic waterfall is just downstream. For more campgrounds, proceed southeast on the main road.

9 km (5.6 mi)
Reach **America Creek Recreation Site #3**, on the right. It has 5 tables near the creek. For one more small campground, proceed east the main road.

20 km (12.4 mi)
Reach **Cold Creek Recreation Site #2**. It has 2 tables.

For MONROE LAKE, now follow the directions below

0 km (0 mi)
Starting southwest on paved Monroe Lake Road, departing Hwy 3. Bear right in 700 meters.

2.3 km (1.4 mi)
Reach a junction. Turn right, staying on pavement, to reach Monroe Lake campground in about 1 km (0.6 mi). Straight on unpaved Lamb Creek road reaches Mineral Lake day-use area in 1.5 km (0.9 mi).

MONROE LAKE RECREATION SITE #31
Overnight / Easy
Elev: 1067 m (3500 ft) / Lake: 51.5 ha
5 tables, gravel boat launch
Accessible by small motorhomes and trailers

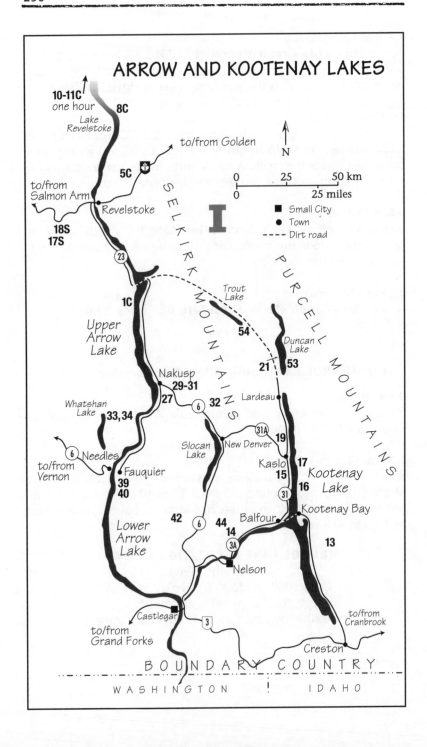

ARROW AND KOOTENAY LAKES

I: Arrow and Kootenay Lakes

Most of these campgrounds are on the Arrow and Kootenay Lake FS Districts recreation map. **C** stands for Columbia FS District. **S** stands for Salmon Arm FS District.

1 C	Eagle Bay
5 C	Tangier Creek
8 C	Carnes Creek
10 C	Pitt Creek
11 C	Potlatch Creek
13	Oliver Lake
14	Six - Mile Lakes
15	Fletcher Falls
16	Pebble Beach
17	Garland Bay
17 S	Wap Lake
18 S	Frog Falls
19	Milford Lake
21	Howser Glayco
27	Box Lake
29	Wilson Lake West
30	Wilson Lake East
31	Little Wilson Lake
32	Beaver Lake
33	Stevens Creek
34	Richy
39	Taite Creek
40	Octopus Creek
42	Little Slocan Lakes
44	Sasquatch Lake
53	Glacier Creek
54	Gerrard

Arrow and Kootenay Lakes

Kootenay Lake and the Purcell Mountains, from Kaslo

Like beads of sweat on straining, bulging muscles, water trickles down from the Kootenay mountain summits. Rivulets gather speed and volume, cascading into the region's inland fiords—great veins of water so deep, cold and clean that lakeshore residents pump it up to their homes and drink it unfiltered.

Upper and Lower Arrow lakes are actually a single reservoir dammed near Castlegar. It stretches 230 km (143 mi) to Revelstoke. Just north of town, the dams and reservoirs resume, with Lake Revelstoke and Kinbasket Lake created in the image of a taffy pull. Their combined length is 346 km (215 mi). Kootenay Lake is 110 km (68 mi) long, 2 to 6 km (1.2 to 3.7 mi) wide, with an additional 30-km (18.6-mi) tentacle reaching to Nelson. Small only by local comparison are 40-km (25-mi) Slocan Lake and 44-km (27.3-mi) Duncan Lake. FS campgrounds on the shores of these oceanic bodies and other lesser lakes are ideal retreats for pondering the big question: explore further, or just stay put?

On such vast liquid spaces, boating becomes travelling. But why restrict yourself to a horizontal plane? This isn't the prairie. You have another option. Up. In this part of B.C., if it's not submerged, it's vertical. Three distinct mountain ranges give the area, generally referred to as the Kootenays, a tightly pleated, accordion topography.

To the west are the gentle, rounded Monashees Mountains. The spikier Selkirks shoulder their way between the Arrow Lakes and Slocan Valley. These ranges fueled gold, silver and copper booms in the 1890s. New Denver, Silverton, Slocan, Sandon and Kaslo began as mining settlements. Farther east, the craggy Purcells separate the Kootenays from the Rocky Mountain Trench. The only way to fully appreciate this land is to ascend the peaks on foot. Read the hiking guide *Don't Waste Your Time in the West Kootenays*. It's described on page 395.

Kootenay towns are small. The land's skyward tilt limits population growth. Skinny lakeshores, slender valleys, and steep slopes grant livable real estate begrudgingly. Only trees flourish in great numbers here. Hospitable forests host mountainside parties, welcoming the usual gang: fir, pine, birch, spruce, larch. In a few isolated nooks, single-variety stands of cedar or hemlock spurn the festivities and refuse to socialize.

To sample the Kootenays from the road, drive or cycle the *Silver Triangle*. Start in Nelson. Follow Hwys 3A and 31 north up the west shore of Kootenay Lake to Kaslo. Turn east onto Hwy 31A and climb over the mountains to New Denver, where you can gaze across Slocan Lake to the Valhallas. Then head south on Hwy 6, through Slocan Valley, back to Hwy 3A and Nelson.

A more adventurous, north-Kootenay loop starts in Kaslo and passes several FS campgrounds. Drive Hwy 31 north, following the northwest shore of Kootenay Lake. Pavement ends near Duncan Lake, but the road proceeding northwest is well maintained. After paralleling the northeast shore of Trout Lake, regain pavement. Curve southwest to Galena Bay, on Upper Arrow Lake. Continue south on Hwy 23, along Upper Arrow's east shore, to Nakusp. From there, a mountainous traverse southeast via Hwy 6 leads to New Denver, on Slocan Lake. Finally, turn east onto Hwy 31A and climb yet more mountains back to Kaslo.

Touring the Kootenays, you'll appreciate the shortcuts that ferries provide across the formidable lakes. But in summer, the prelude to a carefree crossing is usually a frustrating delay in a long line of vehicles waiting to board. You might have to hang out—are you sitting down?—for up to two hours.

On Kootenay Lake, a ferry shuttles between Balfour on the west shore and Kootenay Bay on the east. Departures are every 50 minutes in summer. The Balfour schedule is 6 a.m. to 12:20 a.m. The Kootenay Bay schedule is 6:50 a.m. to 1 a.m. The 9-km (5.6-mi) crossing takes 40 minutes.

On Upper Arrow Lake, a ferry links Galena Bay on the east shore with Shelter Bay on the west. Departures are every hour. The Galena Bay schedule is 5:30 a.m. to 10:30 p.m., plus 12:30 a.m. The Shelter Bay schedule is 5 a.m. to midnight. The 5-km (3-mi) crossing takes 30 minutes.

NEAR REVELSTOKE

Three campgrounds close to Trans-Canada Hwy 1 are convenient for a brief overnight stop en route to or from the Kootenays or Rockies. Frog Falls and Wap Lake campgrounds are west of Revelstoke, south of Three Valley Gap. Tangier River campground is just east of Mt. Revelstoke National Park.

FROG FALLS and WAP LAKE

If you're heading west on Hwy 1 from Revelstoke

Set your tripometer to 0 midway across the Columbia River bridge, on the west side of Revelstoke. Proceed west on Hwy 1. At 19 km (11.8 mi) pass Three Valley Gap, at the east end of Three Valley Lake. At 21.3 km (13.3 mi) pass the rest area beside Three Valley Lake. At 21.9 km (13.6 mi) turn left (south) onto Three Valley-Mabel Lake FS road (across from a large, paved pullout) and reset your tripometer to 0.

If you're heading northeast on Hwy 1 from Sicamous

Set your tripometer to 0 at the junction of Hwys 1 and 97A, by the Shell and Petro Canada gas stations in Sicamous. Proceed northeast on Hwy 1. At 48.2 km (29.9 mi) cross a bridge at the northwest end of Three Valley Lake. Slow down. At 49.3 km (30.6 mi) turn right (south) onto Three Valley-Mabel Lake FS road (across from a large, paved pullout) and reset your tripometer to 0.

For either approach above, now follow the directions below

0 km (0 mi)
Starting south on Three Valley-Mabel Lake FS road, departing Hwy 1. Ignore spurs forking right and left.

2.7 km (1.7 mi)
Proceed south on the main road.

4.4 km (2.7 mi)
Proceed southwest on the main road for Wap Lake. Turn left, just before the bridge, to quickly reach Frog Falls campground.

FROG FALLS RECREATION SITE #18
Overnight / Easy
5 tables
Accessible by motorhomes and 5th-wheels

Continuing southwest on the main road, passing the turnoff to Frog Falls campground and crossing the bridged creek.

4.7 km (2.9 mi)
Proceed southwest on the main road.

11 km (6.8 mi)
Arrive at Wap Lake campground, beside the road, on the southwest shore. The main road continues south to Mabel Lake, eventually reaching Cottonwood Bay campground (page 268) on the east shore.

WAP LAKE RECREATION SITE #17
Overnight / Easy
Lake: 36 ha
2 tables
Accessible by motorhomes and 5th-wheels

TANGIER RIVER

If you're heading southwest on Hwy 1
from Glacier National Park

Set your tripometer to 0 at the summit of Rogers Pass in Glacier National Park, just west of the Visitors Centre. Proceed southwest on Hwy 1. At 34 km (21.1 mi), immediately before the long, cement bridge over Tangier River, turn right (north) off the highway. Reach Tangier River campground in 0.6 (0.4 mi).

If you're heading northeast on Hwy 1 from Revelstoke

Just east of and above Revelstoke, set your tripometer to 0 where Meadows in the Sky Parkway ascends left (north) into Revelstoke National Park. Proceed northeast on Hwy 1. At 34 km (21 mi) pass Canyon Hot Springs. At 34.7 km (21.5 mi), immediately after the long, cement bridge over Tangier River, turn left (north) off the highway. Reach Tangier River campground in 0.6 (0.4 mi).

Tangier River is a good base for exploring nearby Revelstoke National Park. The campground is in mature forest. It's pretty, but shaded and cool. The roaring river muffles highway and train noise.

TANGIER RIVER RECREATION SITE #6
Weekend / Easy
12 tables
Accessible by small motorhomes and trailers

LAKE REVELSTOKE & KINBASKET LAKE

Hwy 23 glides north from Revelstoke, following the east shore of Lake Revelstoke—a 130-km (80-mi) long reservoir at 570 m (1870 ft) elevation. At its north end is 242-m (795-ft) high Mica Dam, BC Hydro's third largest power producer and North America's biggest earth-filled dam. Behind it is yet another reservoir: 216-km (134-mi) long Kinbasket Lake. It covers 41,590 hectares at 755 m (2476 ft) elevation. Beyond are the glacier-mantled Rocky Mountains. Lake Revelstoke has two FS campgrounds reached via paved road. Kinbasket Lake has one campground just beyond where pavement ends.

The first campground on Lake Revelstoke, **Carnes Creek**, is about a half-hour drive from Hwy 1. It's provincial-park quality. North of it is a trail ascending to an alpine ridge on Standard Peak, where the mountain-and-glacier vista is spectacular. **Pitt Creek** is the next campground on Lake Revelstoke. It's nearly an hour's drive beyond Carnes. **Potlatch Creek**, the campground on Kinbasket Lake, is near road's end, about a two-hour drive from Hwy 1.

Looking at a map, you might assume this is lonely, wild country. It's not. Most of the forest within sight has been logged intensely. Mica Dam and the paved road ensure a light but steady flow of vehicles. Something else a highway map won't show you is that the immediate topography is rather dull. You won't be admiring grand mountains along the way. The view across Kinbasket Lake is impressive, but it doesn't justify the long drive. You're a boater? Hot to explore Kinbasket Lake? Come on up. All the campgrounds have boat launches. And just beyond Potlatch, you'll find a multi-season, cement boat launch at **Sprague Bay**, where the FS intends to develop another campground.

0 km (0 mi)
Starting north on Hwy 23, departing Trans-Canada Hwy 1 just east of the Columbia River bridge in Revelstoke.

35 km (21.7 mi)
Proceed north for Kinbasket Lake. Turn left, just after crossing Carnes Creek bridge, for Carnes Creek campground on Lake Revelstoke.

CARNES CREEK RECREATION SITE #8
Weekend / Easy
15 well-spaced campsites with tables, boat launch
Accessible by motorhomes and 5th wheels

50 km (31 mi)
Proceed north for Kinbasket Lake. Turn right to reach Standard Peak trailhead in about 15 km (9.3 mi). The ascent is rough but passable in a 2WD car. The trail leads about 11 km (6.8 mi) gaining 600 m (1970 ft) to a cabin in Keystone-Standard Basin.

135 km (83.7 mi)
Proceed north for Kinbasket Lake. Turn left for Pitt Creek campground on Lake Revelstoke.

PITT CREEK RECREATION SITE #10
Weekend / Easy
6 tables, rough boat launch
Accessible by motorhomes and 5th-wheels

140 km (86.8 mi)
Proceed through the village of Mica Creek.

148 km (91.8 mi)
Pass Mica Dam. Pavement ends. Proceed on Redrock FS road.

150.5 km (93.3 mi)
Reach Potlatch Creek campground on Kinbasket Lake, on the left. Proceed generally east, following the south shore, for Sprague Bay.

POTLATCH CREEK RECREATION SITE #11
Weekend / Easy
15 well-spaced campsites with tables, boat launch
Accessible by motorhomes and 5th-wheels

159 km (98.6 mi)
Turn left (northwest) for Sprague Bay.

162.8 km (101 mi)
Reach the multi-season, cement boat launch at Sprague Bay.

REVELSTOKE TO FAUQUIER

Upper and Lower Arrow Lakes are clutched in a long, narrow, steep-walled valley. The two names imply that these are individual lakes. It's actually a single, monster reservoir covering 49,128 hectares. The elevation is approximately 445 m (1460 ft). The water level fluctuates radically. As it drops, sand and cobblestone beaches grow. At its lowest, a lakeside walk can stretch into a journey. In summer, swimming is not a frigid

Lower Arrow Lake

endurance test. Despite endless undeveloped shoreline, FS campgrounds are few.

On Upper Arrow Lake's west shore, south of Shelter Bay ferry, **Eagle Bay** is Columbia FS District's premier campground. A thoughtful layout and well-spaced campsites give it a provincial-park feel. It's accessible by motorhomes and 5th-wheels.

On Lower Arrow Lake's east shore, south of Fauquier, are small campgrounds at **Taite and Octopus creeks**. Taite is off the main road, shaded by conifers, but it's not on the creek. Octopus is in the open, beside the road but also next to the boisterous creek. The up-and-down access road is 2WD-passable, but could jostle a few screws loose on a Winnebago. Don't drag anything bigger than a modest trailer to Taite. The campsites at Octopus will accommodate truck-and-camper rigs, but that's about it.

Whatshan Lake is west of Lower Arrow Lake, just north of Needles. You can reach it from Hwy 6, near the Needles-Fauquier ferry (page 302), or by crossing Lower Arrow Lake on the Arrow Park ferry (page 305). Whatshan is 19 km (12 mi) long, 1.3 km (0.8 mi) wide, and covers 1733 hectares. It would be considered big if it weren't overshadowed by gigantic Lower Arrow Lake. The elevation at Whatshan is 655 m (2148 ft). There are two camp-grounds—Stevens Creek and Richy—shaded by white pines at the lake's north end. Both have sand and pea-gravel beaches. Summertime water temperature is pleasant for swimming. Stevens accommodates big RVs, if you can stand the long, rattling approach. Richy is smaller and densely treed, limiting vehicle size to truck-and-camper rigs.

For EAGLE BAY, now follow the directions below

From Revelstoke, drive Hwy 23 south 50 km (31 mi), along Upper Arrow Lake's west shore, toward Shelter Bay ferry termi-nal. Just before the terminal, turn right (southwest) onto Shelter Bay FS road and set your tripometer to 0. Stay on the main road following the shore. At 9.5 km (5.9 mi) turn left to reach Eagle Bay campground on Upper Arrow Lake.

EAGLE BAY RECREATION SITE #1
Weekend / Easy
15 tables, 3 tent pads, pebble beach, communal fire ring
cement boat launch
Accessible by motorhomes and 5th-wheels

For TAITE and OCTOPUS CREEKS,
now follow the directions below

Drive Hwy 6 to Fauquier, on the east shore of Lower Arrow Lake. It's south of Nakusp, east of Vernon. If you're crossing on the Needles-Fauquier ferry, drive 0.5 km (0.3 mi) up from the lake after disembarking. Set your tripometer to 0 in Fauquier, at Applegrove Road.

0 km (0 mi)
Starting south on initially-paved Applegrove Road, departing Hwy 6 in Fauquier at the sign GAS AND LODGING. Pass Arrow Lake Motel. Pavement soon ends. Proceed south on Lower Fauquier Road.

3 km (1.8 mi)
The road levels, following power lines.

10.1 km (6.3 mi)
Proceed south for Octopus Creek. Turn right, just before the bridge over Taite Creek, and descend on a narrow, tree-enclosed spur to reach Taite Creek campground in 0.8 km (0.5 mi).

TAITE CREEK RECREATION SITE #39
Weekend / Moderate
3 tables, boat launch, beach at low water
Accessible by small motorhomes and trailers

Continuing south on the main road, now called Octopus Creek FS road, passing the turnoff to Taite Creek campground.

Octopus Creek and Lower Arrow Lake

17.2 km (10.6 mi)
Arrive at Octopus Creek campground. One table is beside the creek, the other is within sight and sound of it.

OCTOPUS CREEK RECREATION SITE #40
Weekend / Difficult
2 tables, boat launch
Too small for motorhomes and trailers

For WHATSHAN LAKE, now follow the directions below
If you're approaching from the south, near Needles

From the rest area, just above the Needles ferry terminal, drive Hwy 6 northwest 4.4 km (2.7 mi). Just before the highway switchbacks south, turn right (north) onto Whatshan Lake Road and reset your tripometer to 0.

0 km (0 mi)
Starting north on Whatshan Lake Road.

1.6 km (1 mi)
Turn right onto Whatshan FS road, also signed WHATSHAN ACCESS ROAD-REVELSTOKE ARROW PARK.

2.5 km (1.6 mi)
Stay left. Your general direction of travel all the way to the campgrounds will be north, roughly following Whatshan Lake's east shore.

4.2 km (2.6 mi)
Whatshan Lake is visible on the left.

14.1 km (8.7 mi)
Stay left.

15.7 km (9.7 mi)
Proceed straight.

16.3 km (10.1 mi)
Cross a bridge over White Grouse Creek.

17.4 km (10.8 mi)
Proceed straight, passing Branch 5 road at the KM 30 sign.

24 km (14.9 mi)
Reach a junction. Right is signed STEVENS CREEK, REVELSTOKE, ARROW PARK. Fork left for Richy and Stevens Creek campgrounds.

24.2 km (15 mi)
Proceed north for Stevens Creek campground. Just before a culvert, turn left for Richy campground.

RICHY RECREATION SITE #34
Destination / Difficult (due only to distance)
5 tables, boat launch, dock
Too small for motorhomes and trailers

~

25.9 km (16.1 mi)
Turn left for Stevens Creek campground. Whatshan Peak is visible across the lake. The pinnacles along the Monashee spine are visible northwest.

STEVENS CREEK RECREATION SITE #33
Destination / Difficult (due only to distance)
11 tables, boat launch, dock
Accessible by motorhomes and 5th-wheels

Low-tech inter-camper communication system

If you're approaching from the east, via Arrow Park ferry

Reach the Arrow Park ferry, on Lower Arrow Lake's east shore, by driving Hwy 6 about 22 km (13.6 mi) southwest from Nakusp, or about 14.3 km (8.9 mi) north from Burton. The cable ferry operates daily, on demand, 5 a.m. to 10:30 p.m. Set your tripometer to 0 after disembarking on the west shore and turning left (east).

0 km (0 mi)
Starting east on Lower Mosquito Road. After a detour skirting a washout, resume on the main road. Follow signs for Stevens Creek and Pass.

6 km (3.7 mi)
Cross Mosquito Creek bridge and turn right onto Branch 20 road.

9 km (5.6 mi)
Reach a fork. Go left (west). Follow signs for Stevens Creek and Pass.

10.5 km (6.5 mi)
Go right and ascend on Stevens Road.

20.8 km (13 mi)
Reach a junction. Turn right onto Branch 1.

22.3 km (13.8 mi)
Turn hard left (south) onto Whatshan FS road, following the northeast shore of Whatshan Lake.

23.6 km (14.6 mi)
Turn right for **Stevens Creek campground**; read page 304 for details. Proceed straight (south) for Richy campground.

25.3 km (15.7 mi)
Just after a culvert, turn right for **Richy campground**; read page 303 for details.

Look for deep-orange wood lilies along West Kootenay roadsides.

NAKUSP TO NEW DENVER

Hwy 6 cuts through the Selkirk Mountains. It links Nakusp, on Upper Arrow Lake, with New Denver, on Slocan Lake. From Nakusp it climbs southeast through a pastoral, suspended valley, soon passing small **Box Lake**.

Shaded in afternoon, Box Lake campground offers asylum from summer sun. The cool hemlock-and-spruce forest shelters baby's breath and luxuriant ferns. Vehicle noise from across the lake occasionally punctures the otherwise secluded atmosphere.

Near Box Lake is the turnoff to deep, narrow, steep-sided **Wilson Lake**. Though small—4.5 km (2.8 mi) long, covering 140 hectares—it has two campgrounds. The elevation is 970 m (3180 ft). The west-shore campground is way too small for anything bigger than a truck-and-camper rig. The east-shore campground is the most scenic, but the access road traverses the rocky bluffs south of the lake. It's a rough 7 km (4.3 mi), passable in a 2WD car or even a small motorhome if you drive slowly, but a more rugged vehicle is preferable.

The backroad to Wilson Lake continues east. It passes campgrounds at **Little Wilson Lake** and tiny **Beaver Lake**. It also accesses a short trail to Wilson Creek Falls. Then it heads south to intersect Hwy 6 at Slocan Lake, just north of New Denver. Driving this backroad in reverse, starting near New Denver, is a long, inefficient way to reach Wilson Lake. Go that way only if you want to explore. The short approach to Wilson Lake is from Hwy 6 near Box Lake.

If you're heading southeast on Hwy 6 from Nakusp

0 km (0 mi)
Starting southeast on Hwy 6, from the junction with Hwy 23 at Nakusp.

6.6 km (4.1 mi)
Proceed southeast on Hwy 6 for Slocan Lake and New Denver. Turn left (east) onto Wilson Lake Road and reset your tripometer to 0 for the short approach to the **Wilson Lakes campgrounds**; directions continue on page 310.

7.7 km (4.8 mi)
Box Lake is visible on the right.

10.3 km (6.4 mi)
Proceed southeast on Hwy 6 for Slocan Lake and New Denver. Turn right (west) and descend (doubling back northwest) to reach Box Lake campground on the southwest shore in 1.9 km (1.2 mi).

BOX LAKE RECREATION SITE #27
Overnight / Easy
Elev: 305 m (1000 ft) / Lake: 71 ha
7 tables, dock, creeklet
Inaccessible by motorhomes and trailers

Continuing southeast on Hwy 6, passing the turnoff to Box Lake campground.

19 km (11.8 mi)
Pass the southeast end of Summit Lake. Goat Range peaks in the Selkirk Range are visible northeast.

32 km (19.8 mi)
Pass Bonanza Road on the right. It leads to Wragge Beach Provincial Park campground on Slocan Lake's northwest shore.

41.4 km (25.7 mi)
Proceed southeast on Hwy 6 for New Denver. Turn left (northeast) onto East Wilson Creek FS road (just after Rosebery Provincial Park and Wilson Creek bridge) and reset your tripometer to 0 for **Wilson Creek Falls, Beaver Lake campground**, and the long approach to the **Wilson lakes campgrounds**; directions continue on page 312.

47 km (29.1 mi)
Reach the junction of Hwys 6 and 31A at the Petro Canada gas station in New Denver, on the northeast shore of Slocan Lake.

If you're heading northwest on Hwy 6 from New Denver

0 km (0 mi)
Starting northwest on Hwy 6 from the junction with Hwy 31A at the Petro Canada gas station in New Denver.

5.6 km (3.5 mi)
Proceed northwest on Hwy 6 for Nakusp and Upper Arrow Lake. Turn right (northeast) onto East Wilson Creek FS road (just before Wilson Creek bridge and Rosebery Provincial Park) and reset your tripometer to 0 for **Wilson Creek Falls, Beaver Lake campground**, and the long approach to the **Wilson lakes campgrounds**; directions continue on page 312.

15 km (9.4 mi)
Pass Bonanza Road on the left. It leads to Wragge Beach Provincial Park campground on Slocan Lake's northwest shore.

28 km (17.4 mi)
Pass the southeast end of Summit Lake.

36.7 km (22.8 mi)
Proceed northwest on Hwy 6 for Nakusp and Upper Arrow Lake. Turn left and descend to reach **Box Lake campground** on the southwest shore in 1.9 km (1.2 mi). Read page 307 for details.

Take Your Brain For a Walk

We all seek relaxation when we go camping. For some, that means plunking down and moving as little as possible. But that's actually not very relaxing. Here's why.

Relaxation has two components: physical and mental. Your body relaxes most deeply after physical exertion. Everyone knows that. What few realize is that the mind also relaxes most deeply after physical exertion.

Even the simple act of walking "pumps up" your brain, as well as your blood vessels and denser nerve connections. It gives your brain a workout and keeps it in shape. Afterward, your thoughts settle and soften, just as your muscles do. The brain is, of course, just a big, complex muscle.

Walking is especially relaxing because it's a cross-patterned movement. Opposite limbs—the arm on one side, the leg on the other—are synchronized. This generates harmonizing electrical activity in your central nervous system. It also tones your nervous and immune systems, reduces stress, increases the flow of oxygen throughout the body, and gives you a sense of strength and well-being.

Definitely bring your lawn chair to the campground. But before you take a load off, take your brain for a walk. Lightweight, high-quality hiking boots are best. Keep a brisk pace. About 45 minutes (4 km / 2.5 mi) a day will ensure you enjoy all the relaxation you came for.

39.3 km (24.4 mi)
The northwest end of Box Lake is visible on the left.

40.4 km (25 mi)
Proceed northwest on Hwy 6 for Nakusp and Upper Arrow Lake. Turn right (east) onto Wilson Lake Road and reset your tripometer to 0 for the short approach to the **Wilson Lakes campgrounds**; directions continue on page 310.

47 km (29.1 mi)
Reach the junction of Hwys 6 and 23 in Nakusp, on the east shore of Upper Arrow Lake.

For the short approach to WILSON LAKE
now follow the directions below

0 km (0 mi)
Starting east on Wilson Lake Road, departing Hwy 6. The ascent follows Wensley Creek upstream and passes a sawmill.

3.2 km (2 mi)
Fork right.

4.5 km (2.8 mi)
Reach the high point on the ascent to Wilson Lake's west end.

5.3 km (3.3 mi)
Go right at the junction.

6.6 km (4.1 mi)
Reach a junction. Turn left and reset your tripometer to 0 for tiny Wilson Lake West campground. Go right on Wilson Creek FS road for Wilson Lake East, Little Wilson Lake and Beaver Lake campgrounds, and to continue the long, backroad drive to Hwy 6 and Slocan Lake. The next 7 km (4.3 mi) are rough where the road climbs over rocky bluffs south of Wilson Lake. A high-clearance vehicle is recommended.

> **0 km (0 mi)**
> Turning left at the 6.6-km (4.1-mi) junction, heading for Wilson Lake West campground.
>
> **0.6 km (0.4 mi)**
> Fork right for the final, steep, rough descent on a narrow spur.
>
> **1 km (0.6 mi)**
> Arrive at tiny Wilson Lake West campground. It's a sliver of land between the shore and the base of a cliff.

WILSON LAKE WEST RECREATION SITE #29
Weekend / Moderate
1 table, fishing float
Inaccessible by motorhomes and trailers

~

Continuing generally east on Wilson Creek FS road from the 6.6-km (4.1-mi) junction, passing the turnoff to Wilson Lake West campground. Stay on the main road, ignoring several right spurs. Before the final steep descent, Wilson Lake East campground is visible below.

14 km (8.7 mi)
Reach Wilson Lake East campground, just after a bridged creek crossing. The campsites ring a large clearing beside the road.

WILSON LAKE EAST RECREATION SITE #30
Weekend / Moderate
4 tables, gravel beach, boat launch
Accessible by small motorhomes and trailers

~

Continuing east on Wilson Creek FS road, passing Wilson Lake East campground.

17 km (10.5 mi)
Proceed southeast on Wilson Creek FS road for Beaver Lake campground, and to continue the long, backroad drive to Hwy 6 and Slocan Lake. Turn right onto a rough spur to reach Little Wilson Lake campground in 0.8 km (0.5 mi). It's open, grassy, near the base of 2350-m (7710-ft) Mount Ferrie.

LITTLE WILSON LAKE RECREATION SITE #31
Weekend / Difficult
Elev: 900 m (2950 ft) / Lake: 27 ha
3 tables, boat launch
Accessible by small motorhomes and trailers

~

Continuing southeast on Wilson Creek FS road, passing the turnoff to Little Wilson Lake campground.

28 km (17.4 mi)
Proceed southeast on Wilson Creek FS road to continue the long, backroad drive to Hwy 6 and Slocan Lake. Turn right to reach forested Beaver Lake campground in 0.4 km (0.25 mi). It's backed by the 2300-m (7545-ft) peaks of the Goat Range.

BEAVER LAKE RECREATION SITE #32
Weekend / Difficult
Elev: 884 m (2900 ft) / Lake: 12 ha
7 tables, level tent sites
Accessible by small motorhomes and trailers

36.5 km (22.6 mi)
Reach a junction just after crossing a bridge over Wilson Creek. Proceed right (south) for Hwy 6 and Slocan Lake. Left (northeast) is a steep, rough, but 2WD-passable spur leading 0.7 km (0.4 mi) to **Wilson Creek Falls** trailhead. It's a 1.5-km (0.9-mi) walk to the falls.

43 km (26.7 mi)
Bear right.

48 km (29.8 mi)
Intersect Hwy 6 near Rosebery Provincial Park and the northeast shore of Slocan Lake. Turn right (northwest) for Nakusp. Turn left (southeast) to reach New Denver in 5.6 km (3.5 mi).

For the long approach to WILSON LAKE now follow the directions below

0 km (0 mi)
Starting northeast on East Wilson Creek Road, departing Hwy 6 near Rosebery Provincial Park and the northeast shore of Slocan Lake.

5 km (3 mi)
Bear left.

11.5 km (7.1 mi)
Reach a junction just before a bridge over Wilson Creek. Proceed left (north) on Wilson Creek FS road for campgrounds at Beaver Lake and the Wilson lakes, and to continue the long, backroad drive to Hwy 6 near Nakusp. Right (northeast) is a steep, rough, but 2WD-passable spur leading 0.7 km (0.4 mi) to **Wilson Creek Falls** trailhead. It's a 1.5-km (0.9-mi) walk to the falls.

20 km (12.4 mi)
Proceed northwest on Wilson Creek FS road for campgrounds at the Wilson lakes, and to continue the long, backroad drive to Hwy 6 near Nakusp. Turn left to reach forested **Beaver Lake campground** in 0.4 km (0.25 mi); read page 312 for details.

31 km (19.2 mi)
Proceed northwest on Wilson Creek FS road for campgrounds at Wilson Lake, and to reach Hwy 6 near Nakusp. Turn left onto a rough spur to reach **Little Wilson Lake campground** in 0.8 km (0.5 mi); read page 311 for details.

34 km (21.1 mi)
Reach **Wilson Lake East campground**, just before a bridged creek crossing; read page 311 for details. Continue generally west on Wilson Creek FS road for Wilson Lake West campground, and to reach Hwy 6 near Nakusp. The next 7 km (4.3 mi) are rough where the road climbs over rocky bluffs south of Wilson Lake. A high-clearance vehicle is recommended. Stay on the main road, ignoring several left spurs.

41.4 km (25.7 mi)
Bear left on Wilson Creek FS road to reach Hwy 6 near Nakusp. Turn right and reset your tripometer to 0 for tiny **Wilson Lake West campground**; directions continue on page 310.

42.7 km (26.5 mi)
Bear left.

46.1 km (28.6 mi)
Bear left.

48 km (29.8 mi)
Intersect Hwy 6. Turn left (southeast) for Slocan Lake and New Denver. Turn right (northwest) to reach Nakusp in 6.5 km (4 mi).

NEW DENVER TO BALFOUR

The few FS campgrounds in this section of the Kootenays are well off pavement, but all are accessible by small motorhomes and trailers. More important, all are near trailheads and serve as basecamps for hikers intrigued by Valhalla and Kokanee

Slocan Lake, from Idaho Peak, above New Denver

Glacier provincial parks. For details about the trails, read the hiking guidebook *Don't Waste Your Time in the West Kootenays*. It's described on page 395.

Southwest of Slocan Lake is a campground at **Little Slocan Lakes** (photo on page 318). It has well-spaced campsites in a birch-and-conifer forest beside a shallow lake. In the nearby Valhallas, the trails to Drinnon Pass and Gimli Ridge are superb. Reach Little Slocan Lakes by turning off Hwy 6 at the village of Slocan (page 316), or farther south at Passmore (page 317).

Southeast of Slocan Lake are two campgrounds: **Sasquatch Lake** and **Six-Mile Lakes**. Hikers will find Sasquatch (from Hwy 6, page 319) convenient to Kokanee Park's Lemon Creek trailhead. Six-Mile can also be reached from Lemon Creek, but another approach (from Hwy 3A, page 320) makes it the closest FS campground to Nelson. From town, it's a 25-minute drive to Six-Mile. Half the distance is on a rocky road with narrow steep sections.

If you're heading south on Hwy 6 from New Denver

0 km (0 mi)
Starting south on Hwy 6, from the junction with Hwy 31A, at the Petro Canada gas station in New Denver, on the northeast shore of Slocan Lake.

4.5 km (2.8 mi)
Proceed south through the village of Silverton, on Slocan Lake.

31.5 km (19.5 mi)
Pass a sign announcing the turn for Drinnon Pass, which is also the north approach to Little Slocan Lakes.

32.5 km (20.2 mi)
Proceed south on Hwy 6 to reach Hwy 3A at Playmor Junction. Turn right (west) onto Gravel Pit Road and reset your tripometer to 0 for the north approach to **Little Slocan Lakes campground**; directions continue on page 316. This is also the south entrance to Slocan village.

38.5 km (23.9 mi)
Proceed south on Hwy 6 to reach Hwy 3A at Playmor Junction. Turn left (east) onto Kennedy Road (just after crossing the Lemon Creek bridge) and reset your tripometer to 0 for **Sasquatch and Six-Mile lakes campgrounds**; directions continue on page 319. This is also the signed access to Kokanee Glacier Provincial Park via Lemon Creek.

62.7 km (38.9 mi)
Proceed south on Hwy 6 to reach Hwy 3A at Playmor Junction. Turn right (northwest) onto Passmore Upper Road (across from a power station) and reset your tripometer to 0 for the south approach to **Little Slocan Lakes campground**; directions continue on page 317.

78 km (48.4 mi)
Intersect Hwy 3A at Playmor Junction. Turn right (south) for Castlegar. Turn left (northeast) for Nelson and Kootenay Lake.

If you're heading north on Hwy 6 from Hwy 3A

0 km (0 mi)
Starting west on Hwy 6, from Hwy 3A at Playmor Junction, between Castlegar and Nelson.

15.4 km (9.5 mi)
Proceed north on Hwy 6 for New Denver. Turn left (northwest) onto Passmore Upper Road (across from a power station) and reset your tripometer to 0 for the south approach to **Little Slocan Lakes campground**; directions continue on page 317.

39.5 km (24.5 mi)
Proceed north on Hwy 6 for New Denver. Turn right (east) onto Kennedy Road (just before the Lemon Creek bridge) and reset your tripometer to 0 for **Sasquatch and Six-Mile lakes campgrounds**; directions continue on page 319. This is also the signed access to Kokanee Glacier Provincial Park via Lemon Creek.

45.5 km (28.2 mi)
Proceed north on Hwy 6 for New Denver. Turn left (west) onto Gravel Pit Road and reset your tripometer to 0 for the north approach to **Little Slocan Lakes campground**; directions continue below. This is also the south entrance to Slocan village, and the signed acccess to Valhalla Provincial Park's Drinnon Pass trailhead.

For the north approach to LITTLE SLOCAN LAKES, now follow the directions below

0 km (0 mi)
Starting west on Gravel Pit Road, departing Hwy 6. Proceed straight and cross the Slocan River bridge.

0.8 km (0.5 mi)
Stay left on Slocan West Road.

1.2 km (0.7 mi)
Cross a bridge over Gwillim Creek.

2.3 km (1.4 mi)
Go right on Little Slocan FS road.

13.2 km (8.1 mi)
Bear left (southwest) for Little Slocan Lakes campground. Turn right onto Bannock Burn FS road for Mulvey Basin (Gimli Ridge) trailhead in the Valhallas.

20.3 km (12.6 mi)
Bear left (south) for Little Slocan Lakes campground. Turn right onto Hoder Creek FS road for Drinnon Pass (Gwillim Lakes) trailhead in the Valhallas.

20.5 km (12.7 mi)
Turn left and descend to reach Little Slocan Lakes campground in 200 meters. A loop road accesses the campsites.

LITTLE SLOCAN LAKES RECREATION SITE #42
Destination / Moderate
Elev: 640 m (2100 ft) / Lake: 1.3 km (0.8 mi) long
6 well-spaced tables, boat launch
Accessible by small motorhomes and trailers

For the south approach to LITTLE SLOCAN LAKES, now follow the directions below

0 km (0 mi)
Starting (northwest) on Passmore Upper Road, departing Hwy 6.

0.3 km (0.2 mi)
Cross a bridge over the Slocan River. Go left to follow the north bank of Little Slocan River upstream, gradually curving north.

3.3 km (2 mi)
Pavement ends.

3.7 km (2.3 mi)
Bear left on Little Slocan FS road.

5.3 km (3.3 mi)
Bear right.

Little Slocan Lake campground

7.5 km (4.7 mi)
Proceed straight on the main road.

9 km (5.6 mi)
Stay right.

13.3 km (8.2 mi)
Proceed straight where Koch Creek FS road forks left.

16.1 km (10 mi) and **23 km (14.3 mi)**
Proceed straight.

24.3 km (15.1 mi)
The first of the Little Slocan Lakes is visible on the right.

25 km (15.5 mi)
Proceed straight (northeast) for the Valhalla trailheads or Slocan Lake. Turn right and descend to reach **Little Slocan Lakes campground** in 200 meters; read page 317 for details.

25.2 km (15.6 mi)
Proceed straight (northeast) for Mulvey Basin (Gimli Ridge) trailhead and Slocan Lake. Turn left onto Hoder Creek FS road for Drinnon Pass (Gwillim Lakes) trailhead in the Valhallas.

32.3 km (20 mi)
Proceed straight (northeast) for Slocan Lake. Turn left onto Bannock Burn FS road for Mulvey Basin (Gimli Ridge) trailhead in the Valhallas.

43.2 km (26.8 mi)
Bear left.

44.3 km (27.5 mi)
Cross a bridge over Gwillim Creek.

44.7 km (27.7 mi)
Go right and cross the Slocan River bridge.

45.5 km (28.2 mi)
Intersect Hwy 6 beside the village of Slocan, at the south end of Slocan Lake. Turn left (north) for New Denver. Turn right (south) to reach Hwy 3A at Playmor Junction.

For SASQUATCH and SIX-MILE LAKES via Hwy 6, now follow the directions below

0 km (0 mi)
Starting east on Kennedy Road, departing Hwy 6. It soon becomes Lemon Creek FS road. Follow signs for Kokanee Glacier Park.

4.7 km (2.9 mi)
Bear right and ascend on the main road.

5.7 km (3.5 mi)
Stay left, still ascending steeply.

7.9 km (4.9 mi) and **9.2 km (5.7 mi)**
Bear left.

10 km (6.2 mi)
Go right.

11.6 km (7.2 mi)
Go left.

14.5 km (9 mi)
Reach a junction. Turn left (north) to reach Kokanee Glacier Park's Lemon Creek trailhead in 2.3 km (1.4 mi). Turn right (southeast) onto Six-Mile Road for campgrounds at Sasquatch and Six-Mile Lakes, and to reach Hwy 3A at Kootenay Lake.

14.9 km (9.2 mi)
Reach Sasquatch Lake campground. Proceed straight (southeast) for Six-Mile Lakes campground, and to reach Hwy 3A.

The tiny lake and campground are beside the road. Warm water allows comfortable swimming in summer. Huckleberry picking is fruitful here in season.

SASQUATCH LAKE RECREATION SITE #44
Overnight / Moderate
Elev: 1024 m (3360 ft)
1 table, 2 campsites
Accessible by small motorhomes and trailers

Continuing southeast on the main road, passing Sasquatch Lake.

18 km (11.2 mi)
Reach **Six-Mile Lakes campground**; read page 321 for details. Proceed straight (southeast) to reach Hwy 3A at Kootenay Lake. The next 3 km (1.9 mi) are rough but passable in a 2WD car.

21 km (13 mi)
Fork left.

31 km (19.2 mi)
Intersect Hwy 3A beside Kootenay Lake's West Arm. Turn left for the Balfour ferry terminal and Kaslo. Turn right for Nelson.

For SIX-MILE and SASQUATCH LAKES via Hwy 3A,
now follow the directions below

If you're heading northeast on Hwy 3A from Nelson

Leaving Nelson, set your tripometer to 0 on the northwest side of the orange bridge spanning Kootenay Lake's West Arm.

Drive Hwy 3A northeast 7.9 km (4.9 mi) then turn left (north) onto Six-Mile Road (just before the blue sign for Duhamel and Willow Bay motels) and reset your tripometer to 0.

If you're heading west on Hwy 3A from Balfour

Leaving the Balfour ferry terminal, turn left (west) on Hwy 3A and set your tripometer to 0. At 22 km (13.6 mi) pass the motel and store at Duhamel and slow down. At 22.4 km (13.9 mi) turn right (north) onto Six-Mile Road and reset your tripometer to 0.

For either approach above, now follow the directions below

0 km (0 mi)
Starting north on Six-Mile Road, departing Hwy 3A.

1.5 km (0.9 mi)
Pavement ends. The road is narrow and rocky as it ascends switchbacks to gain the upper valley.

10 km (6.2 mi)
Fork right. The next 3 km (1.9 mi) are rough but passable in a 2WD car.

13 km (8.1 mi)
Reach Six-Mile Lakes campground. Proceed straight (northwest) for Sasquatch Lake campground.

> Two campsites are next to the road but 10 feet above it. Three more are farther back. A 3-km (1.9 mi) trail rounds the west side of the lakes. It starts south of the campsites, heads northwest, and ends just past the farthest lake.

SIX-MILE LAKES RECREATION SITE #14
Overnight / Moderate
Elev: 1100 m (3608 ft) / Lakes: 2 to 7 ha
4 tables, level tent sites, nature trail
Accessible by small motorhomes and trailers

~

Continuing northwest on Six-Mile Road, passing Six-Mile Lakes campground.

16 km (9.9 mi)

Reach **Sasquatch Lake campground**; read page 320 for details. Proceed straight (northwest) for Hwy 6, or Kokanee Glacier Park's Lemon Creek trailhead.

16.4 km (10.2 mi)

Intersect Lemon Creek FS road. Turn left (west) to reach Hwy 6 in 14.5 km (9 mi). Turn right (north) to reach Kokanee Glacier Park's Lemon Creek trailhead in 2.3 km (1.4 mi).

KOOTENAY LAKE EAST SHORE

On the entire east shore of immense Kootenay Lake, the FS maintains just one campground. It occupies a small, cobblestone crescent beach at **Garland Bay**. At night, the lights of Kaslo, across the lake, add romantic sparkle to this backcountry setting. What Garland often lacks are vacant campsites. It's usually full on summer weekends. Also, there are no hiking trails of significant length nearby. From the Kootenay Bay ferry terminal, Garland's about a 45-minute drive. The entry road descends steeply, so while small motorhomes and trailers can squeeze in, they need muscle to get out.

High above Kootenay Lake's east shore is a campground on Gray Creek Road. It's not much of a campground. But it's quite a road. Starting from Hwy 3A, just south of Crawford Bay, at the anachronistic, metric-free village of Gray Creek, near the certifiably-quaint Gray Creek store (donuts to woodstoves all under one roof), the road traverses the Purcell Mountains. It's rough and steep, with grades up to 14%. But everything from 2WD cars to 5th-wheels can survive it. The east end intersects Hwy 95A just south of Kimberley. Total distance from Kootenay Lake: 85 km (53 mi). Gray Creek Pass elevation: 2065 m (6775 ft). Locals drive it regularly, and it's well maintained. But don't mistake it for a shortcut. Thanks to the miracle of pavement, the circuitous highway will deliver you to Kimberley almost as fast. The highway's also less taxing on you and your machine. It's scenically superior, too. Kootenay Lake is your lovely companion

Ridge roaming above Gray Creek Pass

on the highway south of Gray Creek. Gray Creek Road is as lacklustre as its name implies.

The campground on Gray Creek Road is about 17.2 km (10.7 mi) from Kootenay Lake, at minuscule **Oliver Lake**. It's just a wide spot in the road, with a table on each side. At least the road's rarely driven at night, so you won't be bothered by passing vehicles. And nearby slopes—trailless but hikeable—lead to ridges above Gray Creek Pass. A half-hour of uphill effort will earn you the terrific views that Gray Creek Road fails to deliver.

GARLAND BAY

If you're heading north on Hwy 3A from Creston

From the junction with Hwy 3 at the north end of Creston, drive Hwy 3A north. At 79 km (49 mi) proceed through the village of Crawford Bay. At 83.2 km (51.6 mi), where left descends to the Kootenay Bay ferry terminal, turn right (north) onto Riondel Road and reset your tripometer to 0.

If you're disembarking the ferry at Kootenay Bay

From Balfour (between Nelson and Kaslo, on Kootenay Lake's west shore), take the ferry to the east shore. After disembarking at Kootenay Bay, drive Hwy 3A uphill 1.1 km (0.7 mi). Turn left (north) onto Riondel Road and reset your tripometer to 0.

For either approach above, now follow the directions below

0 km (0 mi)
Starting north on Riondel Road, departing Hwy 3A.

8.9 km (5.5 mi)
Curve left (west) into the village of Riondel.

9.1 km (5.6 mi)
Turn right (north) onto Eastman Avenue, following signs for Riondel campground.

9.8 km (6.1 mi)
Pass Riondel Beach and campground on the left. Proceed straight (north) on Riondel North Road.

13 km (8.1 mi)
Cross Tam O'Shanter Creek bridge. Pavement ends. Proceed straight (north) on Powder Creek FS road.

15.7 km (9.7 mi)
Reach trailhead parking on the left for **Pebble Beach Recreation Site #16**. A 2-km (1.2-mi) trail descends to tent sites above the beach.

16.3 km (10.1 mi)
Proceed straight (north) on the main road where Loki South FS road ascends right. Soon pass a waterfall in a gorge on the right.

18.5 km (11.5 mi)
Proceed straight (north) on the main road, passing a right fork.

21.9 km (13.6 mi)
Pass the KM 9 sign and a private road descending left.

22.2 km (13.8 mi)
After crossing Bernard Creek bridge, turn left and descend to reach Garland Bay campground in 300 meters.

GARLAND BAY CAMPGROUND #17
Destination / Moderate
Elev: 532 m (1745 ft)
Lake: 110 km (68 mi) long, 3 km (1.9 mi) wide here, 42,174 ha
20 tables, boat launch, wharf, sandy beach
Accessible by small motorhomes and trailers

OLIVER LAKE

If you're heading south on Hwy 3A from Kootenay Bay

After disembarking the ferry at Kootenay Bay, on Kootenay Lake's east shore, drive Hwy 3A east to Crawford Bay, then south. At 12.3 km (7.6 mi) pass Gray Creek store and slow down. About 150 meters beyond, turn left (east) onto Oliver Road (before the bridge over Gray Creek) and reset your tripometer to 0.

If you're heading north on Hwy 3A from Creston

From the junction with Hwy 3 at the north end of Creston, drive Hwy 3A north 72 km (44.6 mi) to the community of Gray Creek. About 150 meters after crossing the bridge over Gray Creek, turn right (east) onto Oliver Road (before reaching Gray Creek store) and reset your tripometer to 0.

For either approach above, now follow the directions below

0 km (0 mi)
Starting east on Oliver Road, departing Hwy 3A. Pavement ends.

0.3 km (0.2 mi)
Turn right and cross a bridge over Gray Creek.

0.4 km (0.25 mi)
Stay left and ascend. Immediately switchback left. Stay on the main road, passing minor spurs.

1.3 km (0.8 mi)
Bear left on Gray Creek Pass FS road and descend slightly. Pass a sign MARYSVILLE 84 KM; HWY 95A, KIMBERLEY 88 KM.

7 km (4.3 mi)
Bear right and proceed past the winter snowgate.

16.1 km (10 mi)
Proceed straight and continue ascending.

17.2 km (10.7 mi)
Reach Oliver Lake campground where the road widens. Proceed east for Gray Creek pass and to reach Hwy 95A near Kimberley.

OLIVER LAKE RECREATION SITE #13
Overnight / Difficult
2 tables, 3 campsites, short trail to lake
Accessible by small motorhomes and trailers

18 km (11.2 mi)
Top out on 2065-m (6775-ft) Gray Creek Pass. Proceed generally east another 67 km (41.5 mi) to reach Hwy 95 near Kimberley.

NEAR KASLO

In a province-wide beauty pageant for small towns, Kaslo might take the tiara. Among its many attributes are historic brick buildings. Victorian homes. A downtown with old-world charm. A lovely bay on Kootenay Lake's west shore. And a Purcell or Selkirk mountain view every time you lift your eyes (photo on page 23). Of no consequence to the judges of our fictitious contest, but noteworthy here, are two nearby FS campgrounds.

Fletcher Falls is a pipsqueak campground in a premier setting. It's shoe-horned between the mouth of a creek gorge and the shore of Kootenay Lake. Three groups of campers, a couple day-use visitors, and Fletcher is maxed out. If you can stand the unavoidably social atmosphere, after peeking at the falls you'll enjoy the grand lake-and-mountain view, the broad beach, and the soothing shoosh of the creek. The entry road, just 7 minutes south of Kaslo, is SRN—steep, rough and narrow—with overhanging tree branches. Try it only in a high-clearance, low-profile vehicle. Big rigs are verboten.

About 10 minutes north of Kaslo, you can turn west to begin the 855-m (2800-ft) ascent to **Milford Lake**. The road is passable in a 2WD car, but the steep grades and tight turns will stymie a motorhome or trailer. What you'll find up there is a small campground on a tiny lake, fringed by big timber, in a logged, subalpine bowl. It does not compare to the magnificence of Kootenay Lake. So consider paying to camp (heresy!) at one of the beautiful provincial parks nearby on the great lake: Lost Ledge or Davis Creek. Both are reasonably priced. Directions are on page 329. Or continue driving about 40 minutes farther north to the spacious, scenic, free campgrounds on Duncan Lake (page 328).

For FLETCHER FALLS, now follow the directions below

From the Balfour ferry terminal, drive Hwy 31 north 27 km (16.7 mi) along Kootenay Lake's west shore. Or, from the Mohawk gas station in Kaslo (at the "A" Avenue and 4th Street intersection with a flashing traffic light) drive Hwy 31 south 9.2 km (5.7 mi). From either approach, turn east (toward Kootenay Lake), departing Hwy 31. It's only 0.7 km (0.4 mi) to the campground, but it's a rough, narrow, steep descent. Though passable in a 2WD car, it's wise to scout the road first. Or just park at the road and walk down. Day-use sites with tables are across the bridge from the tiny campground.

FLETCHER FALLS RECREATION SITE #15
Destination / Easy
Elev: 532 m (1745 ft)
Lake: 110 km (68 mi) long, 3.5 km (2.2 mi) wide here, 42,174 ha
3 campsites with tables, 2 day-use tables, cobblestone beach
Inaccessible by motorhomes and trailers

~

For MILFORD LAKE, now follow the directions below

From Hwy 31A in Kaslo (at the "A" Avenue and North Marine Drive intersection, just west of and uphill from downtown) drive Hwy 31 north 9 km (5.6 mi). Turn left (northwest) onto Milford Lake Road and ascend numerous switchbacks to reach Milford Lake campground in about 18 km (11.2 mi).

MILFORD LAKE RECREATION SITE #19
Overnight / Moderate
Elev: 1457 m (4780 ft)
2 tables, 3 campsites
Inaccessible by motorhomes and trailers

DUNCAN LAKE

The tight valley that holds Kootenay Lake in a vice-grip continues north. The upper reaches are filled by Duncan Lake—a 44-km (27.3-mi) long expanse of water that, on the map, appears to be wiggling in the mountains' firm grasp.

Duncan has two provincial-park quality, RV-accessible campgrounds near its south end: Glacier Creek on the east shore, Howser Glayco on the west shore. Bear in mind that "shore" is an impermanent feature here. In spring and fall, the water level plummets, exposing a muddy, stump-studded bottom. In summer, Duncan is full-pool gorgeous.

Glacier Creek campground is a fee-free regional park. It's shaded in a mixed forest of evergreens, aspen and birch, on a small point. Several campsites are near the high-water line. The swimming area, created by a log breakwater, has floating platforms.

Howser Glayco comprises two FS recreation sites: Howser campground, and Glayco Beach day-use area. Howser's campsites are in the trees above a thin strip of sandy beach laden with drift logs. Tenters will be grateful for individual tent sites in a separate, walk-in camping area. Four Squatters Glacier is visible north. Mt. Lavina is southeast, across the lake. The sandy beach at nearby Glayco is broader and has better sun exposure. The swimming area, created by a log breakwater, has a floating platform.

Duncan Lake, from Howser campground

Both Glacier Creek and Howser Glayco are excellent basecamps for hikers. Several nearby trails are among B.C.'s best. MacBeth Icefield (photo on page 335), Monica Meadows, Jumbo Pass, Meadow Mountain, and Silvercup Ridge are a few of the premier alpine destinations nearby. An exciting early-season option is Fry Creek Canyon, south of Johnsons Landing, above the northeast shore of Kootenay Lake. For details, read the hiking guide *Don't Waste Your Time in the West Kootenays.* It's described on page 395.

Approaching Duncan Lake from Galena Bay on Upper Arrow Lake? Read page 333 for directions.

If you're heading north on Hwy 31 from Kaslo

0 km (0 mi)
Starting north on Hwy 31, from Hwy 31A in Kaslo (at the "A" Avenue and North Marine Drive intersection, just west of and uphill from downtown).

9 km (5.6 mi)
Proceed straight (north) on Hwy 31 for Duncan Lake. Left (northwest) on Milford Lake Road leads about 18 km (11.2 mi) to Milford Lake campground; read pages 327 and 328 for details.

23 km (14.3 mi)
Pass Kootenay Lake's Lost Ledge Provincial Park on the right.

28 km (17.4 mi)
Pass Kootenay Lake's Davis Creek Provincial Park on the right.

28.4 km (17.6 mi)
Reach the village of Lardeau, near the north end of Kootenay Lake. Curve left, pass 5th Street, and proceed north on Hwy 31.

34.5 km (21.4 mi)
Reach a junction. Proceed northwest on Hwy 31 for Howser Glayco campground on Duncan Lake's west shore; directions continue on page 331. Turn right (east) onto Argenta Road (signed for Purcell Mountains and Fry Canyon) and reset your tripometer to 0 for Glacier Creek campground on Duncan Lake's east shore.

0 km (0 mi)
Starting east on Argenta Road, departing Hwy 31.

1.5 km (0.9 mi)
Cross the Duncan River bridge. Pavement ends.

2.3 km (1.4 mi)
Reach a junction. Proceed straight (north) for Glacier Creek campground. Right leads south through Argenta to Fry Creek Canyon trailhead.

2.5 km (1.6 mi)
Cross the Hamill Creek bridge.

11.5 km (7.1 mi)
Turn left (west) to reach Glacier Creek campground in 400 meters. Proceed straight (north) another 500 meters, then fork right onto Glacier Creek FS road to access several trailheads in the Purcell Mountains.

GLACIER CREEK RECREATION SITE #53
Destination / Easy
Elev: 577 m (1893 ft)
Lake: 44 km (27.3 mi) long, 1.8 km (1.1 mi) wide, 7200 ha
24 well-spaced tables, boat launch, 3 swimming platforms
Accessible by motorhomes and 5th-wheels

~

Glacier Creek campground on Duncan Lake

Continuing northwest on Hwy 31, passing the turnoff to Glacier Creek campground.

38 km (23.6 mi)
MacBeth Icefield's twin waterfalls are visible northeast.

41.1 km (25.5 mi)
Proceed on pavement, curving left, following the sign for Gerrard and Shelter Bay ferry.

42 km (26 mi)
Pavement ends.

46.8 km (29 mi)
Cross the Lardeau River bridge. Pass several houses.

48.1 km (29.8 mi)
Proceed straight (northwest) on Hwy 31 for Trout Lake. Turn right (east) onto Howser Station Road and reset your tripometer to 0 for Howser campground.

0 km (0 mi)
Starting east on Howser Station Road, departing Hwy 31.

1.2 km (0.7 mi)
Proceed through the community of Howser.

1.9 km (1.2 mi)
Reach a junction. Proceed left for Howser campground. For Glayco Beach day-use area, go right 300 meters, then left another 100 meters.

2.2 km (1.4 mi)
Reach a cement boat launch on the right. Proceed left to enter Howser campground in 100 meters.

2.6 km (1.6 mi)
Reach a parking area on the right for walk-in tent sites. They're beneath wind-sheltering trees, about a meter above the lakeshore. The campground road loops back to the entrance.

HOWSER GLAYCO RECREATION SITE #21
Destination / Easy
Elev: 577 m (1893 ft)
Lake: 44 km (27.3 mi) long, 1.6 km (1 mi) wide here, 7200 ha
5 well-spaced campsites with tables,
4 walk-in tent sites with tables
Accessible by motorhomes and 5th-wheels

Continuing northwest on Hwy 31, passing the turnoff to Howser Glayco campground.

82.4 km (51.1 mi)
Reach the south end of Trout Lake. Turn left onto a spur, then right in 100 meters to enter Gerrard campground. Bear right and cross a bridge over Lardeau River to proceed northwest along the lake.

Gerrard campground was fee-free in 1999. It's part of Goat Range Provincial Park, which protects a remote chunk of the Selkirk Mountains rising abruptly to the east. The campsites are in an abandoned apple orchard, surrounded by lush cedar forest. Grizzly bears forage here, so be extremely wary.

GERRARD CAMPGROUND #54
Weekend / Difficult (due only to distance)
Elev: 715 m (2345 ft) / Lake: 24.5 km (15 mi) long, 2792 ha
5 well-spaced campsites, 4 tables
Accessible by motorhomes and 5th-wheels

Continuing northwest on Hwy 31, passing the turnoff to Gerrard camp-ground. The road becomes narrower and rougher as it winds above the northeast shore of Trout Lake.

110 km (68.2 mi)
Reach the village of Trout Lake, at the lake's northwest end. It's another 28.5 km (17.7 mi)—half of it paved—to Galena Bay ferry terminal on Upper Arrow Lake.

~

If you're heading to Duncan Lake
from Galena Bay on Upper Arrow Lake

0 km (0 mi)
Starting south on Hwy 23 from Galena Bay ferry terminal. Ascend briefly then turn left (northeast) onto Hwy 31 where Hwy 23 proceeds south to Nakusp.

28.5 km (17.7 mi)
Reach the village of Trout Lake, on the lake's northwest end.

56 km (34.7 mi)
After crossing a bridge over Lardeau River, at the southeast end of Trout Lake, proceed southeast on Hwy 31 for Duncan Lake, Kootenay Lake and Kaslo. Turn right to quickly reach **Gerrard campground**; read the bottom of page 332 and the top of this page for details.

90.3 km (56 mi)
Reach a junction. Proceed south on Hwy 31 for Glacier Creek campground on Duncan Lake, or to reach Kootenay Lake and Kaslo. Turn left and reset your tripometer to 0 for **Howser Glayco campground** on Duncan Lake; directions continue on the bottom of page 331.

104 km (64.5 mi)
Reach a junction. Proceed south on Hwy 31 for Kootenay Lake and Kaslo. Turn left and reset your tripometer to 0 for **Glacier Creek campground** on Duncan Lake; directions continue on page 330.

129.5 km (80.3 mi)
Proceed south on Hwy 31 for Kaslo. Right (northwest) on Milford Lake Road leads about 18 km (11.2 mi) to **Milford Lake campground**; read pages 327 and 328 for details.

138.5 km (86 mi)
Reach a junction with Hwy 31A in Kaslo. Turn right (west) for New Denver. Hwy 31 descends left (east) into downtown, then continues south along Kootenay Lake's west shore to the Balfour ferry terminal. From there, Hwy 3A leads southwest to Nelson.

Premier Hikes in BC *and* Don't Waste Your Time in the West Kootenays, *described on page 394, will guide you to magnificent scenery. They include the MacBeth Icefield trail, which begins east of Duncan Lake.*

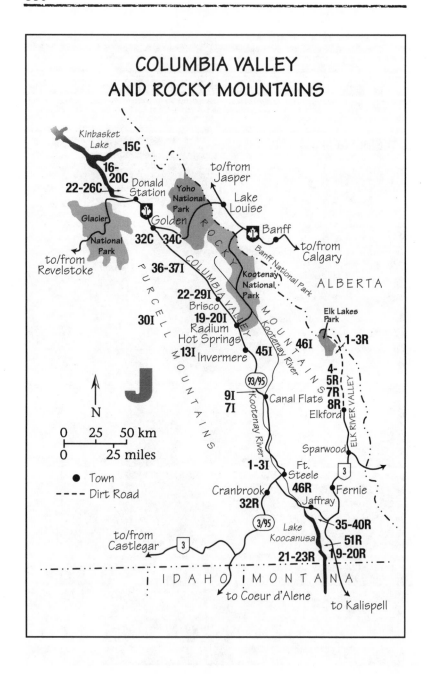

COLUMBIA VALLEY
AND ROCKY MOUNTAINS

Kinbasket Lake **15C**

16-20C

22-26C Donald Station

to/from Jasper

Yoho National Park

Lake Louise

Glacier National Park

Golden

32C **34C**

Banff

to/from Calgary

to/from Revelstoke

36-37I

Kootenay National Park

ALBERTA

22-29I Brisco

30I **19-20I** Radium Hot Springs

Elk Lakes Park

46I **1-3R**

13I Invermere

45I

4-5R
7R
8R

N

0   25   50 km

0   25 miles

• Town

---- Dirt Road

9I
7I

93/95

Canal Flats

Elkford

Kootenay River

Sparwood

1-3I

Ft. Steele

3

46R Fernie

Cranbrook

32R Jaffray

3/95 Lake Koocanusa

35-40R

51R

to/from Castlegar 3

21-23R **19-20R**

IDAHO   MONTANA

to Coeur d'Alene

to Kalispell

J: Columbia Valley and Rocky Mountains

The letter indicates which FS district the campground is in. **C** stands for Columbia FS District. **I** stands for Invermere FS District. **R** stands for Cranbrook FS District.

1I	Tamarack Lake	23C	Blackwater Creek
1R	Upper Elk River	23I	Twin Lakes
2I	Johnson Lake	23R	Englishman Creek
2R	Tobermory Creek	24I	Botts Lake
3I	Larchwood Lake	25C	Bluewater Creek
3R	Riverside	25I	Cub Lake
4R	Weary Creek	26C	Waitabit Creek
5R	Aldridge Creek	26I	Jade Lake
7I	Findlay Creek	27I	Cleland Lake
7R	Blue Lake	28I	Topaz Lake
8R	Krivensky Farm	29I	Cartwright Lake
9I	Whitetail Lake	30I	Bugaboo-Septet
13I	Stockdale Creek	32C	Cedar Lake
15C	Valenciennes River	32R	Palmer Bar Lake
16C	Bush Arm	34C	Hunter Creek
17C	Esplanade Bay	35R	Kikomun Creek
19C	Help Lake	36I	Mitten Lake
19I	Hall Lake	36R	Rock Creek
19R	Loon Lake	37I	Bittern Lake
20C	Blackwater Lake	38R	North Star Lake
20I	Leadqueen Lake	39R	Wapiti Lake
20R	Edwards Lake	40R	Tie Lake
21R	Gold Bay	45I	Horseshoe Rapids
22C	Susan Lake	46I	Palliser-Albert
22I	Dunbar Lake	46R	Horseshoe Lake
22R	Gold Creek	51R	Dorr

Columbia Valley and Rocky Mountains

Columbia River, at Bluewater Creek campground

At the foot of the Canadian Rockies is a heap of adjectives. They were fresh and vivid once. Now they're dull clichés, worn out in countless attempts to express the beauty of this singular mountain range. You have to experience for yourself what all those words fail to convey. The campgrounds described here will serve you on the journey.

The heart of this chapter is the Columbia Valley. It's part of the Rocky Mountain Trench—a 1,600-km (922-mi) long depression just west of and parallel to the Rockies. Mid-valley, between Golden and Invermere, the term *trench* seems especially apt. The Purcells tower to the east, the Rockies to the west.

The valley's natural artery is the Columbia River. Extensive wetlands created by the broad river make the valley an important flyway for migratory birds. The valley's man-made artery is Hwy 93/95. It transports windshield tourists in migratory numbers. Many of the five million people who visit the Rockies each year drive this highway nonstop. Once inside the famous national parks, they're confronted with CAMPGROUND FULL signs. Yet just outside the parks, some FS campgrounds are never full. And several in the Purcells are near trails leading to national-park quality scenery.

At either end of the Columbia Valley, the Rocky Mountain Trench broadens. The scenic intensity wanes. North of Golden are FS campgrounds near an octopus tentacle of Kinbasket Lake. South of Invermere, where it's sunnier and drier, you'll find many more FS campgrounds in gentle foothills carpeted with grassland and sprinkled with open forests of pine and fir.

NORTH OF GOLDEN

North of Golden, where the Trans-Canada turns west toward Glacier National Park, two FS campgrounds are conveniently close to the highway. Waitabit Creek campground is large, well maintained, but next to a busy logging road. Bluewater Creek campground is small, more isolated, on the fast-flowing Columbia River, which helps muffle the sound of nearby passing trains.

A few tiny campgrounds along Bush River FS road (the main logging haul route) are acceptable at night, but they're miserable places to hang out during the day. Industrial traffic is lighter near Susan Lake campground.

Farther north, the combined efforts of the Blackwater Range (east) and the Esplanade Range (west) fail to muster any scenic oomph. Voracious logging has further humiliated these lowly mountains. The land looks exhausted.

Beyond is Kinbasket Lake, a Columbia River reservoir created by Mica Dam. It's huge: 216 km (134 mi) long, covering 41,590 hectares. The elevation is 755 m (2476 ft). The water level fluctuates wildly, but mid-June to September it should be high. The lake's visual appeal rises and falls with the water. Esplanade Bay campground is on a bluff, with a commanding view over Kinbasket Lake's Columbia Reach. Icy peaks are visible in the distance.

Extend your tour of Kinbasket Lake by braving the rocky, dusty logging road to the far east end of Bush Arm, where the Valenciennes River carries meltwater from Banff National Park's Lyell Glacier. You'll find a small, riverside campground here, and a short canyon-probing trail.

If you're heading north on Hwy 1 from Golden

From Golden, drive Trans-Canada Hwy 1 north 26 km (16.1 mi). Shortly before crossing the Columbia River bridge, turn right (north) onto Donald Road and reset your tripometer to 0.

If you're heading east on Hwy 1 from Glacier National Park

From the north edge of Glacier National Park, descend on Trans-Canada Hwy 1 northeast into the Columbia River Valley. Kinbasket Lake's Columbia Reach is visible left (north). Eventually cross the Columbia River bridge. Just 300 meters beyond, cross a large bridge over the railway at Donald Station. About 500 meters farther, turn left (north) onto Donald Road and set your tripometer to 0.

For either approach above, now follow the directions below

0 km (0 mi)
Starting north on Donald Road.

0.7 km (0.4 mi)
Reach a 3-way junction. Follow the dirt road in the middle. Left enters the mill. Right is paved.

1.3 km (0.8 mi)
Proceed straight and descend. Cross a bridge over Waitabit Creek.

2 km (1.2 mi)
Proceed straight (north) for more campgrounds. Turn left to enter Waitabit Creek campground in 100 meters. It's just below the main road.

WAITABIT CREEK RECREATION SITE #26
Weekend / Easy
12 well-spaced tables, more campsites, level tent sites
Accessible by small motorhomes and trailers

Continuing north on the main road, passing the turnoff to Waitabit Creek campground.

4.1 km (2.5 mi)
Proceed straight (north) for more campgrounds. Turn left (west) to reach Bluewater Creek campground in 2 km (1.2 mi); beware of the damaged bridge ahead. The campsites are on the Columbia River.

BLUEWATER CREEK RECREATION SITE #25
Weekend / Easy
2 tables, more campsites
Accessible by small motorhomes and trailers

Continuing north on the main road, passing the turnoff to Bluewater Creek campground.

7.6 km (4.7 mi)
Pass clearcuts.

8.5 km (5.3 mi)
Cross a bridged creek and pass an **overnight pullout** with a table.

12 km (7.4 mi)
Proceed straight (north) on the main road where Bush-Bluewater FS road forks right.

13 km (8 mi)
Proceed straight (north) on the main road for more campgrounds.
Turn left (west) onto Susan Lake FS road and reset your tripometer
to 0 for campgrounds at Blackwater Creek and Susan Lake.

0 km (0 mi)
Starting west on Susan Lake FS road.

1 km (0.6 mi)
Reach **Blackwater Creek Recreation Site #23**. It has
one table beside the road, next to the bridge

5 km (3 mi)
Bear left on the main road.

6 km (3.7 mi)
Turn right to quickly reach Susan Lake campground

SUSAN LAKE RECREATION SITE #22
Weekend / Moderate
Elev: 1524 m (5000 ft) / Lake: 45 ha
3 tables, day-use area for boat-trailer parking
Accessible by small motorhomes and trailers

~

*Continuing north on the main road, passing the turnoff to Blackwater
Creek and Susan Lake campgrounds.*

24.3 km (15.1 mi)
Reach Blackwater Lake campground. It's just off the main road,
on a creek, surrounded by clearcuts. A few young trees provide
no shade.

BLACKWATER LAKE RECREATION SITE #20
Weekend / Moderate
Elev: 970 m (3182 ft) / Lake: 14.5 ha
4 tables, wheelchair-accessible fishing ramp and toilet
Accessible by small motorhomes and trailers

~

29.6 km (18.4 mi)
Proceed straight (north) on the main road for more campgrounds. Turn left (west) to quickly reach Help Lake campground. Beware of the ditch ahead. The lake is tiny, but the grassy campground shaded by cedars is pleasant.

HELP LAKE RECREATION SITE #19
Weekend / Moderate
2 tables, cartop boat launch
Accessible by small motorhomes and trailers

Continuing north on the main road, passing the turnoff to Help Lake campground.

35 km (21.7 mi)
Pass the Giant Cedars interpretive trail on the left. It has one table for day-use.

39 km (24.2 mi)
Proceed straight (north) on the main road for more campgrounds. Turn left (west), at the bottom of a big hill, to reach Esplanade Bay campground in about 6.5 km (4 mi). After crossing a bridge over Succor Creek, descend numerous switchbacks. Go left at the FS sign, then left again to arrive.

ESPLANADE BAY RECREATION SITE #17
Weekend / Difficult (due only to distance)
12 tables, multi-season boat launch
Accessible by small motorhomes and trailers

Continuing north on the main road, passing the turnoff to Esplanade Bay campground.

44.3 km (27.5 mi)
Go right at the junction.

49.3 km (30.5 mi)
Proceed southeast, then east on the main road for remote campgrounds. Turn left for Bush Arm campground.

BUSH ARM RECREATION SITE #16
Weekend / Difficult (due only to distance)
4 tables, multi-season boat launch
Accessible by small motorhomes and trailers

Where the main road turns north and crosses Bush Arm, bear right and continue generally east to reach **Valenciennes River Recreation Site #15**, about 73 km (45 mi) from Hwy 1. The small, treed campground is near the confluence of Bush and Valenciennes rivers. A 2-km (1.2-mi) trail probes the canyon upstream.

After crossing Bush Arm, the main road continues generally northwest, following the shore of Kinbasket Lake, eventually reaching two more small, very remote, lakeside campgrounds: **Caribou Creek Recreation Site #14**, and **Sullivan Bay Recreation Site #13**.

Kicking Horse River at Hunter Creek campground

NEAR GOLDEN

The small but agreeable campground at tiny Cedar Lake is a fifteen-minute drive west of Golden. It has a sandy beach and a shallow area where kids can play. The campsites are well-spaced in trees. This is also a popular day-use area. For more seclusion, tuck you tent under one arm, your sleeping bag under the other, and walk 1 km (0.6 mi) to the tenters-only camping area.

For a quiet night's sleep just off Hwy 1, try Hunter Creek. It's a large, scenic clearing beside the rowdy Kicking Horse River, 20 km (12.4 mi) east of Golden, near Yoho National Park's west boundary. The campground is frequently used by rafting companies, and the FS no longer maintains it, but you can still camp here. Just don't disturb the rafters' tarp-covered tables. The FS intends to develop a new campground nearby.

CEDAR LAKE

If you're heading east or west on Hwy 1

From Trans-Canada Hwy 1, take the exit into Golden. After looping off the overpass, turn left. Turn left again onto 7th Street North (signed for Whitetooth Ski Area) and set your tripometer to 0.

If you're heading north on Hwy 95 from Radium

After entering Golden's business district, cross the Columbia River bridge. Just beyond, reach a Petro Canada gas station where 9th and 10th Avenues intersect. Proceed north on 10th Avenue another 450 meters. Turn left onto 7th Street North (signed for Whitetooth Ski Area) and set your tripometer to 0.

For either approach above, now follow the directions below

0 km (0 mi)
Starting on 7th Street North. In 400 meters curve right (north) and follow the Columbia River.

1.5 km (0.9 mi)
Cross railroad tracks.

1.8 km (1.1 mi)
Proceed on Dogtooth FS road.

2.1 km (1.3 mi)
Curve left, still on pavement. In 100 meters cross the bridge to the Columbia River's west bank.

2.7 km (1.7 mi)
Go left onto Dogtooth Canyon FS road. Pavement ends.

4.8 km (3 mi)
Stay right on the main road.

5.8 km (3.6 mi)
Stay left on the main road.

9 km (5.6 mi)
Go left at the T-junction. Right leads to the ski area.

10.4 km (6.4 mi)
Proceed straight, passing a left spur road.

10.7 km (6.6 mi)
Go left, then immediately fork right. This stretch can be very muddy.

11 km (6.8 mi)
Arrive at Cedar Lake campground. The boat launch is left (electric motors only). Campsites are 200 meters to the right.

CEDAR LAKE RECREATION SITE #32
Weekend / Moderate
Elev: 1036 m (3400 ft) / Lake: 5 ha
3 tables, 4 campsites, walk-in tent sites
sandy beach, boat launch
Too small for motorhomes and trailers

~

HUNTER CREEK

If you're heading northwest on Hwy 1
from Yoho National Park

Set your tripometer to 0 at the large brown sign with yellow letters that says you're leaving Yoho National Park. Proceed northwest 6.5 km (4 mi). Immediately after the small, unsigned, cement-walled bridge over Hunter Creek, turn left onto a narrow road and reset your tripometer to 0. It's also after the second white sign with red letters: FROST WARNING. A green highway sign here says: GOLDEN 26, REVELSTOKE 172, RADIUM 129.

If you're heading southeast on Hwy 1 from Golden

Set your tripometer to 0 at the junction of Hwys 1 and 95, by the big exit sign for Golden. Ascend the steep hill. At 14.4 km (8.9 mi) cross the second bridge over the Kicking Horse River. At 17 km (10.6 mi) pass a truck brake-check pullout on the left. At 19.6 km (12.2 mi) turn right onto a narrow road and reset your tripometer to 0. It's immediately before the small, unsigned, cement-walled bridge over Hunter Creek. The bridge bears a yellow & black warning sign. It's also before the second white sign with red letters: FROST WARNING.

For either approach above, now follow the directions below

0 km (0 mi)
Departing Hwy 1. Descend steeply on broken pavement, then dirt.

1.1 km (0.7 mi)
Stay left.

1.2 km (0.8 mi)
Arrive at Hunter Creek campground.

HUNTER CREEK RECREATION SITE #34
Overnight / Easy
1 table, many more campsites, grassy tent sites
Inaccessible by motorhomes and trailers

Bugaboo Spires, from Bugaboo-Septet campground

GOLDEN TO RADIUM HOT SPRINGS

The FS campgrounds in this stretch of the Columbia Valley are all west of Hwy 95. A few, like Bugaboo-Septet and Stockdale Creek, are in grizzly-bear habitat. Be cautious. Read *B.C. Stands for Bear Country* (page 27).

Mitten Lake (page 351) is the largest in the area. It also has the biggest campground and best mountain view. It's about a 15-minute drive from the village of Parson. On a blazing hot summer day, it's worth the trip just to go swimming. The water temperature is pleasant. Access is easy for small motorhomes and trailers.

About a 1-hour drive from Brisco are the famous Bugaboo Spires, in the Purcell Mountains. The granite monoliths shoot skyward, thousands of feet above the surrounding glaciers. Just outside Bugaboo Provincial Park, the FS maintains **Bugaboo-Septet** campground (page 353). It has an excellent view of the celebrated spires. Several hiking trails are nearby; all lead to tremendous vantage points. Get a BC Parks brochure for general information. *Premier Hikes in B.C.*, described on page 394, will guide you to Conrad Kain Hut, Cobalt Lake, and Chalice Ridge. Big RVs can survive the long access road to the Bugaboos, but the FS campground is too small for them.

On the benchland between Brisco and the Bugaboos, the outstanding campground is at easily-accessible **Cartwright Lake**. Though the view is east to the Rockies, hikers basecamping here will head west to the Bugaboos, Templeton Lake, or Septet Pass (up Frances Creek FS road). Of the two Cartwright camping areas, the north shore offers more privacy than the west shore. Both accommodate small motorhomes and trailers.

Near Cartwright are a dozen other campgrounds on smaller (6- to 43-hectare) **benchland lakes** in mature pine and fir forest. Cleland Lake has a view of the Rockies. Teal-coloured Dunbar Lake has a view of the Purcells. Shallow, reedy Hall Lake has wheelchair-accessible facilities including a dock and observation trail. Big RVs will encounter difficulties at, or en route to, most of these tiny campgrounds. The directions on page 356 will guide you through the rat's nest of narrow, sometimes very muddy roads. Suggestion: If you get confused during your benchland wanderings, follow the frequently signed Bugaboo-Cartwright or Westside roads north to intersect Bugaboo Creek FS road, then turn right (east) to reach Hwy 93.

Yet another hikers' haven is **Stockdale Creek**. The campground is virtually viewless, but nearby trails more than compensate. Lake of the Hanging Glacier—a 2.5-km (1.6-mi) long glacier-fed lake beneath dramatic cliffs—is blow-your-mind beautiful. The 16-km (9.9-mi) roundtrip hike gains 710 m (2330 ft). The trail up Farnham Creek to Commander Glacier is another exciting option. Stockdale Creek campground is too small for motorhomes and trailers.

If you're heading southeast on Hwy 95 from Golden

0 km (0 mi)
Starting southeast on Hwy 95, from 9th Street (the last traffic light) in Golden.

1.2 km (0.7 mi)
Cross the long bridge next to the railroad yard.

34 km (21.1 mi)
Pass the general store and post office in Parson.

35.7 km (22.1 mi)
Proceed southeast on Hwy 95 for Radium Hot Springs. Turn right (west) onto Spillamacheen FS road for **Mitten Lake campground**; directions continue on page 351.

77 km (47.7 mi)
Proceed southeast on Hwy 95 for Radium Hot Springs. Turn right (west) onto Brisco Road for **Bugaboo-Septet campground** and **benchland lakes campgrounds** including **Cartwright Lake**; directions continue on page 353. The turn is signed for Bugaboo Glacier Provincial Park.

105 km (65.1 mi)
Reach the junction of Hwys 95 and 93 in Radium Hot Springs. Turn right (west) onto Forsters Landing Road for **Stockdale Creek campground**; directions continue on page 363. Turn left (northeast) onto Hwy 93 for Kootenay National Park. Proceed south on Hwy 93/95 for Invermere and Cranbrook.

If you're heading northwest on Hwy 95 from Radium Hot Springs

0 km (0 mi)
Starting northwest on Hwy 95 from the junction with Hwy 93 in Radium Hot Springs. For **Stockdale Creek campground**, go west at this junction onto Forsters Landing Road; directions continue on page 363.

28 km (17.4 mi)
Proceed northwest on Hwy 95 for Golden. Turn left (west) onto Brisco Road for **Bugaboo-Septet campground** and **benchland lakes campgrounds** including **Cartwright Lake**; directions continue on page 353. The turn is signed for Bugaboo Glacier Provincial Park.

69.3 km (43 mi)
Proceed northwest on Hwy 95 for Golden. Turn left (west) onto Spillamacheen FS road for **Mitten Lake campground**; directions continue on page 351.

71 km (44 mi)
Pass the general store and post office in Parson.

Mitten Lake and the Purcell Mountains

105 km (65 mi)
Reach 9th Street (the last traffic light) in Golden. Proceed north through town to intersect Trans-Canada Hwy 1.

For MITTEN LAKE, now follow the directions below

0 km (0 mi)
Starting west on Spillamacheen FS road, departing Hwy 95. Cross railroad tracks, then several bridges over the Columbia River and wetlands.

1.6 km (1 mi)
Proceed straight on the main road. Soon begin ascending.

3.5 km (2.2 mi)
Curve left where Aspen Road is right.

4.2 km (2.6 mi)
Proceed straight on the main road.

5.5 km (3.4 mi)
Bear right.

6.2 km (3.8 mi)
Bear left.

7.1 km (4.4 mi)
Turn left onto Mitten Lake Road.

7.3 km (4.5 mi)
Fork left immediately after the yellow KM 7 sign.

9.6 km (6 mi) and **10 km (6.2 mi)**
Bear left, passing right spurs.

11.3 km (7 mi)
Bear right.

15.2 km (9.4 mi)
Reach a junction. Go left for Mitten Lake campground. Turn right to reach **Bittern Lake Recreation Site #37** (tiny lake, dock, 1 table) in 0.8 km (0.5 mi). It's too small for motorhomes and trailers.

18 km (11.2 mi)
Mitten Lake and the Purcell Mountains are visible.

18.3 km (11.3 mi)
Pass an **overnight pullout** on the right, beside the lake.

18.5 km (11.4 mi)
Reach the first Mitten Lake campsite, beside the road.

18.9 km (11.7 mi)
Bear right and descend.

19.5 km (12.1 mi)
Arrive at Mitten Lake's main camping area.

MITTEN LAKE RECREATION SITE #36
Weekend / Moderate
Elev: 996 m (3267 ft) / Lake: 1.4 km (0.8 mi) long, 60 ha
12 campsites with tables, boat launch, dock
Accessible by small motorhomes and trailers

For CARTWRIGHT LAKE and BUGABOO-SEPTET, now follow the directions below

Bugaboo area trailheads and campgrounds are infamous for car-eating porcupines. Seriously. Under cover of darkness, these nocturnal varmints munch tires, hoses and fan belts. Their voracious appetite for rubber could leave you stranded. Thwart the porcs by wrapping chicken wire around your vehicle and securing it with rocks and pieces of wood. Chicken wire is supplied at Bugaboo-Septet campground and Conrad Kain Hut trailhead. Moth balls liberally scattered under and around a vehicle are also rumoured to keep the rascals away.

0 km (0 mi)
Starting west on Brisco Road, departing Hwy 95. Proceed toward the mill.

0.5 km (0.3 mi)
Turn right (north) along the railroad tracks. Soon curve west again and cross two bridged channels of the Columbia River.

3.5 km (2.2 mi)
Reach a junction. Turn right, following the sign BUGABOO 45 KM.

5 km (3 mi)
Reach a junction and trail info sign. Go left, ascending steeply.

6.4 km (4 mi)
Go right on Bugaboo Creek FS road. You've completed most of the ascent from the valley floor. The road improves.

7 km (4.3 mi)
Reach a junction. Proceed right on the better road for Cartwright Lake and Bugaboo-Septet campgrounds. Turn left onto Brisco West - Westside Road and reset your tripometer to 0 for campgrounds at several small benchland lakes; directions continue on page 356.

7.1 km (4.4 mi)
Proceed on the middle fork: Bugaboo Creek FS road.

8.5 km (5.3 mi) and **9.6 km (6 mi)**
Stay straight on the main road.

18.6 km (11.5 mi)
Proceed right (west) for Bugaboo-Septet campground; directions continue on page 355. Turn left (south) onto Bugaboo-Cartwright FS road and reset your tripometer to 0 for Cartwright Lake campgrounds.

0 km (0 mi)
Starting south on Bugaboo-Cartwright FS road, heading for Cartwright Lake.

1.4 km (0.9 mi) and **3 km (1.9 mi)**
Stay straight (southeast) on the main road.

4.4 km (2.7 mi)
Proceed straight (southeast) through the intersection (passing the KM 16 sign) for Cartwright Lake. Right leads to Templeton Lake trailhead.

5.3 km (3.3 mi)
Proceed straight (southeast) on the main road for Cartwright Lake's west campground. Turn left (east) and descend to reach Cartwright Lake's north campground in 0.9 km (0.5 mi). One table is near the entry. Reach six more in the next 300 meters.

CARTWRIGHT LAKE NORTH RECREATION SITE #29
Weekend / Moderate
Elev: 1190 m (3903 ft) / Lake: 1 km (0.6 mi) long, 43 ha
7 tables, dock, boat launch
Accessible by small motorhomes and trailers

Continuing southeast on the main road, passing the turnoff to Cartwright Lake's north campground.

5.6 km (3.5 mi)
Proceed straight (southeast) on the main road.

6.3 km (3.9 mi)
Turn left (east) and descend to reach Cartwright Lake's west campground in 300 meters. Four campsites are on the shore. Two secluded campsites are behind the main area.

CARTWRIGHT LAKE WEST RECREATION SITE #29
Weekend / Moderate
12 tables, dock, boat launch
Accessible by small motorhomes and trailers

Continuing west on Bugaboo Creek FS road from the 18.6-km (11.5-mi) junction, passing the turnoff to Cartwright Lake campgrounds.

20.9 km (13 mi)
Cross a bridged creek.

21.2 km (13.1 mi)
Proceed straight.

23.4 km (14.5 mi)
Bear left.

23.8 km (14.8 mi)
Stay left, along the creek.

40.2 km (24.9 mi)
Reach Bugaboo Falls overlook.

43.3 km (26.8 mi)
Reach a junction. Proceed left (south) for Bugaboo-Septet campground. Right (west) leads to the Conrad Kain Hut and Cobalt Lake trailheads.

44 km (27.3 mi)
Reach a junction. For Bugaboo-Septet campground, turn left (east) and cross the bridge over Bugaboo Creek. Bugaboo Creek FS road continues right (south), soon passing a lodge en route to Bugaboo Pass trailhead.

44.1 km (27.35 mi)
Reach a fork just beyond the bridge. Turn left (north) for Bugaboo-Septet campground. Right (south) leads to Chalice Creek trailhead.

44.3 km (27.5 mi)
Turn left to reach Bugaboo-Septet campground in 100 meters.

The generator from the nearby lodge is audible, but Bugaboo Creek does its best to compete. The campsites are just above the creek. The ridge to the east blocks early morning sunlight.

BUGABOO-SEPTET RECREATION SITE #30
Destination / Difficult (due only to distance)
Elev: 1500 m (4920 ft)
4 tables
Inaccessible by motorhomes and trailers

For BENCHLAND LAKES, now follow the directions below

0 km (0 mi)
Starting south on Brisco West - Westside Road, departing Bugaboo Creek FS road at the 7-km (4.3-mi) junction. Bear left in 100 meters. At 200 meters cross a bridged creek.

0.6 km (0.4 mi)
Bear left on Brisco West - Westside Road for Twin and Dunbar lakes; directions continue on page 357. Turn right onto Cleland Lake FS road and reset your tripometer to 0 for Cleland Lake.

Cleland Lake

0 km (0 mi)
Starting on Cleland Lake FS road.

1.8 km (1.1 mi) and **2.2 km (1.4 mi)**
Bear left and ascend.

2.5 km (1.6 mi)
Proceed straight for Cleland Lake. Left is a steep, rough, narrow road to **Cub Lake Recreation Site #25**. The lake and campground are tiny.

2.6 km (1.6 mi)
Bear left.

2.8 km (1.7 mi)
Reach a junction at Cleland Lake. Go right or left for Cleland Lake campsites. The rough road left continues to Jade Lake campground.

CLELAND LAKE RECREATION SITE #27
Weekend / Moderate
Elev: 1158 m (3798 ft) / Lake: 24 ha
3 tables, 2 docks
Accessible by small motorhomes and trailers

3.8 km (2.4 mi)
Reach **Jade Lake Recreation Site #26**. The lake and campground are tiny.

Continuing left on Brisco West - Westside Road from the 0.6-km (0.4-mi) junction, heading for Twin and Dunbar lakes.

1 km (0.6 mi)
Bear right.

1.1 km (0.7 mi)
Bear left.

1.7 km (4.3 mi)
Bear right.

3.5 km (2.2 mi)
Bear left.

6.1 km (3.8 mi)
Reach a junction and sign: BRISCO WEST. Go left.

6.3 km (3.9 mi)
Cross a bridged creek.

6.4 km (4 mi)
Proceed straight (south) for more benchland lakes campgrounds. Right is a narrow, rough, two-track road (small, sturdy
vehicles only) leading to Botts Lake campground.

> In about 300 meters reach a possible campsite in a grassy,
> level clearing beside the creek. At 0.4 km (0.25 mi) reach a
> viewless campsite with a table, backed by a sandy bank. At
> 0.5 km (0.3 mi) arrive at a table on the shore of tiny, reedy
> Botts Lake.

BOTTS LAKE RECREATION SITE #24
Overnight / Difficult
2 tables
Inaccessible by motorhomes and trailers

*Continuing south on the main road, passing the turnoff to Botts Lake
campground.*

7.8 km (4.8 mi)
Proceed straight (south) for more benchland lakes campgrounds. Right is a narrow, two-track road leading about 40
meters to a one-table **campsite** on tiny Twin Lakes. It has a
mountain view. A weir on the nearby creek creates water music.

8.2 km (5.1 mi)
Bear right.

8.6 km (5.3 mi)
Reach a junction. Proceed straight (southwest) on Westside Road
for Hall Lake campground. Turn right (northwest) and reset your
tripometer to 0 for campgrounds at Twin and Dunbar lakes.

0 km (0 mi)
Starting northwest, departing Westside Road. In 200 meters reach Twin Lakes campground beside the road, in ugly trees, at the grim end of the tiny lake. Two campsites are on a bench above the shore, another is across the road.

TWIN LAKES RECREATION SITE #23
Overnight / Difficult
3 tables
Inaccessible by motorhomes and trailers

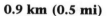

0.9 km (0.5 mi)
Proceed straight and continue ascending.

2 km (1.2 mi)
Arrive at Dunbar Lake campground. It has a mountain view. The campsites are in trees, along the lake, beside the road. There are cabins nearby.

DUNBAR LAKE RECREATION SITE #22
Overnight / Difficult
4 tables
Inaccessible by motorhomes and trailers

Continuing southwest on Westside Road from the 8.6-km (5.3-mi) junction, heading for Hall Lake.

9.4 km (5.8 mi)
Proceed southeast on Westside Road for Hall Lake. Turn right (west) onto a rough, narrow road, go over a steep hill, then turn left (south) to quickly reach **Halfway Lake Recreation Site #21**. The lake and campground are tiny.

11.1 km (6.9 mi)
Reach a junction. Turn right (west) onto Frances Creek FS road for Cartwright Lake, and to rejoin Bugaboo Creek FS road. Proceed left (southeast) on Westside Road and reset your tripometer to 0 for Hall Lake.

Wander at Will

Camp Free is full of detailed directions. Ignore them occasionally. Because when you follow a prescribed route and arrive at an intended destination, you've merely completed a trip. Only an encounter with the unexpected elevates a journey to an adventure.

So wander. Zigzag. Spiral through B.C.'s vast network of back-roads. It will lead you to surprising places, people and experiences that you'd miss by always adhering to ours or anyone else's directions.

Most of us are severely constrained by the expectations of employer, family and society. We need more time free of restrictions, to exuberantly follow our instincts rather than trudge the rut to expected results. When is that possible? More often than we realize. And certainly on a camping trip. Just veer down an unknown road.

Wandering revives youthful curiosity and a carefree spirit. It releases innate creativity. Ironically, it returns the wanderer to exactly where she or he belongs: the present moment. Right here. Right now. A place our future-oriented culture does not honor. Yet the only place anyone can truly, fully live.

0 km (0 mi)
Continuing left (southeast) on Westside Road, heading for Hall Lake.

0.7 km (0.4 mi)
Cross a big cement bridge.

2.8 km (1.7 mi)
Turn left (east) onto a spur road for Hall Lake.

3.4 km (2.1 mi)
Arrive at Hall Lake campground.

HALL LAKE RECREATION SITE #19
Overnight / Difficult (due only to distance)
3 tables, wheelchair-accessible facilities, dock, observation trail
Accessible by small motorhomes and trailers

~

Continuing right (west) on Frances Creek FS road from the 11.1-km (6.9-mi) junction, heading for Cartwright Lake and Bugaboo Creek FS road.

13 km (8.1 mi)
Reach a junction. Proceed straight (northwest) on Bugaboo-Cartwright FS road for Cartwright Lake and Bugaboo Creek FS road. Frances Creek FS road continues left (west). It eventually reaches several trailheads, but in just 100 meters a right spur leads 0.6 km (0.4 mi) to **Leadqueen Lake Recreation Site #20**. It's a single campsite at a reedy widening of a creek, with a mountain view. It's useful for hikers heading to McLean Lake, Tiger Pass or Septet Pass.

14.3 km (8.9 mi)
Bear left.

14.5 km (9 mi)
Pass a KM 45 sign.

15 km (9.3 mi)
Proceed straight (northwest) on the main road.

17.2 km (10.7 mi)
Bear right on the main, upper road.

18.9 km (11.7 mi)
Cross a bridged creek. Proceed straight (northwest) on the main road, passing a minor fork.

20.9 km (13 mi)
Proceed straight (northwest) on the main road to intersect Bugaboo Creek FS road. Turn right (east) to reach **Cartwright Lake's west campground** in 300 meters; read page 355 for details.

21.6 km (13.4 mi)
Proceed straight (northwest) on the main road.

21.9 km (13.6 mi)
Proceed straight (northwest) on the main road to intersect Bugaboo Creek FS road. Turn right (east) to reach **Cartwright Lake's north campground** in 0.9 km (0.5 mi); read page 354 for details.

22.8 km (14.1 mi)
Proceed straight (northwest) through the intersection (passing the KM 16 sign) to intersect Bugaboo Creek FS road. Left leads to Templeton Lake trailhead.

24.2 km (15 mi)
Proceed straight (northwest) on the main road where Bugaboo-Lily FS road forks left.

25.8 km (16 mi)
Proceed straight (north) passing a left fork and the KM 13 sign.

27.2 km (16.9 mi)
Intersect Bugaboo Creek FS road. Turn left (west) for Bugaboo-Septet campground and Bugaboo Provincial Park; directions continue on page 355, from the 18.6-km (11.5-mi) point. Turn right (east) and reset your tripometer to 0 for Hwy 95 at Brisco.

0 km (0 mi)
Starting east on Bugaboo Creek FS road, from the junction with Bugaboo-Cartwright FS road, heading for Hwy 95.

9 km (5.6 mi) and **10.1 km (6.3 mi)**
Bear left on the main road.

11.5 km (7.1 mi)
Proceed straight on the main road and start descending. Pass Westside Road on the right.

11.6 km (7.2 mi)
Stay left.

12.2 km (7.6 mi)
Bear left and continue descending. Slow down as the road narrows and curves sharply.

13.6 km (8.4 mi)
Bear right.

15.1 km (9.4 mi)
Bear left and cross bridged channels of the Columbia River.

18.6 km (11.5 mi)
After skirting the mill, intersect Hwy 95 at Brisco.

For STOCKDALE CREEK, now follow the directions below

From the junction of Hwys 93 & 95 in Radium Hot Springs, drive west onto Forsters Landing Road. In 1.4 km (0.9 mi) reach a junction just before the Slocan Group mill. Set your tripometer to 0 here, so it will be in sync with the KM signs. Horsethief Creek FS road is passable in a 2WD car, but slow down near 41 km (25 mi) where deep waterbars (ditches) cross the road.

0 km (0 mi)
Starting left (west) on Horsethief Creek FS road. Soon cross railroad tracks, then a bridge over the Columbia River.

2.9 km (1.8 mi)
Reach a junction. Stay left on the main road. Steamboat Mountain Road (signed for Red Rock) forks right (north). Ignore all forks until the next major junction.

7 km (4.3 mi)
Proceed straight on the main road, passing a right fork.

9.2 km (5.7 mi)
Reach the KM 9 sign and a major junction with Westside Road. Proceed straight (southwest) on Horsethief Creek FS road, signed for Hanging Glacier. Left leads southeast to Invermere.

13.5 km (8.4 mi)
Go left.

21.5 km (13.3 mi)
Reach the valley bottom, where the road follows Horsethief Creek.

23.2 km (14.4 mi)
Curve left and cross a bridge to the south side of Horsethief Creek.

36 km (22.3 mi)
Bear right where a left (south) fork ascends the McDonald Creek drainage.

39.5 km (24.5 mi)
Proceed southwest on the main road for Lake of the Hanging Glacier trailhead. Turn right, just before the KM 39 sign, to enter Stockdale Creek campground.

STOCKDALE CREEK RECREATION SITE #13
Weekend / Difficult (due only to distance)
Elev: 1300 m (4265 ft)
2 tables, 3 campsites
Accessible by small motorhomes and trailers

41 km (25.4 mi)
The road deteriorates. Slow down. Beware of water bars.

50 km (31 mi)
The road is rough and narrow

50.2 km (31.1 mi)
Arrive at Lake of the Hanging Glacier trailhead.

Kootenay River, from Horseshoe Rapids campground

SOUTH OF KOOTENAY NATIONAL PARK

Twenty minutes of uncommonly smooth, easy, off-pavement driving is all it takes to reach secluded **Horseshoe Rapids** campground on the raging Kootenay River, just south of Kootenay Park. But the small campground is frequented by rafters, kayakers and canoeists. Be glad if you find a vacant campsite. Class II and III rapids make this an ideal river for multi-day canoe trips.

Willing to drive 45 minutes on backroads? Southeast of Horseshoe Rapids, closer to the spine of the Rockies, **Palliser-Albert** is a premier campground at the confluence of the clear, cold Palliser and Albert rivers. It's on the way to Height of the Rockies Provincial Park, so it's handy for hikers.

Horseshoe Rapids and Palliser-Albert are outstanding FS campgrounds in beautiful settings. But camping at either of them should be a supplement to, not a substitute for, time spent in the Rocky Mountain national parks. It's worth paying to camp in the heart of this resplendent mountain range. And hiking there is a must. Read the guidebook *Don't Waste Your Time in the Canadian Rockies*. It's described on page 395.

If you're heading south on Hwy 93 in Kootenay National Park

From McLeod Meadows campground near the south end of Kootenay National Park, drive Hwy 93 south 8 km (5 mi). Before the highway starts ascending, turn left (southeast) onto Settlers Road and reset your tripometer to 0.

If you're heading northeast on Hwy 93 from Radium Hot Springs

From Kootenay National Park's south-entrance toll booth at Radium Hot Springs, drive Hwy 93 northeast 19 km (11.8 mi). At the bottom of the hill, turn right (southeast) onto Settlers Road and reset your tripometer to 0.

For either approach above, now follow the directions below

0 km (0 mi)
Starting southeast on Settlers Road, departing Hwy 93.

11.8 km (7.3 mi)
Cross Kootenay National Park's south boundary.

12.5 km (7.8 mi)
Reach a junction. Turn left (east) onto Kootenay-Palliser Road and reset your tripometer to 0 for Palliser-Albert campground; directions continue below. Bear right and proceed south on Kootenay-Settlers Road for Horseshoe Rapids campground.

18 km (11 mi)
Pass an aspen grove and meadows.

19.2 km (11.9 mi)
Pass a left spur to a possible **overnight pullout** in a meadow.

19.5 km (12.1 mi)
Just after a culvert, turn left and descend on a small, rough road to reach Horseshoe Rapids campground in 0.8 km (0.5 mi). The turn is just before Bear Creek road forks right.

HORSESHOE RAPIDS RECREATION SITE #45
Destination / Moderate
Elev: 1050 m (3445 ft)
2 tables, level tent site on the point
Inaccessible by motorhomes and trailers

Turning left (east) at the 12.5-km (7.8-mi) junction, passing the turnoff to Horseshoe Rapids campground. Reset your tripometer to 0.

0 km (0 mi)
Starting east on Kootenay-Palliser Road, heading for Palliser-Albert campground. Stay left on the main road in 100 meters. Soon cross a bridge over the Kootenay River.

2.2 km (1.4 mi)
Turn right (south) where Cross River FS road forks left.

18.2 km (11.3 mi)
Cross the bridge to the south side of Palliser River and reach a junction. Right (south) leads 7 km (4.3 mi) to **Fenwick Creek Recreation Site #48** just northeast of Fenwick Falls. Turn left

Don't Waste Your Time in the Canadian Rockies, *described on page 395, will guide you to magnificent scenery like this.*

(northeast) on Palliser-Albert FS road for Palliser-Albert camp-ground. Heading east, stay on the main road, ignoring spurs.

26 km (16.1 mi)
Reach a junction near the 40 KM sign. Turn left (north) onto Albert River FS road for Palliser-Albert campground. Proceed straight (east) on Palliser FS road to view Palliser Falls canyon, near the KM 46 sign.

28 km (17.4 mi)
Reach Palliser-Albert campground on the left, just west of the rivers' confluence. Well-spaced campsites are on level terraces in the open pine forest. Proceed north-northeast on the main road for Leman Lake trailhead.

PALLISER-ALBERT RECREATION SITE #46
Weekend / Difficult (due only to distance)
4 tables, 7 campsites, large spaces for RVs
Accessible by small motorhomes and trailers

54 km (33.5 mi)
Reach Leman Lake trailhead, beneath the Royal Group.

FAIRMONT HOT SPRINGS TO KIMBERLEY

This is the south end of the Columbia Valley. The scenery is less compelling here than farther north where the Rockies rise steeper and the valley is narrower. But knowing a little about the area gives it some intrigue.

The easily overlooked hamlet of Canal Flats, for example, is the site of a fascinating phenomenon. It's on a narrow (2-km / 1.2-mi) strip of land separating Columbia Lake (headwaters of the north-bound Columbia River), from the south-bound Kootenay River. Now fast-forward your attention downstream. Each of the rivers, having wandered about 300 km (186 mi) in opposite directions, meet again and get married at Castlegar. Sharing the same name—Columbia River—they go on to achieve great-ness as the fourth longest river in North America. The happy ending to this story takes place in Portland, Oregon, where the Columbia flows peacefully into the Pacific Ocean.

Despite such vast volumes of liquid, this is dry country, and the campgrounds are located on insignificant bodies of water. The Purcells, to the west, catch most of the moisture before it can reach the Columbia Valley. When clouds pass overhead, they're often running on empty. Expect sunshine. In summer, it gets hot enough here to make you wonder if this is really Canada.

As for specific campgrounds, **Findlay Creek** is a nondescript place to spend the night not far from Hwy 93/95. **Whitetail Lake** is weekend worthy, if you can tolerate the rough access road. Whitetail is popular because of its adequate size and fishing reputation. Both Findlay and Whitetail are suitable for small RVs.

Several campgrounds at small lakes near Skookumchuck are close to Hwy 93/95. Consider them for a brief overnighter. **Tamarack** and **Larchwood lakes** are pretty. Tamarack has the better mountain view but a twisty access road—tedious in a car, enjoyable on a mountain bike. Both campgrounds accommodate small RVs.

If you're heading south on Hwy 93/95 from Fairmont Hot Springs

0 km (0 mi)
Starting south on Hwy 93/95 from the Fairmont Hot Springs entry sign.

20.5 km (12.7 mi)
Turn right (west) at the sign BLUE LAKE FOREST CENTRE and reset your tripometer to 0 for **Findlay Creek and Whitetail Lake campgrounds**; directions continue on page 370.

25.5 km (15.8 mi)
Cross the Kootenay River bridge at Canal Flats.

48.5 km (30.1 mi)
Turn right (west) and reset your tripometer to 0 for **Johnson Lake campground**; directions continue on page 372.

54.2 km (33.6 mi)
Cross the Kootenay River bridge just south of Skookumchuck.

55.3 km (34.3 mi)
Turn right (west) onto Farstad Way (toward the pulp mill) and
reset your tripometer to 0 for **campgrounds at Tamarack
and Larchwood lakes**; directions continue on page 372.

66.7 km (41.4 mi)
Reach the junction of Hwys 93/95 and 95A, near Wasa, northeast of Kimberley.

If you're heading north on Hwy 93/95 from near Kimberley

0 km (0 mi)
Starting north on Hwy 93/95, from the junction with Hwy 95A,
near Wasa, northeast of Kimberley.

11.4 km (7.1 mi)
Turn left (west) onto Farstad Way (toward the pulp mill) and
reset your tripometer to 0 for **campgrounds at Tamarack
and Larchwood lakes**; directions continue on page 372.

12.5 km (7.8 mi)
Cross the Kootenay River bridge just south of Skookumchuck.

18.2 km (11.3 mi)
Turn left (west) and reset your tripometer to 0 for **Johnson
Lake campground**; directions continue on page 372.

41.2 km (25.5 mi)
Cross the Kootenay River bridge at Canal Flats.

46.2 km (28.6 mi)
Turn left (west) at the sign BLUE LAKE FOREST CENTRE and reset
your tripometer to 0 for **Findlay Creek and Whitetail Lake
campgrounds**; directions continue below.

66.7 km (41.4 mi)
Reach the Fairmont Hot Springs entry sign.

**For FINDLAY CREEK and WHITETAIL LAKE
now follow the directions below**

0 km (0 mi)
Starting (west) at the sign BLUE LAKE FOREST CENTRE, departing
Hwy 93/95.

0.8 km (0.5 mi)
Pavement ends. Proceed south on Findlay Creek FS road.

2.2 km (1.4 mi)
Proceed straight, passing a left fork.

4.8 km (3 mi)
Pass an **overnight pullout** on the left where a short trail leads
to Findlay Falls.

5.7 km (3.5 mi)
Proceed straight (generally west) where Skookumchuck FS road
forks left.

11.4 km (7.1 mi)
Reach a junction. Proceed straight (west) for Whitetail Lake.
Turn left (south) and reset your tripometer to 0 for Findlay Creek.

0 km (0 mi)
Starting south, heading for Findlay Creek.

0.4 km (0.2 mi)
The campground is visible across the creek.

1.9 km (1.2 mi)
After crossing the bridge, turn left (east) onto a small,
rough road.

3.4 km (2.1 mi)
Arrive at Findlay Creek campground.

FINDLAY CREEK RECREATION SITE #7
Overnight / Moderate
2 tables
Accessible by small motorhomes and trailers

*Continuing west on Findlay Creek FS road, passing the turnoff to Findlay
Creek campground.*

13 km (8.1 mi)
Turn right (northwest).

24 km (14.9 mi)
Near the north end of Whitetail Lake, fork right and curve south to reach the campground in about 1.6 km (1 mi). Proceed another 1 km (0.6) to reach four more campsites with tables.

WHITETAIL LAKE RECREATION SITE #9
Weekend / Moderate
Elev: 1066 m (3495 ft) / Lake: 3.8 km (2.4 mi) long, 157.5 ha
24 tables, boat launch
Accessible by small motorhomes and trailers

For JOHNSON LAKE, now follow the directions below

About 50 meters off Hwy 93/95, the access road forks. Turn left to reach the south camping area in 0.5 km (0.3 mi). Go right 0.8 km (0.5 mi) then turn sharply left to reach the north camping area, on the reedy end of the lake, in another 100 meters.

JOHNSON LAKE RECREATION SITE #2
Overnight / Easy
Elev: 854 m (2800 ft) / Lake: 13.5 ha
4 tables
Accessible by small motorhomes and trailers

For TAMARACK and LARCHWOOD LAKES,
now follow the directions below

0 km (0 mi)
Starting (west) on initially-paved Farstad Way, departing Hwy 93/95.

2 km (1.2 mi)
Turn left onto Torrent Road.

2.6 km (1.6 mi)
Bear right on the main road and cross railroad tracks.

3 km (1.8 mi)
Re-cross the creek and railroad tracks. Pavement ends.

4.6 km (2.9 mi)
Reach a junction. Turn left (southwest) for Tamarack Lake. Turn right (north) and reset your tripometer to 0 for Larchwood Lake.

0 km (0 mi)
Starting north, heading for Larchwood Lake.

3.4 km (2.1 mi)
Bear left, ascending on the main road.

4.4 km (2.7 mi)
Arrive at Larchwood Lake campground. The lake is 200 meters beyond.

LARCHWOOD LAKE RECREATION SITE #3
Weekend / Easy
Elev: 854 m (2800 ft) / Lake: 15.5 ha
3 well-spaced tables
Accessible by small motorhomes and trailers

Continuing southwest at the 4.6-km (2.9-mi) junction, passing the turnoff to Larchwood Lake.

4.9 km (3 mi)
Bear left.

7.4 km (4.6 mi)
Fork right.

8.4 km (5.2 mi)
Arrive at Tamarack Lake campground.

TAMARACK LAKE RECREATION SITE #1
Weekend / Easy
Elev: 883 m (2895 ft) / Lake: 32 ha
2 tables, 3 campsites, dock
Accessible by small motorhomes and trailers

Horseshoe Lake and the Rocky Mountains

NEAR CRANBROOK AND FT. STEELE

Tiny **Palmer Bar Lake** is a convenient place to camp near Cranbrook. It's about a 15-minute drive southwest of town. Though small, the campground is accessible by motorhomes and 5th-wheels.

Southeast of historic Fort Steele, the Rockies leap skyward, giving a lazy camper plenty to look at from the comfort of a folding chair at destination-rated **Horseshoe Lake** campground. A more energetic camper can work-off a pasta lunch by mountain biking the dirt roads ringing the lake. Truly motivated campers can hike a rigorous trail into the Steeples. The trailhead is about 2 km (1.2 mi) south of the lake. Pick up a Steeples Area Trails Map at the Cranbrook FS office. It will also direct you to other, less ambitious hikes. Horseshoe Lake accommodates small motorhomes and trailers.

PALMER BAR LAKE

If you're heading southwest on Hwy 3/95 from Cranbrook

0 km (0 mi)
Starting southwest on Hwy 3/95, from the Tourist Info office across from Jim Smith Road, at the southwest end of Cranbrook.

10 km (6.2 mi)
Turn right onto Moyie River Road.

14 km (8.7 mi)
Bear right.

20 km (12.4 mi)
Arrive at Palmer Bar Lake campground.

PALMER BAR RECREATION SITE #32
Weekend / Easy
4 tables, cartop boat launch
Accessible by motorhomes and 5th-wheels

~

HORSESHOE LAKE

If you're heading south or north on Hwy 93/95

Just 1 km (0.6 mi) north of Fort Steele, turn east onto Wardner—Ft. Steele Road, signed for Norbury Lake Provincial Park. Follow it southeast another 11.5 km (7.1 mi), then turn left (north) at the sign for Horseshoe Lake.

If you're heading northwest on Hwy 3/93 from Jaffray

From Jaffray-Baynes Lake Road in Jaffray, drive Hwy 3/93 northwest 11 km (6.8 mi). Just before the Kootenay River bridge, turn right onto Wardner—Ft. Steele Road, signed for Norbury Lake Provincial Park. Reset your tripometer to 0. At 15 km (9.3 mi) pass the park entrance. At 19 km (11.8 mi) turn right (north) at the sign for Horseshoe Lake.

For either approach above, now follow the directions below

In 300 meters, reach a fork. Campsites are 0.5 km (0.3 mi) in either direction. Right follows the east side of Horseshoe Lake. Left follows the west shore, where the mountain view is better. If you go left, bear left on the upper road, avoiding the sometimes flooded lower road. The lake is ringed by aspen-and-pine forest.

HORSESHOE LAKE RECREATION SITE #46
Destination / Easy
Elev: 854 m (2800 ft) / Lake: 12 ha
12 tables
Accessible by small motorhomes and trailers

JAFFRAY TO ELKO

Looking at a B.C. road map, nobody notices Jaffray (southeast of Cranbrook) and Elko (south of Fernie). Most people aren't even aware of these hamlets when driving right through them on Hwy 3/93. Yet they're significant landmarks for campers. In the gently rolling grassland and open forests between Jaffray and Elko, you'll find several FS campgrounds. Others are farther south, near and on Lake Koocanusa. The scenery is easily shrugged off. But the sun is a reliable fixture in the frequently blue sky. And the campgrounds are peaceful, good for a few days of down-time. Settle in. Ease off the mental accelerator. Nap in the shade. Play music under the trees. Chase your kids through a meadow. Cool off in the creeks and lakes.

Bad news: Cranbrook FS office now charges a per-night camping fee at several campgrounds. North of Hwy 3/93, you'll be asked to crack open your wallet at Tie Lake. Farther south, expect the same lack of hospitality at Loon lake, Englishman Creek and Gold Bay on Lake Koocanusa's west shore, and Dorr on Lake Koocanusa's east shore. If you're a resolute free-camper, like the authors, you'll choose to avoid these campgrounds. But directions are provided here for those who are undeterred by the nominal fee. Your annual BC Camping Pass entitles you to a 50% discount.

Lake Koocanusa is a 110-km (68-mi) long reservoir created by Libby Dam on the Kootenay River in Montana. It averages 1 km (0.6 mi) wide. About half the lake is in Canada. The name was contrived—a combination of Kootenay, Canada, and USA. You won't be taking many photos of this artificial, mundane lake, but Kooc offers a lot of shoreline for boaters to explore. Bear in mind that the water level fluctuates.

WAPITI LAKE

If you're heading southeast on Hwy 3/93 from near Cranbrook

Just northeast of Cranbrook, Hwys 3/95, 93/95, and 3/93 converge. From the junction, drive Hwy 3/93 southeast 26 km (16 mi) to the Kootenay River bridge, just past Wardner. Reset your tripometer to 0 on the bridge, proceed southeast 5.6 km (3.5 mi), then turn right (south) onto paved Rosicky Road. Reset your tripometer to 0.

If you're heading northwest on Hwy 3/93 from Jaffray

From Jaffray-Baynes Lake Road in Jaffray, drive Hwy 3/93 northwest 6 km (3.7 mi). Turn left (south) onto paved Rosicky Road and reset your tripometer to 0.

Wapiti Lake

For either approach above, now follow the directions below

0 km (0 mi)
Starting south on paved Rosicky Road, departing Hwy 3/93.

0.4 km (0.2 mi)
Turn sharply left at the ranch, onto unpaved Shelbourne Road.

1.5 km (0.9 mi)
Turn right at the signpost.

1.6 km (1 mi)
Stay left and continue descending.

2.2 km (1.4 mi)
Reach Wapiti Lake.

2.8 km (1.7 mi)
Arrive at Wapiti Lake campground on the southeast shore.

WAPITI LAKE RECREATION SITE #39
Weekend / Easy
Elev: 777 m (2550 ft) / Lake: 4 ha
5 tables
Accessible by small motorhomes and trailers

MOST JAFFRAY-ELKO CAMPGROUNDS

If you're heading southeast on Hwy 3/93 from Jaffray

0 km (0 mi)
Starting southeast on Hwy 3/93 from Jaffray-Baynes Lake Road in Jaffray. For **North Star Lake campground**, or the **campgrounds near and on Lake Koocanusa's west shore,** go south at this junction onto Jaffray-Baynes Lake Road; directions continue on page 381.

200 meters
Turn left (north) onto Tie Lake Road and reset your tripometer to 0 for **Tie Lake campground**; directions continue on page 384.

5.1 km (3.2 mi)
Pass the lumber mill at Galloway.

12.1 km (7.5 mi)
Turn right (west) onto Rock Lake Road and reset your tripometer to 0 for **Rock Creek campground**; directions continue on page 384.

15.6 km (9.7 mi)
Turn right (southwest) onto Kikomun-Newgate Road and reset your tripometer to 0 for **Kikomun Creek campground**; directions continue on page 382.

17.6 km (10.9 mi)
Reach Elko, where Hwys 3 and 93 split. Proceed straight (northeast) on Hwy 3 for Fernie. Turn right (south) onto Hwy 93 and reset your tripometer to 0 for **Dorr campground on Lake Koocanusa's east shore,** and **campgrounds at Loon and Edwards lakes**; directions continue on page 385.

If you're heading northwest on Hwy 3/93 from Elko

0 km (0 mi)
Starting northwest on Hwy 3/93 from Elko, where Hwys 3 and 93 converge. For **Dorr campground on Lake Koocanusa's east shore**, and **campgrounds at Loon and Edwards lakes**, go south at this junction onto Hwy 93; directions continue on page 385.

2 km (1.2 mi)
Turn left (southwest) onto Kikomun-Newgate Road and reset your tripometer to 0 for **Kikomun Creek** campground, or the **campgrounds near and on Lake Koocanusa's west shore;** directions continue on page 382.

5.5 km (3.4 mi)
Turn left (west) onto Rock Lake Road and reset your tripometer to 0 for **Rock Creek campground**; directions continue on page 384.

12.5 km (7.8 mi)
Pass the lumber mill at Galloway.

17.4 km (10.8 mi)
Turn right (north) onto Tie Lake Road and reset your tripometer to 0 for **Tie Lake campground**; directions continue on page 384.

17.6 km (10.9 mi)
Reach Jaffray. Turn left (south) onto Jaffray-Baynes Lake Road and reset your tripometer to 0 for **North Star Lake campground**; directions continue on page 381.

24.5 km (15.2 mi)
Proceed straight (northwest) on Hwy 3/93 for Cranbrook. Turn left (south) onto paved Rosicky Road and reset your tripometer to 0 for **Wapiti Lake campground**; directions continue on page 378.

North Star Lake

For NORTH STAR LAKE and LAKE KOOCANUSA'S WEST SHORE, now follow the directions below

0 km (0 mi)
Starting south on Jaffray-Baynes Lake Road, departing Hwy 3/93 in Jaffray.

4.7 km (2.9 mi)
Proceed straight (south) for Lake Koocanusa. Turn left (east) to reach North Star Lake campground in 1.8 km (1.1 mi).

NORTH STAR LAKE RECREATION SITE #38
Weekend / Easy
Elev: 847 m (2780 ft) / Lake: 25 ha
9 tables
Accessible by small motorhomes and trailers

Continuing south on the main road, passing the turnoff to North Star Lake campground.

16 km (9.9 mi)

Reach a 4-way junction at the northeast edge of Kikomun Creek Provincial Park. Turn right (west) onto Newgate Road and reset your tripometer to 0 for campgrounds near and on Lake Koocanusa's west shore; directions continue at the bottom.

For KIKOMUN CREEK and LAKE KOOCANUSA'S WEST SHORE, now follow the directions below

0 km (0 mi)

Starting southwest on Kikomun-Newgate Rd, departing Hwy 3/93.

5 km (3 mi)

Proceed straight (southwest) for Lake Koocanusa. Turn right, then bear left at the next two forks, to reach Kikomun Creek campground in 2 km (1.2 mi).

KIKOMUN CREEK RECREATION SITE #35
Weekend / Easy
5 well-spaced tables
Accessible by small motorhomes and trailers

Continuing southwest on Kikomun-Newgate Road, passing the turnoff to Kikomun Creek campground.

7.2 km (4.5 mi)

Reach a 4-way junction at the northeast edge of Kikomun Creek Provincial Park. Proceed straight (west) onto Newgate Road and reset your tripometer to 0 for campgrounds near and on Lake Koocanusa's west shore; directions continue below.

Starting west on Newgate Road, from the junction at the northeast edge of Kikomun Creek Provincial Park, heading for Lake Koocanusa's west shore

0 km (0 mi)

Starting west on Newgate Road, heading for campgrounds near and on Lake Koocanusa's west shore. Soon cross the bridge spanning Lake Koocanusa.

5.6 km (3.5 mi)
Turn left (south), generally following Lake Koocanusa's west shore.

18.6 km (11.5 mi)
Proceed generally south on the main road for Gold Creek and Gold Bay campgrounds. Turn left to reach Englishman Creek campground on Lake Koocanusa in 1 km (0.6 mi).

ENGLISHMAN CREEK RECREATION SITE #23
Weekend / Easy / Overnight Fee
30 tables, 40 campsites, boat launch
Accessible by motorhomes and 5th-wheels

Continuing south on the main road, passing the turnoff to Englishman Creek campground.

26.6 km (16.5 mi)
Reach Gold Creek campground beside the road.

GOLD CREEK RECREATION SITE #22
Weekend / Easy
2 tables
Accessible by motorhomes and 5th-wheels

31.6 km (19.6 mi)
Turn left onto a rough road to reach Gold Bay campground on Lake Koocanusa in 1 km (0.6 mi).

GOLD BAY RECREATION SITE #21
Weekend / Easy / Overnight Fee
9 tables, boat launch
Accessible by motorhomes and 5th-wheels

For TIE LAKE, now follow the directions below

0 km (0 mi)
Starting north on Tie Lake Road, departing Hwy 3/93.

2.7 km (1.7 mi)
Reach a junction. Go right to quickly reach Tie Lake campground on the southeast shore. The road circles the lake.

TIE LAKE RECREATION SITE #40
Weekend / Easy / Overnight Fee
Elev: 850 m (2790 ft) / Lake: 134 ha
12 tables, gravel boat launch, day-use area
Accessible by motorhomes and 5th-wheels

For ROCK CREEK, now follow the directions below

0 km (0 mi)
Starting west on Rock Lake Road, departing Hwy 3/93. The surface is good gravel. Ignore signs for Rock Lake Camp; it's not the FS campground.

1.6 km (1 mi)
Bear left onto a narrow, rough road, where the main road curves right.

3.7 km (2.3 mi)
Reach a 4-way junction and turn right. Soon pass through beautiful meadows.

4.2 km (2.6 mi)
Proceed straight. Pass left and right forks. Descend through forest.

4.6 km (2.9 mi)
Turn left onto a spur to arrive at Rock Creek campground in 100 meters. It's in a forest-fringed meadow beside the languorous creek.

ROCK CREEK RECREATION SITE #36
Weekend / Easy
3 campsites
Inaccessible by motorhomes and 5th-wheels

For LAKE KOOCANUSA'S EAST SHORE and LOON AND EDWARDS LAKES, now follow the directions below

0 km (0 mi)
Starting south on Hwy 93, from the junction of Hwys 3 and 93 at Elko.

13 km (8.1 mi)
Cross a bridge over Elk River.

16 km (9.9 mi)
Proceed straight (southeast) on Hwy 93 for campgrounds at Loon and Edwards lakes. Turn right (southwest) onto Dorr Road and reset your tripometer to 0 for Dorr campground on Lake Koocanusa.

> **0 km (0 mi)**
> Starting southwest on Dorr Road, departing Hwy 93.
>
> **7.7 km (4.8 mi)**
> Turn right (west).
>
> **11.2 km (6.9 mi)**
> Arrive at Dorr campground on Lake Koocanusa.
>
> ### DORR RECREATION SITE #51
> Weekend / Easy / Overnight Fee
> 30 tables, gravel boat launch
> Accessible by motorhomes and 5th-wheels

Continuing southeast on Hwy 93, passing the turnoff to Dorr campground.

24 km (14.9 mi)
Reach the community of Grasmere. Turn right (west) onto Schoolhouse Road and reset your tripometer to 0 for campgrounds at Loon and Edwards lakes.

0 km (0 mi)
Starting west on Schoolhouse Road, departing Hwy 93.

0.4 km (0.2 mi)
Turn left (south) onto Edwards Lake Road for Edwards Lake campground. Turn right (north) onto Loon Lake Road to reach Loon Lake campground at 2 km (1.2 mi). Partially-treed campsites are on the south and west shores.

LOON LAKE RECREATION SITE #19
Weekend / Easy / Overnight Fee
Elev: 802 m (2630 ft) / Lake: 45 ha
30 tables, gravel boat launch
Accessible by motorhomes and 5th-wheels

Continuing left (south) at the 0.4-km (0.2-mi) junction, passing the turnoff to Loon Lake campground.

0.9 km (0.6 mi)
Reach a junction. Make a tight hairpin turn right. Bear left on this road until the lake is visible.

3.4 km (2.1 mi)
Arrive at small Edwards Lake. The first camping area has three tables. Proceed 0.5 km (0.3 mi) along the shore for two more tables.

EDWARDS LAKE RECREATION SITE #20
Weekend / Easy
Elev: 802 m (2630 ft) / Lake: 42.5 ha
5 tables, boat launch
Accessible by motorhomes and 5th-wheels

ELK VALLEY

In the far lower-right-hand corner of B.C., on Hwy 3, is the town of Sparwood. Directly north of Sparwood is Elkford. And north of Elkford is a string of FS campgrounds up Elk River Valley, en route to Elk Lakes Provincial Park. The road is good, the setting is beautiful, the campgrounds are pleasant, and the trail into the park is very rewarding. Allow a full day for the roundtrip hike to Upper Elk Lake, where Rocky Mountain peaks and alpine slopes are visible. Upper Petain Basin is a splendid two-day backpack trip.

Early explorers often saw herds of 100 elk here, hence the name. The valley is also home to mule and white-tail deer, bighorn sheep, mountain goats, and bears—blacks and grizzlies. Read *B.C. Stands for Bear Country* (page 27). Follow all the recommended precautions. And unless you're a hunter, clear out of here on September 1. This big, tranquil valley suddenly seems very small and scary when hunting season begins.

The Elk Valley road is usually snowfree by mid-June and is maintained through September.

If you're heading east or west on Hwy 3 in the southeast corner of B.C.

Drive Hwy 3 to Sparwood. It's 29 km (18 mi) northeast of Fernie, or 18 km (11.2 mi) northwest of the Alberta border. In Sparwood, turn north onto Hwy 43 and follow it 33 km (20.5 mi) to Elkford, where pavement ends. Set your tripometer to 0.

0 km (0 mi)
Starting north on Elk Lakes FS road, from Elkford.

10.5 km (6.5 mi)
Reach **Krivensky Farm Recreation Site #8** on the right. It has 5 tables in a field near the Elk River.

20.8 km (12.9 mi)
Reach **Blue Lake Recreation Site #7** on the left. It has 3 tables on the tiny lake.

39 km (24.2 mi)
Reach **Aldridge Creek Recreation Site #5** on the right. It has 2 tables beside the Elk River.

46.3 km (28.7 mi)
Soon after crossing a bridge to the east side of Elk River, reach **Weary Creek Recreation Site #4** on the left, beside the road. It has 1 table on the river. Just beyond, the FS road intersects Kananaskis Power Line Road. Bear left and proceed north.

58 km (36 mi)
Reach **Riverside Recreation Site #3** on the left. It has 2 tables between the road and the river.

63.5 km (39.4 mi)
Reach **Tobermory Creek Recreation Site #2** on the left. It has 4 tables in open forest. The FS maintains a cabin here for public use. It has 4 bunks and a woodstove. It's available first come, first served.

64.5 km (40 mi)
Reach **Upper Elk River Recreation Site #1** on the left. It has 3 tables beside the Elk River, and a view of meadows and mountainside avalanche chutes.

69 km (42.8 mi)
Reach **Elk Lakes trailhead** at road's end. An easy, 20-minute walk on a level trail leads to tent sites in Elk Lakes Provincial Park.

Forest Service Offices

For information about camping in a particular Forest Service district, speak to the Recreation Specialist. Instead of calling the office direct, dial **Inquiry B.C.** (660-2421 from within Vancouver, 1-800-663-7867 from elsewhere in B.C.). Tell them the name of the office and the phone number. They'll connect you at no charge.

For on-line information about B.C. Forest Service regions, go to **www.for.gov.bc.ca/mof/regdis.htm**

The **hours of operation** for most Forest Service offices are Monday through Friday, 8 a.m. to 12 noon, and 1 p.m. to 4:30 p.m.

VANCOUVER FOREST REGION
ph: (250) 751-7001
fax: (250) 751-7190
2100 Labieux Road
Nanaimo, BC V9T 6E9

Campbell River Forest District
ph: (250) 286-9300
370 Dogwood Street South
Campbell River, BC V9W 6Y7

Chilliwack Forest District
ph: (604) 794-2100
Box 159, 9850 S. McGrath Road
Rosedale, BC V0X 1X0

South Island Forest District
ph: (250) 724-9205
4227 6th Avenue
Port Alberni, BC V9Y 4N1

Port McNeill Forest District
ph: (250) 956-5000
Box 7000, 2291 Mine Road Place
Port McNeill, BC V0N 2R0

Squamish Forest District
ph: (604) 898-2100
42000 Loggers Lane
Squamish, BC V0N 3G0

Sunshine Coast Forest District
ph: (604) 485-0700
7077 Duncan Street
Powell River, BC V8A 1W1

KAMLOOPS FOREST REGION
ph: (250) 828-4131
fax: (250) 828-4154
515 Columbia Street
Kamloops, BC V2C 2T7

Kamloops Forest District
ph: (250) 371-6500
1255 Dalhousie Drive
Kamloops, BC V2C 5Z5

Lillooet Forest District
ph: (250) 256-1200
650 Industrial Place, Bag 700
Lillooet, BC V0K 1V0

Merritt Forest District
ph: (250) 378-8400
Box 4400, Stn. Main
Hwy 5A and Airport Road
Merritt, BC V0K 2B0

Penticton Forest District
ph: 1-800-661-4099;
(250) 490-2200
102 Industrial Place
Penticton, BC V2A 7C8

Salmon Arm Forest District
ph: (250) 833-3400
Bag 100, 790 16th Street NE
Salmon Arm, BC V1E 4S4

Vernon Forest District
ph: (250) 558-1700
2501 14th Avenue
Vernon, BC V1T 8Z1

NELSON FOREST REGION
ph: (250) 354-6200
fax: (250) 354-6250
518 Lake Street
Nelson, BC V1L 4C6

Arrow Forest District
ph: (250) 365-8600
845 Columbia Avenue
Castlegar, BC V1N 1H3

Boundary Forest District
ph: (250) 442-5411
Box 2650, 136 Sagamore Avenue
Grand Forks, BC V0H 1H0

Columbia Forest District
ph: (250) 344-7500
Box 1380, 800 9th Street North
Golden, BC V0A 1H0

Columbia Forest District
ph: (250) 837-7611
Box 9158, RPO #3
1761 Big Eddy Road
Revelstoke, BC V0E 2S0

Cranbrook Forest District
ph: (250) 426-1700
1902 Theatre Road
Cranbrook, BC V1C 4H4

Invermere Forest District
ph: (250) 342-4200
Box 189, 625 4th Street
Invermere, BC V0A 1K0

Kootenay Lake Forest District
ph: (250) 825-1100
1907 Ridgewood Road, RR 1
Nelson, BC V1L 5P4

B.C. Road Map

Modestly priced B.C. road maps are available at Tourist Info Centres in towns and cities throughout the province.

If you live out-of-province, the SuperNatural British Columbia tourism office will mail you a British Columbia Road Map and Parks Guide. Call 1-800-663-6000 from anywhere in North America, (604) 387-1742 from overseas, or (604) 663-6000 from within Vancouver.

REPORT ALL FOREST FIRES TO 1-800-663-5555

B.C. Stands for Best Camping

Camp Free authors Kathy and Craig have free-camped all their lives. While she was still a baby in diapers, Kathy's parents took her camping most weekends. Her earliest memories are of her mother cooking dinner under a tarp draped from the back of the family's pickup while her father listened to the rain. As a boy, Craig was obsessed with fly fishing. He backpacked to remote trout streams, until he realized the joy of hiking and camping is an end in itself and all that fishing gear was just slowing him down. Together, Kathy and Craig have perfected the art of free-camping. Their camping adventures have taken them throughout North America, Europe, Australia and New Zealand. They've driven all kinds of vehicles to all kinds of places in all kinds of weather. It hasn't always been idyllic.

One time, they pitched their tent at midnight on the grounds of an English country manor. They were hitchhiking. Unable to afford a hotel, they had only two choices. A fenced, tussocky paddock crowded with cattle? Or the manor lawn? They knocked at the imposing door to ask permission, but nobody appeared. So they set their travel alarm for 5:30 a.m. The next morning, they packed quickly, left unseen, and walked three kilometers to Stonehenge. They watched it emerge from the fog at sunrise, before anyone else arrived.

Asleep under the stars beside a creek near Payson, Arizona, they were startled by a gang of Hell's Angels in the middle of the night. The bikers roared in, only a few feet from the Copelands' heads, but otherwise weren't a problem. Until morning. After the bikers took off, Craig discovered they'd dumped one of their buddies. He was bleeding and out cold.

Again in Europe, they were exploring the Cairngorm Mountains of northern Scotland. This time they were driving Freida — a rusty, old, Bedford Beagle they'd bought for $93 US. As always, they wanted to camp free. A sign on a dirt road caught their eye: Forestry Personnel Only. They risked it, but couldn't find even a tiny pullout. So they started turning around, backed into a ditch and became hopelessly mired. "Guess this is where we say goodbye to Freida," Craig said. But before they could load their backpacks and start hiking, a forestry official drove up in his truck. After a light rebuke, he towed them out. Feeling lucky, the Copelands splurged that night and paid for a campsite at the national park.

On the Oregon side of the Columbia River Gorge is the Eagle Creek Trail, which the Copelands had just finished hiking. It was so late they decided to camp in their car at the trailhead, but later wished they hadn't. A light directly over their heads woke them up. Another hiker? A policeman? A thief? A murderer? They laid there wondering, zipped into their sleeping bags, stuffed into the back of their car, their hearts pounding with adrenalin. "He's going to break into the car," Kathy whispered. Craig roared like a bear. They saw the flashlight bob away into the night. It was probably a teenage burglar, but they didn't wait to find out. They raced onto the highway and, still dazed, approached the bridge over the Columbia. With Kathy still in her bag and Craig in his underwear, they presented an interesting site to the matron in the toll booth. They eventually fell asleep, parked on a residential street in North Bonneville, Washington.

Now you can understand why Kathy and Craig are thrilled to live in British Columbia. They say it offers the easiest, most enjoyable, most abundant free camping of anyplace they've ever traveled.

Home

Universe is home for earth.
Air is home for wind.
Tree is home for bird.
Meadow is home for flower.
Dirt is home for seed.
Water is home for whale.
Mind is home for idea.
Fire is home for warmth.
Tent is home for camper.
Earth is home for all.

Other Titles from Voice in the Wilderness Press

Look for these and other titles by the Copelands in outdoor shops and book stores. You can also order them by sending a cheque to Voice in the Wilderness Press, P.O. Box 71, Riondel, B.C. V0B 2B0 Canada. The prices include shipping and GST. If you order more than one book or cassette, deduct the following amount from the total cost: CDN $3 for shipments within Canada, or US $3 to the States. Allow 2-3 weeks for delivery in Canada, 3-4 weeks to the States.

Camp Free in B.C. Volume II.........CDN $19   US $16
ISBN: 0-9698016-6-1   1999, 1st edition, 368 pages
Precise directions to over 225 official, free campgrounds accessible by two-wheel drive. Covers central BC, from Trans-Canada Hwy 1, north past Highway 16. Follow exciting backroads through the Shuswap Highlands, East Cariboo, and Chilcotin. Includes sites near Terrace, Smithers, and Prince George.

Bears Beware! Warning Calls You Can Make to Avoid an Encounter...CDN $11   US $9
ISBN 0-9698016-5-3   1998 edition, audio cassette
30 minutes that could save your life. Find out why pepper spray, talking, and bells are not enough. Follow these strategies for safer hiking and camping in bear country.

Premier Hikes™ in British Columbia............CDN $19   US $16
ISBN 0-9698016-8-8   May 2000, 240 pages, 16 pages of colour photos
The only book you need to enjoy the most spectacular, exhilarating hikes in the province. Discerning trail reviews help you choose your trip. Detailed route descriptions keep you on the path. Includes dayhikes and backpack trips. Covers the Coast Mountains, Cascades, Selkirks, Kootenays, and Rockies.

PREMIER   OUTSTANDING   WORTHWHILE   DON'T DO

The Don't Waste Your Time® *hiking guidebook series rates and reviews trails to help you get the most from magnificent wilderness areas. Route descriptions are comprehensive. Includes shoulder-season trips for more hiking opportunities. Offers wisdom on mountain travel.*

Don't Waste Your Time®
in the BC Coast Mountains........CDN $17 US $15
ISBN 0-9698016-3-7   1997 edition, 288 pages
72 hikes in southwest BC, including Vancouver's
North Shore mountains, Garibaldi Provincial Park,
and the Whistler-Pemberton region.

Don't Waste Your Time®
in the Canadian Rockies........CDN $19 US $16
ISBN 0-9698016-4-5   1998 edition, 392 pages
125 hikes in Banff, Jasper, Kootenay, Yoho and Waterton
national parks, plus Mt. Robson and Mt. Assiniboine
provincial parks.

Don't Waste Your Time®
in the North Cascades...............CDN $20 US $17
ISBN 0-89997-182-2   1996 edition, 364 pages
110 hikes in southern BC and northern Washington.
Includes North Cascades National Park, Mt. Baker and
Glacier Peak wilderness areas, plus BC's Manning and
Cathedral parks.

Don't Waste Your Time®
in the West Kootenays.........CDN $19 US $16
ISBN 0-9698016-9-6   April 2000, approx. 320 pages
70 hikes in the Selkirk and Purcell ranges of southeast
B.C. Includes Valhalla, Kokanee Glacier, Goat Range,
West Arm, and St. Mary's Alpine parks.

Receive Your Camping Pass By Mail

To camp free at B.C. Forest Service campgrounds, you must have an annual Camping Pass. A single-night Camping Pass is also available. Camping Passes are sold at sporting goods stores and government agent offices. All funds raised by Camping Pass sales go directly to campground maintenance.

To receive your Camping Pass by mail: (1) Determine the cost by reading the form on the next page. After 2001, call to confirm current prices. (2) Make your cheque payable to the Minister of Finance. (3) Complete the form on the next page and send it, along with your cheque, to **Government Agent, 250 — 455 Columbia Street, Kamloops, B.C. V2C 6K4**. Phone: (250) 828-4540. Fax: (250) 828-4542.

The annual Camping Pass allows an individual, family, or group of six, to enjoy more than 1400 Forest Service campgrounds throughout B.C., at no additional charge, for one year beginning in spring. Only about 30 of the busiest campgrounds charge a modest per-night fee to cover increased maintenance. At those, the annual Camping Pass entitles you to a 50% discount. A single-night Camping Pass allows an individual, family, or group of six, to camp one night at a Forest Service campground.

Forest Service campgrounds operate on a first-come, first-served basis. Your Camping Pass does not guarantee access to campgrounds or reserve campsites. The Forest Service asks that you limit your stay at any one campground to 14 days.

Camping Pass
Registration Form

Name

Street Address

City   Province / State

Postal / Zip Code   Phone

B.C. Forest Service Regions I'll be visiting

☐ Cariboo   ☐ Kamloops

☐ Nelson   ☐ Prince George

☐ Prince Rupert   ☐ Vancouver

My accompanying cheque for CDN $_____ covers the
total amount for the following:

☐ Annual Camping Pass — $27

☐ Seniors Annual Camping Pass — $22

☐ Single Night Camping Pass — $8

☐ Two Single-Night Camping Passes — $16

Mail this form with your cheque to
**Government Agent, 250 — 455 Columbia Street,
Kamloops, B.C. V2C 6K4.**

Camping Pass
Registration Form

Name

Street Address

City   Province / State

Postal / Zip Code   Phone

B.C. Forest Service Regions I'll be visiting

☐ Cariboo   ☐ Kamloops

☐ Nelson   ☐ Prince George

☐ Prince Rupert   ☐ Vancouver

My accompanying cheque for CDN $_____ covers the
total amount for the following:

☐ Annual Camping Pass — $27

☐ Seniors Annual Camping Pass — $22

☐ Single Night Camping Pass — $8

☐ Two Single-Night Camping Passes — $16

Mail this form with your cheque to
**Government Agent, 250 — 455 Columbia Street,
Kamloops, B.C. V2C 6K4**.

Camping Pass
Registration Form

Name _____

Street Address _____

City _____ Province / State _____

Postal / Zip Code _____ Phone _____

B.C. Forest Service Regions I'll be visiting

☐ Cariboo   ☐ Kamloops

☐ Nelson   ☐ Prince George

☐ Prince Rupert   ☐ Vancouver

My accompanying cheque for CDN $_____ covers the total amount for the following:

☐ Annual Camping Pass — $27

☐ Seniors Annual Camping Pass — $22

☐ Single Night Camping Pass — $8

☐ Two Single-Night Camping Passes — $16

Mail this form with your cheque to
**Government Agent, 250 — 455 Columbia Street,
Kamloops, B.C. V2C 6K4.**